FLEXIBLE WORKING PRACTICES

John Stredwick, before joining Luton Business School in 1992, spent over 20 years as a personnel practitioner, including spells in industrial relations at a shipyard in the north-east of England and as a generalist in regional publishing and public-sector contracting. For over 10 years he was head of personnel at a subsidiary of RTZ plc in the home-improvement industry. He currently manages the MSc HRM part-time course and the IPD portfolio at the Business School, and jointly runs one of the IPD reward faculty short courses concerning incentives and variable pay. He has given papers on flexible working and reward subjects at a number of conferences, including an international conference in Singapore, where he also teaches as a visiting lecturer.

Steve Ellis holds a Henley MBA and an MPhil from Putteridge Bury Management Centre. He currently lectures on management and human resources to masters-level students, and has completed HR consultancy projects in the UK, USA and the Far East. Steve worked for both Midland Bank plc and Sheffield County Council prior to entering academia. He is currently developing flexibility policies with organisations in the furniture industry that may be applicable more widely to SMEs in other sectors. He has published articles on management and business strategy for the *Management Development Review*, *TQM Magazine*, *Management Today* and *Training for Quality*. In the 1980s Steve penned a regular monthly column for *Thames Valley Business Magazine*.

Other titles in the series:

The Institute of Personnel and Development is the leading publisher of books and reports for personnel and training professionals, students, and for all those concerned with the effective management and development of people at work. For details of all our titles, please contact the Publishing Department:

tel. 0181-263 3387
fax 0181-263 3850
e-mail publish@ipd.co.uk

The catalogue of all IPD titles can be viewed on the IPD website:
http://www.ipd.co.uk

FLEXIBLE WORKING PRACTICES

Techniques and innovations

John Stredwick and Steve Ellis

INSTITUTE OF PERSONNEL AND DEVELOPMENT

First published in 1998

Design by Paperweight
Typeset by
Fakenham Photosetting Ltd, Fakenham, Norfolk
Printed in Great Britain by
The Cromwell Press, Wiltshire

British Library Cataloguing in Publication Data
A catalogue record for this book is available from the
British Library

ISBN 0-85292-744-4

iD

INSTITUTE OF PERSONNEL
AND DEVELOPMENT

IPD House, Camp Road, London SW19 4UX
Tel: 0181 971 9000   Fax: 0181 263 3333
Registered office as above. Registered Charity No. 1038333
A company limited by guarantee. Registered in England No. 2931892

CONTENTS

ACKNOWLEDGEMENTS

We are very grateful to the large number of people – colleagues, students and practitioners – who helped in many ways with getting this book written and published. Firstly, to Matthew Reisz at the IPD, for all his ideas and encouragement along the route.

We visited a large number of organisations and gratefully acknowledge their co-operation in allowing us to use their experience in the form of cases or in the text. We would like to thank in particular Peter Radcliffe, Carole Holmes, Joanna Simonds, Joyce Nairn, Joanne Roberts, Gill Rothwell, Geraldine O'Connor, Kathy Woodward, Ken Lewis, Stephen Lytton, Graham Hill, Mike Cope and Steve Luckhurst.

Publishing organisations in the field have been particularly helpful in giving permission to reproduce their survey material, including Industrial Relations Services and Income Data Services, as have a number of consultants, including Hewitt Associates.

At Luton Business School our librarian, Audrey Stewart gave us considerable help in our literature searches, and Lyn Barrett gave us assistance with diagrams and illustrations.

Our colleague, Sue Bathmaker, gave invaluable help in drafting Chapter 14 on the psychological contract.

PROLOGUE

In the early 1970s, I joined a 3,000-strong shipbuilding company in Sunderland and obtained my first taste of hard-nosed industrial relations. One particular day in the early weeks stands out in my memory. We had just entered into the annual pay negotiations with our 12 unions and we were giving our first response to the usual claims, presented the week before, for a substantial pay increase, better holidays, overtime, sick pay and a new bonus scheme. Significantly (and ominously, as they were the more militant groups), a number of the unions had handed us their claim, all typed out with an argued justification, rather than simply reading out a list from the back of the traditional cigarette packet. They indicated that they were becoming more progressive, and one of their key points was that they wanted a clear involvement in the decision-making process to secure a good future for their members.

Our response was to talk about flexibility in return for any improvement in pay and conditions. We wanted to bring in a degree of interchangeability between skills and a variety in shift patterns. We wanted to be rid of the various overt fiddles known as 'Spanish practices'. It had not been an easy process to convince the board that changes of this type were necessary as most board members had themselves been steeped in the culture which produced a fierce pride in the separation of historical skills and practices. Some of the directors, including the personnel director, had paid a visit to Japan recently and had begun to realise the necessity of change, but all were not entirely convinced.

Our first meeting was with the boilermakers and we talked about flexibility between, say, the welders and ship-wrights. There was nearly a riot. We met with a passionate defence of their individual skills and how they could not be diluted, how they would not give up their work to anyone else (even those in the same union), and how the so-called 'Spanish practices' had been freely negotiated with management and we could not go backwards. Forgetting for the moment that these 'negotiations' had often taken place immediately prior to a launch or sea trials to allow them to go ahead, we stressed the benefits of flexibility and the need to adopt these strategies to survive. Survival, we were told, was not the issue. It was one of principle – and, in any case, the government would ensure the company's survival.

The same message came back to us in meetings with the other unions – even those professing to have a more progressive outlook: flexibility was not a negotiable issue. Our last meeting was with the staff committee representing managers and supervisors, and this was the most depressing of all. Most had been in the industry for 25 or more years and supervised their own skilled trades. They saw flexibility as a denial of all their work and effort to get into their relatively well-paid positions, and new shift systems as a means to deny them the right to organise, and be paid for, the two extra evening shifts and a Sunday morning (at double time) that they had become used to. They were no more interested in a strategic shift in employment systems. The solution, for their part, was to get much tougher with the unions and embark on a wholesale policy of sacking troublemakers. If this caused delay in finishing the ships, it wouldn't matter – the customers would have to wait.

Our attempts on this occasion therefore met with an equal intransigence from both management and unions. The rest, as they say, is history. We made some cosmetic progress at the edges but not enough of substance to alter the overall performance. The customers were not prepared to wait and opted for Japanese and, later, Korean and Polish shipyards. The Labour government ensured a survival of a diminished sector industry, as did even Margaret Thatcher for a few years in the early 1980s, but by 1986 the shipbuilding industry in Sunderland, which once employed 40,000 men, had closed down completely.

Ironically, it was just outside Sunderland that Nissan decided to build the first transplant Japanese car factory. Peter

Wickens (1987), when recalling the first 10 years of this amazingly successful and influential complex, tells how important the flexibility concept was in all the operations, constituting one of the three core values on which Nissan's culture is based – the others being quality and teamworking (Pickard, 1997). This was extended even to using psychometric tests to identify the attitude of applicants to flexible methods of working.

Upmarket housing and leisure activities now stand in the place of the Sunderland shipyards. Only a small handful of ex-shipyard employees were taken on by Nissan. Many remain out of work to this day.

For someone relatively new to the realities of the personnel environment it was a sobering lesson. A few years on from that early meeting, I moved to a company in the home improvement industry based in the Home Counties which was only 12 years old and which had shown truly remarkable growth. It sold, manufactured and distributed made-to-measure products in a highly competitive environment, and flexibility was at the heart of its business. Nobody questioned the need to make new products, to change factory layouts, to learn more skills or to experiment with shift patterns and reward systems. On the contrary, employees complained if they did not have the opportunity to take part. The customer-oriented culture had been bedded-in at a very early stage, while career-planning and communication systems reinforced that culture. Under this flexible regime, the company prospered for a decade or more.

The bleak contrast between these two organisations stimulated an interest in both the strategic and the operational aspects of flexibility which was shared by my colleague Steve Ellis, whose experience mirrored my own. We welcomed the opportunity to write this book, which is both a description of a range of flexible initiatives and also a prescriptive narrative of best practice and legal warnings. The chapters on teleworking, multi-skilling, empowerment and selling the ideas on flexibility are written by Steve; the remainder are by myself.

Structure of the book

The book is divided into four main sections. The first section contains an introduction to the economic and social context which has brought pressure on organisations to improve their flexibility, followed by an assessment of how widespread flexibility developments have occurred. Also in this chapter are two extended case-studies of organisations that have approached flexibility in an integrated way.

The second section deals with how flexibility is operated by organisations in practice in its various guises. Temporal flexibility schemes are dealt with in a number of chapters. *Annual hours* schemes (Chapter 2), which originated in manufacturing environments, are now being introduced in service environments in a number of forms. *Part-time working* (Chapter 3) now has a huge variety of formats, including job sharing, zero hours and portfolio working. The management of labour force numbers, called *predicting the unpredictable* (Chapter 4), has some of the fastest-growing initiatives in recent years, and the new concepts of complementary worker and interim management are included in this chapter as well as the more conventional subject area of shiftworking. A closely associated subject, *outsourcing*, is the subject of Chapter 7.

Functional flexibility is covered in a further three chapters – and here we deal with all the ways that flexibility in operations have been introduced. Developments in *multi-skilling* are in Chapter 6; some of the more recent innovations in *teleworking and homeworking* in Chapter 5: and the phenomenal growth in *call centres* in Chapter 8.

The third section of the book looks at ways that organisations have attempted to support and encourage the ethos of flexibility in the organisation. Financial flexibility – dealing with the changes in the way employees are flexibly rewarded – is covered in three chapters. *Rewarding individuals* (Chapter 9) looks at skills-based pay, competence-based pay, broadbanded structures and innovative performance-based pay systems. *Rewarding teams* or groups of employees (Chapter 10) examines profit-related pay, gain-sharing and team-based pay. *Flexible benefits* are the subject of Chapter 11. The strides that organisations have made to assist employees to work flexibly are examined in Chapter 12, which deals with policies that can loosely be called 'family-friendly', such as flexitime, career breaks, child-care and elder-care.

The final section looks some of the general difficulties and opportunities that flexible working brings. Chapter 13 examines the issue of *empowerment* of employees while, under the heading of *the psychological contract* (Chapter 14), the changes that are occurring in the relative contract expectations of employees and employers under flexible working arrangements are analysed. Methods of selling flexible working are dealt with in Chapter 15 while we look at future legal changes in Chapter 16.

None of these subjects should be looked at in isolation. The links with others can be very close. For example, outsourcing and the use of temporary employment have strong connections, as do multi-skilling and empowerment. We have attempted to demonstrate that organisations are most successful when they operate an integrated approach, rather than pick-and-match from the flexibility menu. Finally, we have included through each chapter a selection of short case-studies to illustrate how organisations have successfully moved in the direction of flexibility.

References

PICKARD J. 'Tour de force', *People Management*, 17 April 1997, pp. 34–35.

WICKENS P. *The Road to Nissan*. London, Macmillan, 1987.

1 INTRODUCTION

It is 9.15 am on Monday morning, and people are working in many different ways.

- George Fournier has been working on a spare desk at Rank Xerox in the open-plan office hall since he arrived at 8 am. He is the chief executive and he does not have an office. If he wants some privacy, he simply finds a spare meeting room.

- Alice Jones waits at home hoping for the phone to ring. She is on zero hours with a large clearing bank and could do with the work this week. A fortnight ago she had to turn down a couple of days' work because her aged mother was ill: she hopes it will not affect the amount of work the bank will offer.

- Alan Rogers is at home mending the car and hoping that the phone does not ring. He is on an annual hours contract with a paper mill and completed 55 hours on the night shift the previous week. This week he is on reserve for Monday and Tuesday and, if he gets called in because of absence or breakdowns, he will not get paid a penny because it will come out of his reserve hours.

- Duncan Green, with his second cup of coffee, settles down to the computer again. He is on a critical part of a re-programming contract with a tight deadline, and he hopes to complete it and download it to his company by the end of the week. After a two-hour stint he will take the dogs out for a walk down to the canal. He has been a teleworker from his Cotswold home for a software company for two years.

- Vanessa Goodchild is getting ready to catch the first off-peak train to London to work for an environmental charity. She is not employed, but they pay her the train fares and £30 a day expenses for a 10.30 am to 5 pm day. She graduated four months ago and hopes to use this position as a stepping-stone to permanent work. The series of projects she has found stimulating and she could put the geography degree work to good use.

☐ Andy Black is washing the hair of his first customer. He used to be employed by the boss but, a year ago, all six hairdressers became self-employed, renting the chairs and the facilities and keeping all the income and tips. A meeting with his accountant last night seemed to indicate he was making a living, but he was not quite sure that he was doing the right thing.

☐ Angela Manning is on the phone to John, her other job share half, about the assessment centre that she is running and which is due to start in 30 minutes. There are a couple of key facts that John has not made clear in the daybook written up on Friday. Luckily, he is in and able to sort the problems out for her.

☐ Anita Fullick is hard at work in the shed in the garden, soldering costume jewellery. She took up homeworking six months ago and had two days' soldering training in the small engineering company. It is straightforward work and she is turning out the products on time and to the quality they want, although boredom is starting to set in. If she completes 25 today, she will make £35.

☐ Geraldine Parker is waiting in the company reception with her bag packed. The coach is coming in 10 minutes to take her to the airport to catch a plane to Majorca. Two of the company's business centres have won team prizes of a weekend abroad for their overall performance and six of the head office staff are to join the party. The selection of these six was made by lottery: Geraldine's name went into the draw because she made a suggestion on customer service which has been successfully taken up.

☐ Harry Oldford wraps up the area seven team meeting by summing up the key action, the team responsibilities and the agreed objectives before the team moves back to their places on the line. Ten years ago he was a supervisor and told them what to do, but since his appointment as a team-leader this has no longer been the case. After a shaky start, he and the team have learned how to operate in a more open and democratic fashion. A steady flow of improvements has come from the team, Harry helping where necessary to put them into operation and get them working. They have just agreed rosters for the next month with a number of changes from his original draft. The team seem to like taking decisions and he has eventually seen the advantages of a new management style which does away with most orders and instructions.

New labour style: new ways of working – in this book we will be examining all these working systems and more besides. Not all of them are absolutely new. Homeworking supported the early stages of the Industrial Revolution, as did shift-working; part-time and temporary working have been familiar *modi operandi* throughout the twentieth century; while job sharing and flexitime arrived in the 1950s. Others have been visible in one form for some time but have changed their emphasis in recent years – teamworking, multi-skilling and empowerment are cases in point.

Some systems, however, are much more contemporary. Teleworking, annual hours, V-Time, zero hours, gainsharing, flexible benefits, virtual offices and call centres are concepts that have been adopted in a formal way only in the last 20 years in the UK.

These new systems that emphasise the vital nature of working flexibly have throughout been introduced mainly in an incremental way, sometimes tentatively, and rarely in an integrated form. Three stages have been evident:

☐ Firstly, they have been introduced to save money. Outsourcing operations, and recruiting part-timers because they are cheaper than full-timers, are examples.

☐ The second phase has been associated with downsizing. Keeping the headcount low has meant using temporary employees, empowering teams with fewer supervisors, and using annual hours and performance pay to improve productivity from a smaller workforce. Sometimes this has been associated with crisis measures. Examples of this include the threat of closure of the Heinz factory in Wigan (Choat, 1997), where multi-skilling agreements were

achieved only at the last minute through the closure lever-
age, and at Alcan in Lynemouth, where the agreement to
flexible working shifts and other practices pursuaded the
major shareholder to keep the plant open and invest in
new facilities (Pickard, 1997).

□ The final stage is where organisations have seen that these
measures taken during the recession can be effective at all
stages in the business cycle – that they can improve the
total flexibility of the entire operation in an integrated
fashion, leading to a major improvement in the bottom
line: flexibility in internal operations through multi-
skilling and empowerment; using complementary workers
to the full, both inside the company and at a distance; substantial outsourcing operations, including those at the core
of the business; and backing all these processes up with
flexible reward, benefit and communications policies.

A flavour of how an integrated flexible system works can be
shown in two detailed examples of Bedfordshire-based
companies. One is a small organisation, Dutton Engineering,
and the case-study follows in this chapter. The second is a
better-known organisation, Whitbread, which has been no
stranger to flexible practices for many years; the case-study is
to be found in the concluding chapter.

Case-study

DUTTON ENGINEERING

Flexibility: this is crucial in an uncertain and rapidly changing world.
Things will never be the same as they were. Nowadays customers want
choice, at low prices – and we have to be able to provide accordingly,
or they will just go elsewhere. We have to be flexible and grab the
opportunities before the competition does.

Lewis and Lytton (1995), p. 45.

Introduction

On a rather rundown estate on the edge of Sandy in Bedfordshire is
a nondescript industrial building that houses a small sheet-metal
engineering company called Dutton Engineering. You park your car
on the grass field at the back of the building, walk round to the front,
enter through an entryphone system, look in vain for a receptionist,

walk up the stairs, and then join another group of visitors (600 a year on average) from around the world who are trying to get to grips with what is so rather special about this organisation that has only 29 employees.

And it *is* special. Flexible hours, flexible work teams, flexible pay systems – they are all here and all working to the satisfaction of employees and management alike. It is also currently very profitable. Articles appear in national newspapers; Ken Lewis, one of the major shareholders, talks to endless conferences; and there has even been a book written about it.

The book tells the story of how a three-week visit to Japan in 1985 caused Ken to start to transform the method of management and to adapt some of the Japanese concepts to work in the British context. The most important concept was that of *trust*. The Japanese management and employees trusted each other, and companies trusted their suppliers, even their customers. It took over five years but, through a combination of quality-improvement programmes with suppliers and customers, the abolition of the quality department (yes, they do go together!) and a large number of training sessions with his employees, he introduced a series of measures that empowered the employees, brought teamworking to the fore and embedded that sense of trust throughout the organisation and its outside contacts. This reinforces the strong emphasis on the needs of the customer, and especially their needs in quality and delivery terms.

Dutton Engineering

Dutton Engineering is a subcontract manufacturing facility specialising in the fabrication of stainless steel, mild steel and aluminium for a variety of industries from printing to electronics. It won the Wedgewood Trophy for its contribution to the pursuit of excellence in 1994, and the KPMG Motivation Award in 1997. It is a host company for the DTI 'Inside UK Enterprise' national scheme, sharing best-practice ideas with business around the world. The work flow is highly unpredictable with no definable seasonal variations.

As one of the first elements in the 'trust' process, the company in 1989 began the process of 'partnership sourcing' with its customers, followed by the same arrangement with its suppliers in 1991. This, in practice, meant a commitment to single sourcing on a long-term basis. Suppliers are paid within the month, are issued with swipe cards so they can enter the building and fill up bins as necessary, and have even been trained to operate the forklift truck to facilitate swift offload and positioning of supplies.

These changes and those described below have meant that production lead times have been reduced from six weeks to eight hours; reject rates have dropped from 10 per cent to 0.07 per cent and paperwork has been cut by 70 per cent.

Flexibility in working operations

To start with, there are no job descriptions. Employees all have the same title of 'production operative' and they work in one of four teams. They used to be recruited for their skill, and simply used that particular skill. This had two major disadvantages. From the employer's viewpoint, it made him very vulnerable. When an employee was sick, there was nobody to turn to, and when work came in a rush, the employee had rather strong negotiating cards for pay and overtime. From the employee's viewpoint, it was somewhat restrictive and limiting in the work he or she could do.

The pigeon-hole effect led to employees' acting as individuals – carrying out their own work but not caring what happened before or afterwards, and casting the blame on others when anything went wrong. The switch to teamworking meant that this outlook had to change.

A skills audit identified that there were around 10 core skills in the organisation, but that most employees possessed only one or two. A target was set for everybody to have at least three, and the process became highly visible: a skills chart was posted prominently on the wall. When employees found themselves strongly encouraged to develop their skills, they were very co-operative. They enjoyed the process of passing on their skills to others, and they enjoyed learning other skills – seeing another part of the company jigsaw rather than just one piece. They could also understand how one job impinged upon another. If the welder left a great deal of excess weld, the polisher wasted a long time getting it off. Multi-skilling – as well as being more fun than they expected (there was much good-natured ribaldry during the training process from both teachers and students) – was a highly educative process. All took part: Tina, the business manager, learned to weld like the rest.

They needed the skills because the teams were multi-skilled in groups together to meet the needs of the customer – doing a job from start to finish. There were no inspectors because the teams were trusted to complete the work properly and build in quality as they went along. The next stage was further empowerment: teams were encouraged to deal directly with the customer in making the products, rather than consult through the office. Being close to the customer, knowing the quality required and the delivery date, have meant that the teams all know the real needs of the job. The computer in each section tells them immediately the status of each job. The outcome was that they worked closely together to achieve the results.

Under normal control systems, a supervisor would schedule and allocate the work and maintain discipline in the section. With teamworking, the roles had to change. If trust and empowerment were the key, then the teams had to be left to organise these operations for themselves, each taking a different role. The position of supervisor was abandoned, and team leaders who facilitated, rather than instructed, emerged instead.

The two managers had the most difficult part to play in these changes. They had to alter their own role and pass many of the day-to-day responsibilities to the teams. A team member would come with a problem – and would be politely asked to go away and work out a solution, and only to come back if the team were not 100 per cent confident they had got it right. Initially they would come back, but increasingly as team members became more sure of their own judgement, they would simply sort it out themselves. It did not happen overnight: the empowerment was a slow and gradual affair.

They made mistakes – some time and money were lost through those mistakes. But Ken made it clear that these were learning processes and the benefits would outweigh the odd difficulty.

Flexibility in time

Eight years ago, the hours of work were fairly representative of engineering: 7.30 am to 5.45 pm Monday to Thursday – a total of 39 hours. When work was short, the staff were sent into the stores, performed general maintenance tasks or built up stocks for the future. At these times employees were conscious of the situation and stretched work to fill the day, throwing the costings way out. When work came in a rush, they worked Friday and Saturday overtime and even Sunday overtime at enhanced rates, which also put the costs way out.

Feast and famine on fixed hours of work was the formula for uncompetitiveness and there had to be a better way. As the volume of work varied under no set pattern (it was not seasonal in any way), monthly rostering was not possible. Hours had to be truly flexible to meet demand. So after careful evaluation, the system of annual hours was developed.

The annual working requirement became 1,769, which was 52 weeks at 39 hours, less 259 hours for all holidays. In addition, employees would be paid for an additional 160 hours which could be called upon when the business was busy, making a grand total of 1,929 hours. Those hours would also cover sickness, medical appointments and any rework. Overtime beyond these hours would never be authorised. Employees would be paid on a monthly contract, the same every month, and all differences between monthly and hourly paid staff would be abolished. It would be a single-status organisation.

It was made plain that the employees would not necessarily have to work the full hours. If they worked 'smarter' and completed the work in hand early, they could go home. If they were on schedule for the work for the week, they could take the day off. The only overriding requirement was that the teams deliver their products to the customer on time at the right quality. The decision on how to work was left to the teams to make on a democratic basis – the Monday morning team meeting by the 'wipe-board', which set out the tasks and delivery dates, became a decisive feature of the teams' operations.

The incentive, then, was to work co-operatively and skilfully, satisfy the customer, and get more leisure time for a guaranteed salary. The focus switched away from filling in time, getting through the week, to filling in completion dockets and getting through the week's work quickly. Gradually the ideas for improved working methods came forward – layouts, liaison with customers, use of skills – and would be adopted by the teams. *Kaizen* had arrived. Just in case the customer wanted work urgently on a Thursday when the team had finished on a Wednesday, each team had a bleeper carried by one of the team on a rota. If bleeped, it was up to the team member to organise how and when the work would be carried out, even if this meant collecting somebody from the golf course!

A final point was that the system allowed employees the necessary time off for any difficulties at home.

Flexibility in pay

Employees at Dutton are very aware of profitability on contracts and their role in satisfying the customer. To reinforce this further, employees share 20 per cent of the profits on a monthly basis. There are only three individual basic pay rates and no automatic pay increases each year. All the employees decide what is affordable in the given circumstances, taking the profit-sharing into account. When a sudden reduction in orders took place in 1996, all staff agreed to take a reduction in pay, which was reinstated with interest three months later when business just as suddenly shot up. This was only possible because of the mutual trust embedded in the business.

Conclusion

It would be foolhardy to say that Dutton's future is assured. All businesses are so competitive that constant forward planning and innovation is essential to survive. For Dutton, future plans may include a more flexible salary system determined by 360-degree appraisal and the recognition of individual excellence while retaining the core team culture and values. Many other ideas will be considered throughout the company, especially those that emerge from the workforce.

The context of flexibility

The Dutton experience demonstrates an integrated and strategic approach to flexibility led by a chief executive with a clear vision of how that flexibility becomes a clear competitive advantage to the organisation.

The success of the global free enterprise system has led to a fundamental reappraisal of the implications for the labour force in all advanced countries. In the UK, the IPD Position Paper *People Make the Difference* has set out in detail the driving forces and the organisational responses, and how the system has affected the way people are organised and managed (see Table 1, page 10).

The change to a flexibly geared organisation is shown in greater relief in Table 2, page 11. Organisations that have to respond quicker to a notoriously fickle consumer will need to set up an organisational structure that allows speedy changes: one that is flatter and less hierarchical. To obtain a more responsive workforce, they need to be positioned closer to the customer, empowered to take the necessary actions to get the desired results, and trained in all the practical and people-based skills to assist achieving those ends. Flexibility is required both *vertically* and *horizontally*. In the vertical sense, employees carry out work which could be regarded as above their job, such as supervisory or managerial aspects, and work below their level, such as cleaning up or helping out in routine

Table I
COMPETITION – THE DRIVING FORCES AND CRITICAL SUCCESS FACTORS

The driving forces
- [ ] customers demanding products and services increasingly customised to their needs, with satisfaction standards increasingly established by global competition
- [ ] reductions in international trade barriers leading to new overseas competitors, particularly in Pacific rim countries, in mature production and service sectors
- [ ] technology which is changing rapidly and easily transferable
- [ ] public sector financial constraints, political pressures for higher value for money and privatisation or market testing.

How organisations are responding
- [ ] highly differentiated goods and services
- [ ] *flexibility from people and technology*
- [ ] customer-led organisations
- [ ] quicker response times, 'step' change and continuous improvements of products, processes and services
- [ ] investing in and developing the core competencies of people.

How this is affecting the way people are organised and managed
- [ ] decentralisation and development of decision-taking
- [ ] slimmer and flatter management structures
- [ ] *Development of a flexible workforce*
- [ ] total quality and lean organisation initiatives
- [ ] more project-based and cross-functional initiatives and teamworking
- [ ] empowered rather than command structures
- [ ] partnership approach to supplier links.

What this means for employees
- [ ] customer-orientation to meet the needs of both internal and external customers
- [ ] greater self-management and responsibility for individuals and teams
- [ ] contributing to the continuous improvement of processes, products and services
- [ ] commitment to personal training, development and *adaptability*.

Adapted from: IPD Position Paper *People Make The Difference*, 1994.

tasks. This is often referred to as 'going beyond contract' or 'doing whatever is needed to get the job done properly on time'. In the horizontal sense, employees' skills and knowledge are stretched to cover a variety of activities in their area. Examples are in areas like multi-skilling in manufacturing, such as at Vauxhall, where employees carry out a wide range of assembly and routine maintenance work on the line, or in insurance,

Table 2

FROM TRADITIONAL TO FLEXIBLY-GEARED ORGANISATION

From	Towards
limited competition, long runs	more intense competition, short runs
low risk-taking	high-risk innovation
centralised control	decentralised empowerment
product-driven systems	customer-driven systems
double staff just in case	deliver just in time with just right staff
employees as a factor of production	employees as a valuable resource
maximum task breakdown	wider task responsibility
fixed tasks	continuous improvement
narrow-focus skills for life	multiple broad-skilling for the present
work at the same level	work at any level
quality rework	right first time
problem-solving	problem prevention
fixed organisational resources	flexible internal/external resources
measuring output	measuring contribution
rewarding service and loyalty	rewarding achievement and focus
fixed hours of work	flexible time system

where employees in one department deal with new business, claims and settlements, rather than have the work split, Weber-style, into three separate operating departments.

In the enthusiastic analysis of flexibility in the early 1980s, it was the work by John Atkinson and his colleagues at the Institute of Manpower Studies that produced the seminal and much-quoted model depicting the divisions between 'core' and 'peripheral' workforces. Under this model (see Figure 1 overleaf), the *core* workers are full-time permanent career employees whose security is won at the cost of accepting 'functional' flexibility both in the short term (multi-skilling, multi-responsibilities) as well as in the longer term (career changes, lateral movements). Their terms and conditions reflect their importance with a raft of benefits and salary increases depending on their achievements and those of the team and the organisation.

The *first peripheral* group enjoy less job security and access to career opportunities, and their jobs are 'plug-in' ones, not skills specific to the firm. The organisation looks to the marketplace to fill these jobs, many of which are filled by women, and numerical flexibility is achieved by the normal wastage which tends to be fairly high.

Figure 1
CORE AND PERIPHERAL WORKFORCES

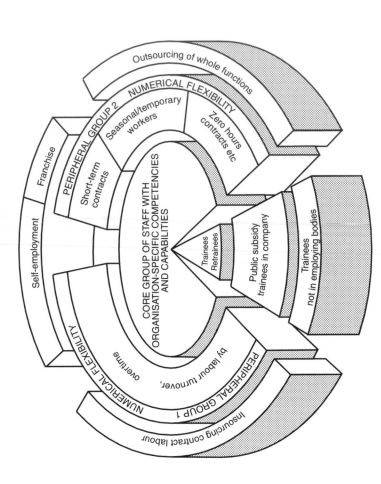

Outsourcing of whole functions

NUMERICAL FLEXIBILITY

PERIPHERAL GROUP 2

Seasonal/temporary workers

Zero hours contracts etc

Short-term contracts

Franchise

Self-employment

CORE GROUP OF STAFF WITH ORGANISATION-SPECIFIC COMPETENCIES AND CAPABILITIES

Trainees Retrainees

Public subsidy trainees in company

Trainees not in employing bodies

by labour turnover,

overtime

PERIPHERAL GROUP 1

NUMERICAL FLEXIBILITY

Insourcing contract labour

Source: Atkinson J. and Meager N. 'Is flexibility a flash in the pan?' *Personnel Management*, September 1986, pp. 26–9. Adapted with permission by Professor Ian Purcell

The *second peripheral* group is an extension of the first, with much part-time working, twilight shifts, zero-hour and short-term contracts which maximise flexibility. Such terms and conditions in general minimise organisational commitment to the employee, job security and career development.

External groups give additional support to numerical flexibility by filling positions that are very mundane, like office cleaning, or very specialised, including IT areas, on a contract or self-employed basis. Here there is also encouragement to greater functional flexibility as a result of the greater commitment of the self-employed to get the work done profitably within the terms of the contract. Sometimes they are insourced by bringing in short-term labour either directly or through agencies. Increasingly, whole departments are being outsourced completely.

Alongside this is the extended use of trainees who bring with them some form of public subsidy through the latest re-badging of government schemes (Jobstart, YTS, etc) to help young people, females re-entering the labour force after bringing up families, and the unemployed, to get back to work.

Despite the popularity of this model, it does not fit every situation in practice. Part-timers, for example, may be at the heart of a company's operations. This is certainly true at McDonald's and at many call centres and, increasingly, in management job-shares. A project manager on a short-term contract for implementing a new IT system may well be one of the most important employees working in the organisation for that period.

Distinguishing the core of the business from the periphery is becoming an escalating philosophical argument. British Airways, for example, were quite prepared to outsource both their cabin crew operations and their aircraft maintenance squads, which led to the damaging strike in the summer of 1997. 'If it moves, we will outsource it', were the reported comments of one senior executive. Local authorities continue to expand the market-testing process, identifying operations, such as whole personnel departments, which were previously seen as rooted in the core.

Flexibility – myth or reality?

There have been a number of surveys in the last few years

that throw light on the reality of the movement towards flexible working. All point to a patchy but consistent growth in the use of flexible practices, although few organisations appear to be moving in this direction for strategic reasons.

A report by the Policy Studies Institute (Casey *et al*, 1997) drew evidence from the Labour Force Survey (LFS) and a number of case-studies and came to the conclusion that there had been a substantial increase in the use of flexible working time over the previous decade, and that more than half of all employees now worked variable hours every week. There had also been a proliferation in the number of people working part-time or on a temporary basis, and a growth – though at a slower rate – in the use of subcontractors. The overall expansion had taken place chiefly in larger establishments.

Flexibility in Practice, a report commissioned by the Equal Opportunities Commission (Neathey and Hurstfield, 1995), found that employers were making increasing demands on all employees to become more flexible, both in working flexible hours and in functional flexibility, although the greatest emphasis was on flexibility in part-time working.

In the Department of Employment Research publication *Labour Market Flexibility* (Beatson, 1995), strong evidence was adduced of manufacturing employers' taking steps to improve flexibility: by 1990, managers in more than two thirds of workplaces felt there were no constraints on their ability to organise work as they saw fit.

Our own survey of 90 organisations in Hertfordshire, Bedfordshire and Buckinghamshire found that the majority of employers were increasing the adoption of flexible working practices and expected to move further in that direction in the near future.

There are, however, mixed signals about the widespread nature of the totality and integration of flexible practices. Hunter and MacInnes (1991) found little evidence of a comprehensive and systematic drive towards the 'flexible firm' in the companies they analysed. Most of their companies made considerable use of various forms of flexible working, but few embraced the ideas of Handy and other gurus who, according to Wilsher (1996),

> visualised a post-modern business structure consisting of little
> more than a small elite core of professional managers, presid-

ing over an essentially ad-hoc temporary workforce and a string of outsourcing subcontractors.

On the other hand, Proctor *et al* (1994) argue that the lack of devised and written strategy, based on conscious and deliberate decisions at the highest level, on flexible working changes does not necessarily mean that strategic change (in its widest sense) does not exist. Strategy in this area should be regarded much more as a continuing pattern of change where incremental movements in various flexible areas add up to a much wider driving force.

If the leaders of industry and commerce are to be believed, increasing flexibility is becoming a key factor in reducing operating costs in response to competitive pressures. A report by the Institute of Management and Manpower plc (1995), based on a survey of 146 senior directors, found that all forms of alternative work patterns were due to increase: 80 per cent of respondents predicted an increase in flexible working, and 70 per cent an increase specifically in contracting out.

A further report was commissioned by the Department for Education and Employment from the Centre for Research in Employment and Technology in Europe (Rajan *et al*, 1997) which confirmed that the trend towards greater flexibility is likely to continue for the rest of the decade. Further findings included the widening wage differentials underpinned by performance-related pay, the role played by flexibility in the early fall in unemployment in the current recovery arising from the ability of organisations in the UK to take on and lay off staff comparatively easily, and the rising skills gaps. This always features as recovery gathers pace, but the special needs brought by the emphasis on flexibility, especially in the IT area, have accentuated the gaps. So great is the expected gap that the Confederation of British Industry commissioned a report into flexible labour markets (CBI, 1996) pointing out the vital importance of the issue of who pays for the training of atypical workers.

So the evidence is strong all round that the move to greater flexibility is gathering pace, and that organisations see it as a means of achieving competitive advantage. Employees are not always fully co-operative in these ventures. As indicated in the

Prologue, unions may find it difficult to budge from their entrenched positions regarding the nature of jobs, hours of work and where the work should take place. A crisis may persuade them to change or the carrots of better pay and terms and conditions may do so. The 1998 Vauxhall Agreement is an example of the threat of closure bringing agreement on a range of flexibility elements. Often, the ability and willingness of employers to move operations geographically, sometimes overseas, convinces employees that they have little choice and must simply obtain the best deal they can get.

References

BEATSON M. *Labour Market Flexibility*. London, Employment Department, 1995.

CASEY B., METCALF H. and MILLWARD N. *Employers' Use of Flexible Labour*. London, Policy Studies Institute, 1997.

CHOAT I. 'Heinz secures flexibility', *Personnel Today*. 18 September 1997, p. 9.

CONFEDERATION OF BRITISH INDUSTRY. *Flexible Labour Markets*. London, CBI, 1996.

HUNTER L. and MACINNIS S. 'Employers and labour flexibility: the evidence from case studies.' *Employment Gazette*. June 1991, pp. 307–15.

Institute of Management. *Survey of Long-term Employment Strategies*. London, IOM, 1995.

LEWIS K. and LYTTON S. *How to Transform Your Company and Enjoy It*. Chalford, Management Books 2000, 1995.

NEATHEY F. and HURSTFIELD J. *Flexibility in Practice*. London, Equal Opportunities Commission, 1995.

PICKARD J. 'Tour de force', *People Management*. 17 April 1997, pp. 34–35.

PROCTOR S., ROWLINSON M., McARDLE L., HASSARD J. and FORRESTER P. 'Flexibility, politics and strategy: in Defense of the Model of the flexible firm'. *Work, Employment and Society*. Vol. 8, No. 2, 1994, pp. 221–242.

RAJAN A., VAN EUPEN P. and JASPERS A. 'Britain's Flexible Labour Market: what next?' *Labour Market Trends*. May 1997, pp. 171–172.

WILSHER P. 'Flexible Workers or Spare Bodies?' *Human Resources*. Jul/Aug 1996, pp. 32–33.

2 ANNUAL HOURS

Introduction

A few years ago, Frigoscandia, based in Norfolk, was faced by a growing problem – quite literally: 700 employees were finding it increasingly difficult to process, freeze and pack up to 75,000 tons of fresh vegetables and chips within the limited harvest period and yet provide an efficient storage and distribution service to large supermarkets and other customers for the remainder of the year.

The answer was not simply to take on large numbers of temporary employees in the summer months. Although flexible, this labour needed training and considerable supervision. It was not always possible to pinpoint precisely the harvest dates or the size of the harvest from one year to another. A sizeable core of skilled employees needed to be retained throughout the year to process imported rice and vegetables and to service customers' requirements. The crux was that the hours in the summer would always be considerably in excess of those in the remaining months. The problem was that employees were on a contract of 37.5 hours per week, summer and winter. They were willing to work extra hours, which averaged as much as 62 in some years, with individual weeks of 84 hours not uncommon, but these hours would be on overtime at premium rates. Come October, there was not the work to keep all the workforce fully occupied for 37.5 hours. Then they heard about annual hours.

Within three months, their methods of operation had altered fundamentally. Labour costs had reduced and scheduling was operated far more efficiently. More surprisingly, employees were more committed and morale was far higher. Shareholders received higher profits and customers a more professional and reliable service. It was clear that there was something rather unusual about a system that appeared to benefit all stakeholders in the business.

Background

The Scandinavians are credited with the first formal large-scale introduction of an annual hours scheme in 1977 when the Swedish paper board industry produced an innovative system to cover 24-hour seven-day-a-week working at their paper mills. The chemicals industry and other continuous-process industries moved tentatively into this unknown territory, often through extensive national union negotiations.

Schemes began to appear in the UK in the early 1980s but were at first slow to develop. An ACAS survey in 1988 found that only 3 per cent of employees were working under a formal scheme, but this had risen to 9 per cent (2 million employees) by the time of the 1993 Labour Force Survey which included most teaching staff. Evidence from more recent surveys has indicated that this level is being exceeded as schemes become more popular and versatile.

The context for annual hours

Schemes have been traditionally associated with a manufacturing context. The majority of schemes still take place either where seasonal operations occur, such as in cheese processing (Express Foods) or television manufacturing (Matsushita), or where production is required around the clock, seven days a week (Continental Can). In these situations detailed rostering is required, usually some weeks or months ahead, to ensure that labour is evenly distributed to meet the foreseen requirements. A key feature is to reduce or totally eliminate the level of overtime.

It is now clear, however, that annual hours schemes are beginning to spread to more unusual domains, particularly in the service sector. Manchester Airport's scheme began in 1992 and covers around 200 engineering supervisors, technicians and operatives. Yorkshire TV and ITN have both operated schemes since the late 1980s, covering a combined total of 1,000 employees. Northallerton National Health Trust has extended a scheme to the nursing force, and a number of local authorities, including Wrekin and Strathkelvin District Councils, have responded to the efficiency needs of compulsory competitive tendering by introducing schemes in seasonal services such as leisure centres and grounds maintenance. A number of schemes have started in the transport sector. The European Passenger Service started the Channel Tunnel operation with annual hours contracts for its operating staff. London, Tilbury and Southend Rail, one of the newly privatised train-operating companies, operates a scheme of annual hours together with performance-related pay and flexible benefits.

As detailed in Chapter 1, such schemes are rarely introduced as a 'stand-alone' initiative. In the majority of cases it is part of a wider integrative process of change, incorporating a raft of HRM initiatives. For example, at Lever Brothers, the scheme formed part of the 1992 'Horizon 2000' agreement which harmonised terms and conditions of employment and included the implementation of an integrated pay and grading system and performance-related pay. Similarly, at Bristol and West Building Society it was included within the 1991 package called 'Towards 2000' aimed at harmonising conditions for employees working in three different sectors of the organisation – estate agent, building society and financial adviser. Welsh Water introduced the 1991 'Partnership Agreement' which, alongside annual hours, gave single-status single-table negotiating and a unified pay structure.

How a scheme works

The essential feature of a scheme is, as the name suggests, the replacement of a weekly-hours contract with one that covers the whole year. Instead of a 38-hour week, an employee may, for example, be on a contract of 1,976 hours for the year. The pay system is also changed so that the employee receives a fixed monthly payment, no matter how many shifts are worked during that month. How much the pay system changes is discussed later. That is the easy part.

Alongside this change is an evaluation of the basic labour requirement for all the operations involved. This does not

Table 3
CALCULATING ANNUAL HOURS

Annual hours total		1,976
Rostered hours 150 shifts at 10 hours	1,500	
Holidays, including public holidays	228	1,728
Reserve hours		248
Training hours	60	
Hours on call	188	248

equate with the existing manning levels. It is a careful analysis of the labour required *if the operation runs completely smoothly*: no absenteeism, no machine breakdowns, no supply or quality problems, no industrial relations problems, no accidents, and no acts of God. In the majority of cases, this evaluation takes place with the help of consultants, although in establishments where there is a high level of trust, the operational managers will carry out the analysis themselves. It is such a crucial activity and so central to the success of the entire scheme that the estimates have to be right. The usual British system of sorting out problems through overtime is not a solution under annual hours because the aim is to eliminate all overtime. Any absenteeism or disruption of any sort which affects the work scheduling has to be remedied by the system of reserve hours.

The annual hours will then be divided into sections (see example in Table 3).

Rostered hours

If the labour requirements for the year are reasonably foreseeable, as they might be on an oil rig or in the chemical industry on long-term supplier contracts, then an employee's hours will be rostered for the year. In this example, the 150 shifts could be worked on the basis of working alternate weeks, with six shifts on one week and none the next. A more complex shift pattern, spreading the hours over days and nights, is shown in Table 4.

A key feature is that the amount of leisure time is extended by concertinaing the working time into a shorter period.

If the labour requirements are less predictable, as in seasonal operations, they may be allocated on the basis of a

Table 4

EXAMPLE OF FIVE-CREW THREE-SHIFT SYSTEM UNDER ANNUAL HOURS

Week of cycle	1	2	3	4	5
	m t w t f s s	m t w t f s s	m t w t f s s	m t w t f s s	m t w t f s s
Crew					
A	m a a – – n n	n m m a a – –	– – – – – – –	– n n m m a a	a – – n n m m
B	n m m a a – –	– – – – – – –	– n n m m a a	a – – n n m m	m a a – – n n
C	– – – – – – –	– n n m m a a	a – – n n m m	m a a – – n n	n m m a a – –
D	– n n m m a a	a – – n n m m	m a a – – n n	n m m a a – –	– – – – – – –
E	a – – n n m m	m a a – – n n	n m m a a – –	– – – – – – –	– n n m m a –

m = morning   a = afternoons   n = nights

general indication – such as 42 hours in summer and 30 hours in winter, and then scheduled one or two months ahead in detail as the business requirements are clarified.

Holidays

These are fixed under the normal rules that apply in the establishments, although we will see later that more flexibility is allowed to change them by mutual agreement.

Reserve hours

It is these hours that define the scheme. These hours are to be used when necessary for a number of reasons. Firstly, they can be used for training. We have seen that teamworking and multi-skilling are often an integral part of the changes implemented simultaneously with annual hours, so some of the reserve hours are used to train operatives in alternative tasks on their shift which qualify them to become more flexible. There may be training in new systems introduced to aid efficiency and improve quality. Time may be spent in gaining a better understanding of associated functions, such as dealing with suppliers or the distribution system. All this training is to enable an employee to respond quicker and more co-operatively to any problems that arise.

Secondly, they can be used to cover for absenteeism or for any difficulty that confronts a shift. Employees will be rostered to be on call in case they are required. In these circumstances they will have to be available to be at the work site within an hour or so. They do not get paid anything extra for attending work on these occasions because it is all included in the monthly wage.

If the scheme works well, a situation will emerge where those reserve hours are not all used. The number of times employees need to be called in drops as absenteeism, machine breakdowns and materials supply problems fall. That is the main objective of the scheme and one that defines the most successful schemes.

Inducements to employees

Employees are usually sceptical when new working practices are proposed. For those who work considerable overtime, annual hours is bad news. When complex rosters with 24-hour working are announced, it presents problems for employees with a regular weekly social commitment. For supervisors and managers who rule through the carrot of overtime, there has to be a fundamental change in their outlook on good management practice.

For many employees, however, there are some immediate benefits. They get a guaranteed income each month which assists in obtaining mortgages and other credit. Their rosters are set out in advance, and they know when they are on call and when they are completely at leisure. They would welcome the change to the scheme without any further inducement.

Both these groups tend to be minorities, though, and it is the bulk of employees in the middle who work some overtime and have some commitments that has to be convinced. There is also a third party to consider in some cases – namely, the trade union. Overtime has always been a thorn in the side of trade unions. Although many of their members enjoy the opportunity to work overtime and press for union help in negotiating improved overtime conditions, unions see overtime as a barrier to employment. They can see a group of their members out of work and trying to exist on social security at the same time as they see other members working excessive hours and earning high wages. Trade unions have given full support to European legislation that limits hours, such as the limits to drivers' hours in the 1970s and the more recent Working Time Directive.

The introduction of annual hours therefore presents no problems of principle for trade unions. Quite the contrary: it is welcomed with considerable enthusiasm as reflecting good union practice. All that is left to negotiate are the terms and conditions. Because these are specific to the work site, to the rostering system and to the methods of working, the union is not often faced with problems over national or local practices or parity with other local firms. The dangers associated with trendsetting agreements is therefore much reduced. Unions and management, with only terms and conditions to agree, rarely have too much trouble in coming to an amicable agreement.

The agreements usually have at least two parts. There is some *reduction in the weekly hours* with no loss of earnings. It may be quite small – from 38 to 37.5 hours – or it may be bolder, stretching the reduction over three years from 38 to as low as 36. When Peugeot introduced their scheme in 1997, they reduced the working year by 20 hours and also added an additional day of holiday. This is the principal bargaining point for the trade union. Since the late 1980s, employers have fought very hard against any reduction in the working week because one hour off the week is equivalent to a pay increase of almost 3 per cent. At a time of low inflation, this is a huge concession. They have also been aware that there is no great support for reducing hours as such from the employees unless it gives them the chance to work more hours at overtime rates. Introducing annual hours, however, presents an opportunity to meet union aspirations and to get valuable proven concessions in return. Taking an hour off the week to 37 hours would mean a revision in the original calculation to that shown in Table 5.

The rostered hours and holidays do not change: it is simply the number of reserve hours that reduces. Because the aim is to try to avoid working reserve hours in any case, that may not be crucial to the organisation. In fact, it may be a concession that costs nothing.

Table 5

ANNUAL HOURS SYSTEM WITH A REDUCTION OF ONE HOUR A WEEK

Annual hours total		1,924
Rostered hours 150 shifts at 10 hours	1,500	
Holidays, including public holidays	228	1,728
Reserve hours		196

The second element may be *a one-off inducement to accept the scheme*. This may be an across-the-board payment of, say, £250, or it may be related to the amount of actual overtime earnings by individual employees over the previous period, say, two years. How it is paid depends a great deal on the number of high overtime earners, their importance to the organisation and their influence amongst their peers. If they are few in number and have little influence, the payment is likely to be across the board to generate general agreement to the scheme. If they are influential or a sizeable proportion of employees, they are likely to get a more sympathetic ear and the payments may be more variable.

There may be other items in the agreement. The way holidays are rostered and how they can be traded may become much more flexible. Decisions on leave for dental appointments, seeing solicitors, etc may be delegated to local managers rather than be a detailed centrally-determined policy. There may also be an offer of voluntary redundancy. Agreements often include a time-related guarantee of no compulsory redundancies through implementing the scheme.

Another option is to make further concessions dependent upon the success of the scheme, leaving a year or so for it to bed in and prove its cost-effectiveness.

Key benefits of the scheme
Saving in labour costs

Overtime operation is extremely costly. For ITN, the overtime bill prior to annual hours was a crippling 21 per cent of staff costs – and this is not unusual. But there is a more subtle hidden cost. For the average operator the temptation of overtime is difficult to resist. Overtime is usually paid at time-and-a-half (double time on Sundays) so employees can add a sizeable chunk to their wages at the expense of a few hours' extra work.

Studies have found that overtime is habit-forming: the employees' expenditure patterns can start to match the expectations that overtime will be regular. A reasonably high level of sickness and absenteeism on the part of their colleagues will give regular attenders overtime opportunities.

They will be sympathetic to the difficulties of their absent colleagues. That machines break down or that critical supplies run out is unfortunate for the company schedules but lucky for the operators. It is not far to the next step, which is for the operators to assist in creating the overtime: going just a little bit slower, ensuring more rejections of poor-quality work, for example. Add on a little bit of absenteeism by themselves, and this will provide overtime for their workmates as a quid pro quo.

Furthermore, it is not unusual for the traditional supervisors to be paid overtime and to covertly support this general approach, thereby guaranteeing overtime payments for themselves. All this operates against the interest of the employer and increases organisational costs.

Annual hours puts a stop to all this. The elimination of overtime costs creates a substantial saving and more than makes up for the increase in basic pay and any other inducements offered to gain acceptance to the scheme. Another saving is in the reduction in the workforce which can be associated with the scheme. The average overall labour cost saving under annual hours is estimated at around half the overtime costs. In the case of ITN, this was as high as 10 per cent of overall labour costs.[1]

Improving commitment

Because overtime is eliminated completely, it does not take long for employees to realise that their way to gain under the scheme is to protect their reserve hours. If not called in for those 196 reserve hours in Table 5 (page 23), they will have gained the equivalent of an extra five weeks' holiday or more. To be certain that they are not called in, they need to make sure that they are not required in the workplace. They need the elimination of absenteeism and sickness, of machine breakdowns and poor materials supply. They need production schedules to be met on time. To achieve these goals, they need to work closely with their team-mates to ensure that any problems on a shift are overcome. Self-development by gaining new skills is vital so that they can step into the place of an absent colleague rather than calling in a replacement.

This change of attitude means that the objectives of the

employers and the employees are aligned. They both want high production levels, good-quality, on-time delivery. This is clearly demonstrated in the Siemens GEC scheme (see the case-study on page 30).

Reducing absenteeism

Absenteeism diminishes for two reasons. Firstly, the increased sense of commitment leads to employees taking time off only when they are truly ill. Secondly, there is peer pressure to conform to high levels of attendance. When an employee is absent, it may be necessary for a colleague to be called in under the reserve hours scheme and the employee will not be the most popular person in this circumstance! There have been a number of examples of a team's demanding action from management against a colleague with a poor attendance record.

Improved health and safety

It cannot be good for the long-term health of employees to work 55 or 60 hours a week, nor can it lead to efficient working. There is also an increased emphasis on employees taking regular leisure and relaxation time. Moreover, there is anecdotal evidence that the number of accidents is reduced under annual hours. This may be simply because employees have their eye on the ball and because they know that an accident in the workplace can lead to other employees being called in to help solve the inevitable production problems that accidents bring.

Improved teamworking and co-operation

Associated with increased employee commitment, there is evidence that employees work together better as a team and use their empowerment effectively. This may show itself in covering for an absent colleague, in arranging swaps on rotas or on holidays, or in implementing more ideas which improve the work systems. This has been a key feature of the Queen's Hospital scheme (see the case-study on page 32). Teams are often given responsibility for organising their own breaks, for liaising on materials supply with purchasing departments, and for carrying out basic maintenance on

their machinery rather than waiting for a specialist maintenance mechanic.

Difficulties encountered

There are always teething troubles whenever new schemes
have been introduced, and annual hours is no exception. The
working hours and rotas can be complex and may need fine-
tuning. For employees with children, the call-outs to use their
reserve hours can create problems for child care, which may be
awkward or even impossible to arrange at short notice. This
has been a particular problem at ITN, and special rostering and
payment arrangements have been made in these cases.

There can be minor difficulties associated with employees
who start and leave during the course of an annual hours year,
especially one which operates seasonally. The issue of paying
back hours in these cases is a thorny one. The same applies in
the case of an employee who takes maternity leave during a
slack period and comes back to work more hours for the rest
of the year. Introducing changes in shift patterns part-way
through a year can also present difficulties.

Having said this, there are surprisingly few reported major
problems with the scheme's operation. Moreover, very few
schemes are started and then abandoned; when this happens
it is usually due to a shift in the marketplace.

Variations in schemes

Very few schemes are identical. New variations appear on a
regular basis in two areas.

Choice of contract hours

In a number of schemes, employees can choose their total
annual hours and be paid accordingly. For example, installation engineers at Siemens GEC may choose between four
levels of hours, ranging from 2,520 down to the standard
number of hours at 1,920. There is even a part-time option
at 800 hours. This has allowed high-performing, reliable
engineers to continue to have the opportunity of higher
earnings.

Customer advisers at Alliance and Leicester have a choice of 787 or 936 hours per year as part-time employees, with working patterns agreed one month in advance. Saturdays and Sundays can be included in the work patterns.

There are other examples of employees who have a choice of hours in the service sector. ITN offers three levels above and below the standard hours, and Bristol and West offer four part-time options.

Quarterly reserve hours

Rather than having a year-long bank of reserve hours, some companies have shorter periods. For example, Elida Gibbs' aerosol factory divides the year into four quarters, and any reserve hours unused at the end of the quarter are written off. A similar arrangement operates at Lever Brothers over a four-month period.

Success rate

The IPM survey of annual hours in 1993 reported that nearly all the organisations involved were extremely satisfied with the introduction of their schemes and had no wish to return to their previous systems of working. As part of an overall package of employment changes, it had proved to be a valuable vehicle for changing attitudes and methods of work, and one that continued to work over the years.

However, not all schemes work smoothly from the start. The first annualised hours scheme for train drivers – introduced at LTS Rail in 1996 – produced an increase in productivity of 30 per cent in its first year, but there has been some reported union opposition from ASLEF to plans on the part of the company to extend drivers' hours. ASLEF has campaigned to restrict drivers' hours to a maximum of 37 a week, but the company and many of the drivers have indicated that they wish more extensive hours to be incorporated for those drivers that want to work longer hours (*Personnel Today*, 1997).

Successful introduction: ten key points

☐ Do not attempt to introduce a scheme unless your business has sufficient signs of labour utilisation slackness, such as periods of laying-off and permanent overtime, which indicate that a considerable saving can be made.

☐ Work with line managers to agree the base line of working, especially the absolute minimum number of employees required to run a shift or service operation efficiently without sickness or any other disrupting factors.

☐ Do not allow line managers to include any additional factors when calculating base manning, no matter how hard they argue their necessity.

☐ Involve members of the work teams in the planning for the scheme. They are far more likely to promote a scheme which they have helped plan.

☐ Consider who are the winners and losers in the scheme, and ensure that there is some appropriate compensation for losers who may be influential in obtaining the scheme's acceptance.

☐ Ensure that you include in the calculations opportunities for employees to benefit by working more 'smartly' and thereby working fewer hours. Make sure that there are a number of bank hours that will not be used if the operations run smoothly.

☐ Be prepared for redundancies, which are usually associated with the introduction of the scheme: have a voluntary scheme or robust criteria for selection prepared in case voluntary redundancies do not produce sufficient numbers.

☐ Carefully evaluate the scheme each month to ensure it is working smoothly.

☐ Get feedback from employees on a regular basis and be prepared to change the scheme, especially where ideas arise from the employees themselves.

☐ Communicate the successes of the scheme to the employees on a regular basis.

ANNUAL HOURS AT SIEMENS GEC

The need for change

Siemens GEC is the leading independent supplier of business equipment in the UK, manufacturing, selling, installing and maintaining telecommunications equipment. A combination of increased market competition, falling prices and increased service demands from potential customers brought a reappraisal in the early 1990s of installation working methods.

Surveys had shown that customers specifically wanted telecom installations to take place outside working hours, minimising disruption to their businesses, rather than having to fit in with the installation department's conventional 9–5 Monday-to-Friday schedules. The company could not afford excessive overtime payments so a new system of operation was required.

Having ruled out a complex shift system covering weekends together with a proposal to enlist part-time employees for out-of-schedule installations, a project group of 12 installation engineers, chosen from the 70-strong team for their innovative outlook and ability to cascade the scheme to their colleagues, worked with Graham Bayliss, national manager, to come up with a working scheme of annualised hours.

'It was not intended to be seen as an imposed change handed down from on high by management, consultants and the HR department,' explained Graham. 'It was a genuine attempt to get the engineers to help create a scheme that was viable, acceptable and disaster-proof.'

The outline scheme that emerged was accepted by management and the engineers' union MSF, who were in agreement with the fundamental objective of creating a good salary without excessively long hours. The scheme was introduced in 1993.

How the scheme works

Engineers had seven choices of annual hours they could work – from 1,800 to 2,520 – which reflected the original basic hours (1,800) up to 15 hours of overtime (2,520). That maximum was still well below the regular excessive overtime worked by some engineers. Having chosen the hours that suited his or her particular requirement, each engineer was guaranteed the work level for the year and received the same pay each month. The team (usually two engineers) would then be allocated work that had a fixed number of hours calculated at the contract price. It was then up to the teams to negotiate installation arrangements with the customer and, in conjunction with their controllers, to ensure that the materials and equipment were in place at the right time. They then proceeded to carry out the work, and they would be credited with the allocated hours no matter how long the job took – as long, of course, as it was completed to the customer's satisfaction.

Winners in the new scheme

For the engineers, the scheme has meant a higher guaranteed monthly salary that replaces a variable overtime element which was unpensionable. They are also empowered to plan their own working time, which has often given them more leisure opportunities – how much has depended on their own levels of productivity and quality. They certainly have fewer excuses for non-completion on time because they are closely involved in ordering materials and equipment.

For the organisation, labour costs are far more predictable and there are very few cost overruns. Nor does every hour an engineer works have to be logged. Customer requirements are met more closely, and first-time quality measures have improved sharply. Saturday and Sunday are regarded as normal working days. Engineers now see that their interests lie in planning the work and progressing it smoothly and efficiently, which coincides precisely with the company's interests. Previously, overruns and overtime may on occasions have suited the engineer's pockets but it certainly did not suit the company's profit statement.

Teething problems have inevitably arisen. It has been necessary, for example, to sort out a fair and efficient system of dealing with installation problems that are not the fault of the engineers which penalises neither side. Allowances are given only in exceptional situations because a certain number of contingent hours are built into the price. So far, not many serious arguments have occurred here. A more serious problem emerged at an early stage when it became evident as engineers chose their hours that a small degree of de-manning was required. This was overcome through transfers and a few redundancies – but it was not the best start they had envisaged.

By 1997, the scheme had proved very successful. Sickness had dropped by two-thirds, productive time had increased by 14 per cent, and staff turnover had been reduced to less than 3 per cent. The best improvement has been in the company's measure of on-time performance, which has jumped above 90 per cent and is still rising. So successful has it been that it has now been adopted as best practice for the Siemans GEC Communications Systems business and is being introduced throughout their UK operations.

This case has been extracted from Stredwick, J. 'Time on the line', *Flexible Working*, September 1997, pp. 23–24.

ANNUAL HOURS AT 'QUEEN'S HOSPITAL'

Opened in the early 1990s, 'Queen's Hospital' is a private hospital for acute patients built in the grounds of a large NHS hospital. It has 33 beds and 140 permanent staff. Two multi-speciality wards treat both day-case and longer-stay patients, and a consulting room suite operates six days a week from 8 am to 9 pm.

For the first few years of operation, nursing staff worked an informal flexible rostering system. The rosters were issued two to four weeks ahead, and requests for changes in the rosters for personal or domestic reasons were dealt with sympathetically by department heads. In those circumstances, when roster swaps could not be arranged 'bank' nurses were brought in.

In 1996, a further development took place. 'Queen's Hospital' is part of a larger health-care group and a system of annual hours had been gradually pioneered at a number of units within the group, with considerable success. After full consultation with the staff, the system was introduced for those staff that wished to transfer onto the new arrangement immediately and for all new recruits.

How it works

Staff are contracted onto full-time hours at 1,950 per annum or at various levels of part-time hours – 936 is a popular level. They are issued with a provisional rota for each month and each employee indicates any areas of difficulty or any time when he or she would be available and willing to work extra. The department head then looks at revisions that may be necessary, confirms swaps that can be easily made, and allocates efficient extra manning based on indicated willingness to work. During any month, the workload may suddenly increase (if, say, bad weather produces more orthopaedic work) and staff who had indicated availability may be asked to work. Sometimes the workload may drop owing to, say, cancelled operations, and when this happens the staff on the shift are asked if they would prefer not to work that day.

The year runs from January to December, and a running total of the hours worked is kept for each employee: nobody exceeds their contracted annual hours' total. Employees may choose to make themselves available for extra work from January to March and then work fewer hours in the summer months or take an extra week of holiday. It may happen in the course of the year that one or two employees regularly work for more than their provisional shift hours. If it looks as though they may be heading towards exceeding the annual hours total, they may be paid overtime for those excess hours instead, and the number of hours may be deducted from the annual hours. (This arrangement is not common, however.)

Anne Jones has been nursing director at 'Queen's Hospital' since it opened and has seen the scheme develop. 'The key to the scheme is the recognition that Queen's Hospital is everybody's hospital. Everybody needs to work with and for each other to make sure that it is successful. Without that genuine belief, the flexibility would become one-sided. Either the hospital would make excessive demands on the staff to work shifts and rotas against their will, or the staff would exploit the system just for their own benefit. Neither of these is happening.'

One of the other key points is the need to have a multi-skilled nursing force, well able to perform extended roles in, say, venepuncture or ECG recordings, because it is essential that the skills mix on the shifts is correct. Without these skills – and 'Queen's Hospital' strongly supports professional development for each employee – the flexibility would be more limited in practice.

Achievements of the scheme

For 'Queen's Hospital', the staffing levels are always on-line to meet the needs of the hospital's workload. In the case of traditional shift patterns, if the workload is reduced for any reason, the nursing staff on that shift are under-utilised and resources are wasted: the over-manning involved can be very costly. When a situation of reduced workload occurs under annual hours, the roster is reduced accordingly. The staff then work shifts when they are fully needed.

From the employees' viewpoint, it gives them a degree of flexibility to fit their shifts to their domestic and private commitments within an environment that is consciously aimed at accommodating their needs.

Finally, Anne feels that 'It helps being quite a small unit so that everybody knows each other. Often they will help out with each other's child-care needs, for example. Certainly they can see that the scheme is operated fairly for all concerned, which can be difficult in much larger NHS hospitals where rumours can circulate about unfair practices. The department heads, who also work under the scheme, find it successful and it presents them with few problems. Certainly, the principles of the scheme can easily be transferred to any NHS setting as long as the will to make it work is there.'

The name 'Queen's Hospital' has been used in this case-study for reasons of confidentiality. It is not its real name.

Postscript

For Frigoscandia the scheme has been a considerable success since its introduction in 1989. It has not remained unchanged, however, and they have not been wholly successful in eliminating all overtime. The culprits here are the major supermarkets. Frigoscandia can deal with the vagaries of harvesting and storage through their flexible rostering system, which is accepted and understood by the employees. What has proved more difficult to deal with are the ever-tightening demands of supermarkets for supply and delivery of their frozen products. What used to be a two-day order has now become a 10-hour order as the supplies kept in the supermarkets have been cut to the bone. Come a couple of hot days and the customer will within hours require large quantities of specified ice-cream, and other frozen goods pallets which are sure to be at the most awkward part of the massive storage depot. The reserve hours system finds difficulty coping with this, and a small amount of overtime is creeping back. It should be possible to give some forecast of the supermarkets' demands and to adjust the storage and labour requirements accordingly. Frigoscandia are working on it.

References and further reading

ABBS C. and CHARLTON D. 'The rewards of annual hours', *Management Services*, November 1991, pp. 16–20.
CARRINGTON L. 'Counting the years', *Personnel Today*, 25 June 1991, pp. 40–41.

Foster A. 'Annual hours', *Human Resources*, Jan/Feb 1995, p. 13.

Fowler A. 'How to operate an annual hours contract', *Personnel Management*, April 1994, pp. 26–27.

Hutchinson S. *Annual Hours Working in the UK*. London, IPD, 1993.

Hutchinson S. 'The changing face of annual labour', *Personnel Management*, April 1993, pp. 42–47.

IDS Study 544. *Annual Hours*. London, December 1993.

Personnel Today. 'Train driver hours plan hits buffers', 31 July 1997, p. 1.

Pickard J. 'Annual Hours: a year of living dangerously', *Personnel Management*, August 1991, pp. 39–43.

More information can be obtained from Philip Lynch Associates, Eagle Star House, 69 The Mount, York, North Yorkshire, YO2 2AX.

End note

1 ICI have reported a saving of £2 million a year since absence has been reduced from 7 per cent to 4 per cent.

3 LONGER HOURS, SHORTER HOURS: INNOVATIVE FORMS OF PART-TIME WORKING

Introduction

In the previous chapter, the necessity for competitive organisations to meet customers' key requirements on availability was stressed. We see examples of this around us constantly. Many garages are now open 24 hours a day, seven days a week; shops compete with the large retail chains to open later each day; the battle over Sunday trading was won in 1995 by the Retail Consortium, one of the most influential of pressure groups, and trading on that day has now grown to equal the trading of a normal midweek day. Even manufacturers and wholesalers must be willing and able to service urgent materials and product needs outside of normal hours – which explains why the M25 on a weekend is burdened with many more lorries than 10 years ago. When the clearing banks stopped opening on Saturday in the 1970s, they little suspected that what many regarded as a cosy cartel would be swept away in the mid-1980s by the de-regulation revolution which allowed building societies to compete and which brought back longer opening hours with a vengeance.

The vast increase in telephone services has led to greater opportunities to link up with customers. Barclaycard offers a round-the-clock service with information, not just to deal with emergencies caused by lost cards. Each time there is a privatisation share offer or a mutual insurance or building society 'goes public', customers are offered a full extended-hours telephone service to answer enquiries. Call centres –

dealt with in Chapter 8 – are a permanent extension of this phenomenon, allowing customers to choose when they want service.

Increasingly, and often irritatingly, we are offered services out of hours. Double-glazing canvassers call from their office with 'special offers' attempting to fix appointments for their sales representative. Itinerant freezer vans with irresistible luxury items ply suburban roads, calling at the key selling hour (between 6 pm and 7 pm).

Strategies for staffing these longer hours have been various. In Chapter 2 we saw the value of annual hours in this context. Other strategies include overtime and shiftworking, which are dealt with in Chapter 4. The key strategy, however, is the effective and innovative use of *part-time working*, which is the subject of this chapter. This includes job sharing and zero-hours schemes.

The origins and development of part-time working

The hotel and catering industries were the first to identify the problem when post-Second-World-War full employment became an established fact. As the demand for eating out grew, the industry was faced by a crisis: it was not possible to recruit full-time staff for their generally low-paid jobs, in particular because the peaks were in the evening, at weekends and during holiday seasons. The solution – part-time working – rapidly spread to retailing and, rather more gradually, into all forms of service industries. By 1986, 90 per cent of all part-time employees were to be found in the service sector, and part-timers made up over 60 per cent of hotel and catering staff and over 45 per cent of retailing staff. Because service industries have been the growth industries (unlike manufacturing where part-time working has been far less prevalent), the overall increase in part-time working has been extensive, as shown in Table 6.

For women the rise was substantial in the 1960s and 1970s, as the growing respectability of the married woman's part-time job became established. The proportion had steadied at around the mid-40 per cent mark by the 1990s. This may be due to other cultural developments, including the

Table 6
PART-TIME WORKERS (IN THOUSANDS) 1951 TO 1997

	1951	1961	1971	1975	1986	1997
Male part-timers	139	149	584	697	843	982
% of male employees	1.9	2.0	4.4	5.3	6.7	8.3
Female part-timers	417	2,060	2,757	3,551	4,108	4,728
% of female employees	6.0	25.8	33.6	42.2	47.1	44.3
Total part-timers	556	2,209	3,341	4,248	4,951	5,710
% of all employees	2.7	9.8	15.5	19.1	23.6	25.0

increased take-up of the 'return-to-work' right after maternity leave and the continuing decline in the average number of children, both of which have encouraged more full-time jobs.

For men, part-time jobs have shown a more solid growth only in the 1990s. The shake-out from the recession in the early 1990s led to a demand for a part-time job first by older men to augment their early pension, and second by men in their forties and fifties for whom obtaining a full-time job proved problematical and the requirements of the benefit system propelled them towards a part-time job which was all that was available.

Continuing on the supply side, the huge increase in higher education take-up has meant a pool of over one million full-time students for whom the reduction in local authority grants made it necessary to acquire a part-time job for some or all of the course.

Downshifting, V-Time and portfolio workers

There are three other areas which, although apparently still small in the number of participants, are becoming a subject of interest.

Firstly, employees are *downshifting*. Examples range from prominent businessmen who leave their chief executive posts and collect a range of part-time non-executive positions, to aspiring writers who move to a part-time position to try to complete their novel, or to one part of a 'dinki' (dual income, no kids) duo for whom part-time earnings in accounting, consultancy or law allows a broader social scene for both parties. There is also the situation in which a voluntary interest (charity, sport or pressure group) demands more time and energy than can be spared from a full-time position. A survey from the Henley Centre for Forecasting reported in 1996 that as many as 6 per cent of Britons had downshifted over the previous 12 months, and another 6 per cent were planning to do so.

In the few examples of formal schemes that are sometimes called *Voluntarily Reduced Work Time* (V-Time), employees trade income for time off over a fixed period of time. It is not uncommon in the United States but very rare in the UK.

Abbey National plc offer such a scheme to their staff, allowing them to reduce their hours for an agreed period of between six months and five years. Staff must have had three years' service and an 'effective' or better rating for the previous two years to be eligible. They can use this period for caring responsibilities or for studying or for other short-term personal commitments. If V-Time is for a period of 12 months or less, full-time work in the same job is guaranteed, provided that it still exists in a full-time capacity. If V-Time is for more than 12 months, the jobholder will, at the end of the agreed period, automatically be shortlisted for jobs at the same level (possibly in another department) when a suitable vacancy arises. During the period of V-Time, pay and benefits are paid pro rata.

Sheffield City Council is another organisation that offers this option, but other examples are very thin on the ground. There are, however, many informal arrangements made in organisations to the effect employees are allowed to go part-time for a period to accommodate a special domestic situation before reverting to full-time work again.

The third area is that of the *portfolio workers* – those with more than one part-time position – as defined by Handy (1994). Hard facts are difficult to come by here but the 1994 Labour Force Survey showed that 3.4 per cent of men and 5.2 per cent of women admitted to a second job – more than double the percentage of 20 years earlier. In the *Sunday Times* (Coles, 1997), examples were given of men who had taken up a combination of part-time positions rather than a full-time job. One combined lecturing and business development in eastern Europe, consultancy in performance management, a marketing role with the European Aluminium Association, and deputy chairmanship of a grant-maintained school. This was through choice rather than by necessity, for he had been offered a number of full-time positions through headhunters. The main reason he gave for accepting this revised working lifestyle was 'the flexibility to take up activities that appealed, rather than having to do certain things as regularly as clockwork in a corporate environment'.

For the employers concerned, it is of no importance how many jobs their part-time employees take on as long as their commitment and performance are as required. Another example of an interesting portfolio combination is the case-study below.

Case-study

KATHERINE WOODWARD: PORTFOLIO WORKER

In 1996 Katherine Woodward was development director at BPC Ltd (one of the UK's largest printing groups), following a career which had encompassed both general and specialist areas in information technology and publishing.

A series of changes, including the restructuring of her current organisation, coincided with her children starting secondary school and the end of her mortgage repayments. This created the backcloth against which she considered alternative career options and decided to set up her own consultancy. To avoid the isolation that she felt was a risk after working in a large organisation, she combined her new business activity with lecturing at Harlow College, which occupied two afternoons and evenings per week.

Soon afterwards she was approached by the Astron Group, one of her clients, to join their fast-growing group of companies as human resource director. The organisation employed 400 staff in a variety of printing and logistics activities. She declined the position on a full-time basis but agreed to provide cover until they could recruit a suitable candidate.

Several months went by without success until the chief executive, David Mitchell, discussed with her the option of staying on in the role. He accepted that she would continue to work at Harlow College and would occasionally consult for other organisations. They agreed that she would work for two and a half days a week, which might occasionally be at weekends. She would receive 50 per cent of the market rate for the role, including a company car, free medical insurance, a pension and the benefits sometimes reserved for full-time employees.

It is not all roses, of course. Trying to match the objectives and priorities of both jobs is not easy, she would be the first to admit. 'It is a constant juggle of priorities and requires tolerance from both employers,' she says.

Organisation-wise, she has fixed times of work in Harlow on Wednesday and Thursday afternoons, and the remainder of her responsibilities at both locations are fitted into the remaining time. She tells her boss at both locations what her appointments are for the following week and keeps in close contact during working hours. She is, she admits, a slave to her mobile phone. Sometimes she wonders if she learned her maths wrong at school and 0.5 + 0.5 actually equals 1.3.

For the continuing heavy demands there are high compensations. She feels she is in control, and this relieves much of the stress. Some of the work, particularly the college work, can be carried out at home, and the total pay and benefit package is very respectable. The college work also aids her personal development, and she is able to be both an academic and a practitioner at the same time rather than a practitioner who dabbles in a little lecturing or an academic out of touch with the real world.

European comparisons

The latest broadly comparative figures for other countries (OECD, 1994) show that the UK has one of the highest proportions of part-time workers, at 23.5 per cent of total employment, exceeded only by Holland, Norway and Australia. France (12.7 per cent) and Germany (14.1 per cent) are some distance behind.

In considering these statistics, there is always the strong possibility that the amount of part-time working may be underestimated because of the so-called 'black economy' by which payments are made in cash, no records kept and few questions asked. It is not in the interests of the 'employee', who is avoiding tax and National Insurance contributions and may also be claiming benefits, or the 'employer' who is avoiding taxes and National Insurance for these transactions to be recorded in any survey. One report estimated that as much as £2 billion worth of benefits are illegally obtained each year by claimants who are working in the black economy.

Where part-time working is prominent

Statistics from the 1994 Labour Force Survey show that the service sector has the highest proportion of part-time working, particularly in retail distribution (men 16 per cent, women 60 per cent). The proportion in manufacturing and the construction industry remained comparatively low, at less than 5 per cent for men and similarly low for women. This was reflected in occupational statistics, where the proportion of women in sales (77 per cent) and personal services such as hairdressing (63 per cent) greatly exceeded skilled craftspersons (20 per cent) or managers (19 per cent). For clerical and secretarial workers, just over one-third of women were part-time. For men, the highest proportions were in sales (36 per cent), security (15 per cent) and teaching (10 per cent).

Categories of part-time working

Part-time work can be divided into three broad categories: *classical, supplementary* and *substitution* (Syrett, 1983).

Classical part-time jobs are posts where the nature of the job requires that only a few hours a day have to be worked, usually on a fixed basis. Such posts include school midday meal supervisors, lollipop ladies, cleaning staff, gardeners, care visitors, child-minders and many bar staff (although the derestriction of opening hours has changed the picture here).

Supplementary part-time jobs are those used in association with full-time jobs to improve the efficiency of the full-time operation. To cover peak periods is an obvious example of such a requirement as instanced in Saturday jobs in a betting shop, hairdressing or in retailing, or weekend jobs in leisure centres. Housebuilders employ site negotiators on Saturdays and/or Sundays. In a number of businesses the weekly flow is uneven, with greater pressure on certain days. Part-timers may be recruited for, say, Monday and Tuesday or Thursday and Friday only.

Some businesses make the *flexibility* quite specific. Briggens House Hotel, in Hertfordshire, advertises for casual housekeeping staff stating that 'hours will be as required, depending on business levels within the hotel'. Broxbourne Council Leisure Services recruit part-time staff for weekend and evening work on 'an as-and-when basis, with sessions between three and eight hours'. Alliance and Leicester takes on part-time customer advisers at 16 hours a week, but makes it plain they will be required to work longer hours on occasions by mutual agreement.

Substitution part-time jobs represent situations where an organisation has decided as a matter of strategy that part-timers will be recruited to replace full-time staff. Burtons are a prime example here. The Burton Group created a considerable stir in 1993 by announcing that they would reduce their full-time workforce by 2,000 jobs and replace at least half of these jobs with 3,000 part-time jobs. Earlier initiatives included that of the Forte Hotel Group in which 1,500 full-time employees were given the choice of a part-time job or redundancy. The biggest driving forces here are the greater availability of part-time applicants and the reduction of costs, particularly if employees work short hours which take them below the National Insurance contribution lower limit (Huddart, 1993).

Innovative ideas

Asda, the supermarket giant, in August 1997 announced plans to put all their retail staff on 15 hours a week minimum contract to try to improve staff loyalty. David Smith, personnel director, considered that employees on very short hours tend to feel detached and that, at around 15 hours, staff are able to put more into the business. It was bound to lead to increased costs because employees who work more than 15 hours receive pay above the National Insurance threshold, currently at £61 a week. Since July 1996, a variety of flexible schemes have been advertised to staff in all Asda stores and offices. These have included job coupling, by which employees who wish to increase their hours can take on a second part-time job, such as 10 hours in the bakery added to 12 hours at the checkout. Shift swaps can also be easily arranged if an employee pins a card to the noticeboard. And flexibility is offered to student employees who can cut their hours or stop work altogether while preparing for examinations, and who can work at another Asda store while at home during vacations. Staff turnover has dropped by 3 per cent since the introduction of these arrangements (*Flexible Working*, 1997).

Another example in this area is detailed in a case-study in the chapter on outsourcing (Chapter 7) which describes how the Astron Group have contracted with a variety of employees who want to work limited hours.

Zero hours

A more recent development in part-time work is the concept of zero hours in which the employees are *not guaranteed any work at all* but in some way are required to be available as and when the employer requires them. In some cases, the employees may have the right to refuse work when offered.

A survey by Katherine Cave (1997) found 36 organisations that used such systems, the majority of which were in retailing (16 out of 54 that responded), but there were also strong representations in health authorities (7 out of 8) and in catering (6 out of 18). Six of the organisations had over 1,000 employees working on this basis, split evenly between retailing, catering and the Health Service. This method of staffing can be crucial to the organisation, as demonstrated in one example where 45 per cent of all staff work under these terms; a further 16 had more than 10 per cent of their staff in this category.

The reasons that zero hours were introduced were:

- □ 94 per cent   ability to deal with fluctuations of work
- □ 80 per cent   creation of a pool from which employees could be moved into permanent work
- □ 75 per cent   enhanced flexibility in planning
- □ 54 per cent   cost saving
- □ 19 per cent   legal reasons.

The cost saving related to two areas: paying for staff only when they were required by the business; and saving on benefits that would apply to staff who worked on a normal contract. (This latter is dealt with under the next heading *Legal situation*.)

The type of work varied between organisations. Much of it was unskilled or semi-skilled, such as packing, clerical or delivery. However, in the Health Service and local authorities, skilled and professional workers such as nurses, dieticians and radiographers were on zero hours. In the financial sector, there was an example of mortgage and pension assistants. The number of hours actually worked varied greatly, with no minimum, and extending in one example up to 60 hours. Employers were reluctant or found it difficult to compute an average.

One of the key factors of interest relating to these contracts is the degree of mutuality. This has two parts: the obligation of employers to offer work, and the right of employees to refuse the work offered. All seven employers who provided documentation made it clear that there was no obligation on the employer to offer work. Concerning refusal, only one employer said that there was no right to refuse, but 21 others made it clear that employees had to make themselves available for particular times and that sanctions would be taken if the employees often refused. Some made the number of refusals allowed quite specific at one, two or three before warnings would take place or before removal from the payroll.

The number of hours for which an employee has to be available varies. Kings Oak Hospital, part of the BMI Healthcare group of private hospitals, has between 20 and 30 'bank' staff who are available from two or three hours a week to more than 20. Some are early-retired nurses and auxiliaries who are happy to work from January to April but may then want a break for two or three months in the summer. Others are content to be called in for a few weeks over the summer months only – each employee has a different situation.

At Middlesex University, library assistants are employed on a stand-by arrangement. They are guaranteed 3.5 hours per month: otherwise, they are on call as part of a stand-by panel on rates the same as full-time staff.

Elsewhere, zero-hours arrangements have been common for many years in catering (weddings, for example) and in corporate hospitality, some of which is contracted under employed terms and some as self-employed or simply 'black economy' cash payments.

Union criticism of zero hours has been widespread. The bank workers' union BIFU has claimed that increasingly casualised employment practices are turning bank workers into a new exploited class (Overell, 1997). Following the reduction of 130,000 employees in total in the banking industry in the 1990s due to cutbacks in the branch network and to new technology, the union claims that banks have no intention of creating permanent jobs. This is supported in part by a statement by Alan Grant, assistant director of personnel at Barclays, that: 'Our primary responsibility is to our permanent staff. It would be dishonest to take people on for jobs we knew were about to disappear.'

Legal situation

There have been two recent cases concerning zero-hours employees which demonstrate the grey legal area in which it operates.

Carmichael and Lees v National Power plc, May 1996, EAT unreported.

Two women had been working as guides showing visitors round a power station for six years, working up to 25 hours a week on a 'casual as required' basis. The tribunal decided that they had the right to refuse work, and because this meant there was no mutuality of obligation it was held that they were *not* employees and could not claim a statutory statement of particulars (or unfair dismissal or redundancy rights, of course). The tribunal decision was reversed by the Court of Appeal in March 1998, which found that the 'casual as required' arrangement led to an implied obligation that work would be offered and accepted.

Clark v Oxfordshire Area Health Authority, May 1996, EAT unreported.

Mrs Clark was a bank nurse employed on a casual basis with no guarantee that work would be provided. She had been provided with a detailed 'statement of employment', and the tribunal placed great reliance on this document when coming to the decision that she *was* an employee – it referred to rights and obligations akin to those of employment and indicated a considerable element of control by the employer. Again reversing the original tribunal decision, the Court of Appeal found in December 1997 that Mrs Clark was only an employee for each 'single engagement' at the hospital. This was based on the belief that there were no obligations to offer work and that Mrs Clark had the right to refuse any work offered.

Although the two cases are factually very similar, it was the nature of the documentation and the implied mutuality that caused the results to be different.

The factors that courts take into account when reaching a decision on the status of the employee are:

☐ *mutuality* – As in the second case above, an overriding right to refuse without comeback would indicate that no employment relationship exists. It has to be said that in most current zero-hours contracts the right to refuse is severely circumscribed, which would indicate a tendency towards an employment relationship – particularly if there is a strong indication of a minimum number of hours to be worked over a week, month or year.

☐ *degree of control* – Zero-hour workers who are also circumscribed by clear company rules, procedures and systems which are identical to those of employees in the organisation are likely to be regarded as employees. It is a collection of freedoms – such as different starting and finishing times or exclusions from dress codes – that would indicate a non-employment relationship.

☐ *documentation* – Although not conclusive (tribunals look behind the formal agreements to see where the true relationship lies), the existence of a laid-down agreement which looks the same as the agreement for employees would, as in the Clark case above, bend towards an employment relationship.

☐ *inclusion* – If zero-hours staff are included in activities such as training and social events at the workplace, this could tip the balance towards employment.

It cannot be said that zero-hours workers either have or do not have full legal employment rights – it depends entirely on the individual circumstances – a most unsatisfactory situation.[1]

What makes the issue so vital is that employers may be misguided if they see zero-hours contracts as a way to avoid the employment regulation and to exclude zero-hours workers from some of the normal benefits given to employees, such as holiday pay, sickness benefit, clothing allowances and pension rights. Their zero-hours workers could be regarded at law as part-time employees. Because the vast majority of them are female, their employer could be breaking the law by discriminating against such part-time employees. The employer would have to show that this indirect discrimination was objective and related to the requirements of the business. This would not be an easy matter to demonstrate.

The Labour Party made clear its disapproval of zero-hours contracts prior to the 1997 general election and is committed to legislation. This may take a form similar to that in Ireland which provides that employees may not be subject to zero-hours contracts without compensation. Broadly, this means that if an employee is not required to work for at least 25 per cent of the time for which the contract may require him or her to be available for work, the employee will still be entitled to payment for 25 per cent of the contract hours or 15 hours, whichever is the lesser.

Summing up the benefits

The reasons given for introducing the scheme make the benefits to employers clear. They have much greater use of flexibility to match the labour required directly to the needs of the business and to suit unpredictable trading patterns. If business falls off one week, they do not need to pay staff they do not need; if business suddenly increases, they have an immediate pool of labour on which to call. Flexibility and a degree of cost-saving are firm advantages.

The benefits to the employees are not so easy to spot. Some are happy to work on a casual basis on which work appears from time to time, just as occurs with temporary agency work. Others use it as a step on the ladder to obtain a permanent job in the same organisation or as a way of getting back into employment after a long break without the major commitment of a permanent job or the constant change caused by working for an agency.[2]

Table 7

PERCENTAGE OF JOBSHARE IN OCCUPATIONS, 1993

Occupation	Men	Women	All
Clerical and secretarial	0.1	3.0	2.3
Personal, protective occupations	0.7	1.9	1.5
Associate professional and technical	0.4	2.0	1.2
Professional	0.4	2.5	1.1
Sales	0.5	1.4	1.1
Management and administration	0.1	0.4	0.3
All	0.3	1.9	1.1

Source: Labour Force Survey, 1993.

Job sharing

Job sharing is an easy concept to understand, is relatively straightforward to implement, and has gradually been extended to most walks of life over the past 20 years. It describes a situation where two or more people share one full-time job, dividing the pay, holidays and other benefits between them in proportion to the number of hours they each work. The 1997 Labour Force Survey indicated that 0.9 per cent of employees worked under a job-share arrangement, of which 85 per cent were women, down from 1.1 in 1993. Table 7 shows the breakdown in terms of occupation in 1993.

Job sharing is most widespread in distribution, catering, banking and other services; there is little evidence of it in manufacturing. Half of all job sharers work in public administration, education, health and other public services. It is not a new concept, having been operated for telephonists when the telephone industry was part of the Post Office in the 1950s. Barclays Bank began to employ some secretarial and administrative staff on a system of alternate weeks known as twinning in the 1940s, and Everest Double Glazing were employing filing clerks on a job-share basis in the late 1970s.

Other examples in the public sector have included probation officers in the London Probation Service and health visitors at East Suffolk Health Authority.

Reasons for introduction

To *retain staff* is the principal reason given by employers. Employees who start families often want to return to their jobs on a part-time basis, which is often not possible unless a second person is recruited to make it up to a full-time job. Without such an arrangement, the employee either has to struggle to perform the full-time job and go through the often traumatic demands, or the employee leaves, and the skills and experience are lost to the organisation. Job sharing is also a way of satisfying employees who may wish, for personal reasons, to switch to part-time working, and of doing so without the employer's incurring the full recruitment and training costs.

To *reduce turnover* is also often quoted where it has been difficult to recruit and keep employees to tedious, pressurised or unpopular low-level jobs. Because of a larger pool of potential part-time employees, job-sharing arrangements make these positions more attractive.

A by-product of such schemes has been *a lower level of absenteeism*. This is not just because part-time employees generally have better attendance records (they can fix medical appointments outside working hours more easily, for example) but because arrangements are often made that if one employee is off sick, another may be able to step into the breach. Because job sharers in general like the scheme, they want it to work, and low absenteeism is a measure of showing that it is working.

Job sharers often divide the day into two with a small overlap or handover period, so there is often *a high level of continuity*. This can also apply in holiday periods where at least one employee is available all the time. Two employees may also bring a wider range of skills between them and be able to organise themselves to use those skills to the full.

At time of unexpected peak loads, two job sharers could *both work at the same time*, arranging time off as appropriate. This would be financially advantageous because any extra hours worked would not be at enhanced rates unless the hours worked in the week or month exceeded the equivalent full-time hours.

All this can lead to *higher productivity*, with a pair of well-focused, hardworking employees using their skills to good advantage.

Other reasons quoted which can apply to all part-timers include:

☐ tapping a wider employment pool

□ greater effort by the employee because the weekly period is shorter

□ contributing to the organisation's equal opportunities policy (see more details in the section on family-friendly policies, page 229).

Benefits to job sharers

The most obvious benefit is *the occupancy of a suitable part-time position* where only an unobtainable full-time post was available previously. An attraction of the arrangement can be *the pleasure of working closely together with another employee* to achieve the objectives of the job. The planning and successful execution of such arrangements which leaves managers, customers (and occasionally the job sharers' staff) satisfied with the outcome can be a source of considerable pride. It possesses the additional cachet of a shared challenge.

There may also be the flexibility that allows either party to *take days off when they want them* outside of a normal pattern in the knowledge that they are being covered. Holiday arrangements over longer periods can also be made to great advantage. In teaching, for example, it is possible for one employee to take a week's holiday during termtime (therefore off-peak and cheaper) while being covered by the other employee: an advantage not possible contractually for full-time teachers.

Difficulties that may be encountered

Not all managers welcome the arrangement with open arms. It has always been a rule of thumb that management difficulties increase in direct ratio to the number of direct staff reporting to them. Managing a pair of employees on one job who are rarely at work together can cause some complications, and if it goes wrong it is the manager who has to pick up the pieces. For some hard-pressed managers job sharing can appear to be an unnecessary complication, except in the most routine of operations.

There will probably be *double the amount of appraisals, wages queries and employee records to maintain*. Similarly, communications with customers, internal and external, can present potential problems. We all like to work with one person we know and it can create confusion unless excellent detailed records are kept of agreements, promises and arrangements.

The more complex the job that is being shared, the greater the potential for misunderstandings – and the need for a joint memory may lead to *more administration than for one job*. For example, if the job of contracts manager in a housebuilding company was shared, would the contracts be split between the parties (meaning that communications about a particular contract could take place for only half the time) or should they be shared over all contracts (meaning substantial and effective communications would be needed between the two job sharers)?

Difficulties can occur over policy decision-taking. If there is a crucial meeting with, say, executives or other managers in the organisation, who should attend – one of the job sharers or both? It is possible to conceive of internal political situations where negotiations would be preferred with one of the job sharers rather than with the other. Should job sharers also share the blame when things go wrong? A mature relationship is required between the parties to avoid blame offloading and to focus on solving problems and avoiding future difficulties. Not all employees would be happy with this situation.

Some job sharers have revealed that *their actual hours are much longer than they are paid for*. The handover is often longer than scheduled and extra calls inside and outside normal hours are the norm to overcome the communications difficulties in the workplace.

Making a job-sharing scheme work
Establishing a policy
Either using a pilot scheme within the organisation or drawing from experience elsewhere, it is essential to achieve an enabling agreement in the organisation whereby employees have the right to propose a job-share arrangement. This should be incorporated as part of an equal opportunities policy. Experience has shown that job-share arrangements that have been proposed and carefully thought through by employees are the ones most likely to succeed, so these need

to be encouraged at the earliest stage. Once the policy is established, it needs to be communicated to the workforce. Newsletters, briefing groups, notices, e-mail are all media to be used if appropriate.

Setting up the arrangement

Assuming that the proposals come from employees, there are several essential factors:

☐ There must be full agreement from the line manager (enthusiastic approval, not mere acquiescence).

☐ Arrangements need to be made on a term basis, for either six months or a year, in case there are insuperable unseen problems. After that time, they can be agreed as 'permanent'.

☐ The proposal should be costed thoroughly and should set out how any responsibilities are to be divided.

☐ Details of holidays, location (including the arrangements for sharing a desk and phone), specific hours and control systems must all be included.

The personnel manager should act as a facilitator in helping employees put forward proposals, and getting them to find ways round potential problems by balancing realism with enthusiasm.

There are two schools of thought on how to ensure a successful growth of job sharing in the organisation. One school says that there should be a high-profile job share, perhaps involving a manager's job, which would then act as a role model for all employees. If successful, it should certainly work this way – but it is also a risky strategy. The evidence to date is sketchy but it is clear that more problems emerge the further up the hierarchy the job share takes place. They can certainly be overcome given goodwill and determination: it is probably unwise, however, to try to go for the 'big bang' at the start.

The other school encourages successful job sharing at the lower hierarchies at first, and then a gradual and careful move up the levels – so that if one does not work the concept is not damned. In fact, a failure would give a good opportunity to review and build on the successful features. An example of a successful job share at a high level is at University College Hospital, which is featured in the case-study below.

Case-study

JOB SHARING AT UNIVERSITY COLLEGE HOSPITAL

The highest-profile example so far has been the appointment of two job sharers for the position of personnel director at University College Hospital, London, a position Peter Rankin and Sandra Meadows obtained in May 1994 as the only job-share proposal from a total of 70 applications. They had worked with each other in various capacities for nearly 20 years, and both wanted the opportunity to continue forms of consultancy at the same time as being involved in an operational position. Sandra had, in fact, combined a part-time personnel directorship with consultancy work in her previous position.

They were both employed for three days a week, with one day overlap, but both have found it difficult not to put in a lot of extra time. Part of their communication system is to keep a day-book in which each writes down every detail of information and gossip that the other may have missed. They do not have standard days each week but swap around so employees deal with whoever is available for any and every problem. One of the major advantages as they see it is that each paper they write on specific issues, policies or problems is of a high standard thanks to the cross-fertilisation of the two minds thinking them through.

Source: Huddart 1994.

Working arrangements

Sharing a job can take place in three main ways (although others are feasible):

- [] mornings and afternoons (either fixed or alternating)
- [] three days and two days, or two and a half days each (sequentially or alternating)
- [] week and week about.

East Hertfordshire Council operates a job-share arrangement for a number of jobs including taxi licensing and enforcement officers who work three days and two days. All three options can work well, and which way to work should be by preferred option of the parties involved rather than by overall company policy.

The contractual requirements must be clearly set out, particularly those relating to additional hours required by the manager (what circumstances, how much notice, etc) and to how 'empowered' the job sharers are to change working arrangements. For East Hertfordshire Council job-share positions it is made clear in relation to each job whether any evening or weekend work may be required on top of the standard job-share hours.

Recruiting and training

With a new scheme, it is often the case that one employee wishes to job share so that a second has then to be recruited and trained. Unlike normal recruitment, there is the additional complication of obtaining third-party approval to the process – but this is crucial: if the two employees do not get on well, the arrangement will never succeed.

Setting up systems, especially computer records

The special systems that apply here are communications and record-keeping so that the amount of confusion and misunderstanding is kept to a minimum. The systems will vary depending on the jobs and the organisation.

Publicising the arrangement

It is vital that everybody who may be affected by the arrangement is informed carefully as to its commencement – and given the opportunity to ask questions and point out last-minute pitfalls!

Many of these aspects were addressed thoroughly in the Luton Borough Council scheme described below.

Case-study

JOB SHARING AT LUTON BOROUGH COUNCIL

Luton Borough Council includes a form of encouragement to job sharing under its equal opportunities policy and currently has around 10 positions under job share. These include:

☐ reception/enquiry clerks, housing benefit

☐ enquiry clerk, local taxation

☐ enforcement officer, environmental health

☐ payments manager, housing benefit

Denise Clarke, personnel officer at the Council, carried out an internal survey of the operation of the scheme in 1993, talking to the job sharers (who were all female), their managers and five managers with no experience of job sharing who could give an independent view.

Some of the key findings were as follows:

Reasons for job sharing

Seventy five per cent of the job sharers wanted additional time for child-care responsibilities, one had a family illness, one wanted to devote more time to voluntary work, and one simply wanted more time to herself. Two-thirds of the job shares were set up when an employee returned from maternity leave.

Seeking agreement

There were few difficulties in setting up the lower-graded jobs, but obtaining the managers' support for setting up two more senior positions proved tricky. It took 10 weeks of meetings with officers and union representatives before agreement was reached and the concerns of the managers overcome.

Hours of work

There was a mix of mornings/afternoons and two-and-a-half day weeks.

Continuity

Special arrangements had to be made in positions where continuity was vital. Extra attention had to be paid to record-keeping. Detailed notes were left for each partner, and calls between the two during the day or in the evening were quite frequent.

On-going difficulties

None of the job sharers reported any difficulties once initial agreement was reached and the contractual arrangements were clarified.

Management perspective

Eighty per cent of the managers mentioned some additional costs in recruiting, training and supervising the arrangement. The greatest concern here came from the manager involved in a direct service organisation where costs were crucial. Four out of the five independent managers indicated that they would oppose job sharing for senior positions, particularly where complex case-work was involved and where serious consequences would occur if there were misunderstandings or maladministration (for example, in children's work). Another objection came from external clients who preferred to deal with one person.

A number of managers were happy to deal with a small percentage of job shares but were loath to extend the arrangements too far. They recognised the considerable advantages for the employees concerned as well as the benefits to the Council.

The legal situation relating to part-time working

The legal situation for part-time staff (which include job sharers) has changed considerably over the past five years following a number of high-profile legal decisions.

The most significant was the House of Lords' decision in *R v Secretary of State for Employment ex parte Equal Opportunities Commission* to the effect that the weekly hours threshold provisions for part-timers were incompatible with Article 119 of the Treaty of Rome. The government accordingly removed those provisions in 1995. Until then, part-timers who worked less than eight hours a week had no protection from unfair dismissal or redundancies rights under the Employment Protection Consolidation Act (EPCA) 1978. Those working for more than eight hours but less than 16 hours needed five years' service to achieve the same rights as full-timers. Part-timers, no matter what their hours, currently need two years' service to achieve employment rights under EPCA 1978.

In 1995 the European Court of Justice indicated that the exclusion of part-timers from pension schemes could amount to indirect discrimination, although organisations could still attempt to argue an 'objective justification' in special cases – for example, where the additional costs of administering and paying large numbers of small pensions is excessive in relation to the benefits received. This argument has still to be tested.

One interesting decision that did not go the way of part-timers concerned *overtime payments*. The European Court of Justice decided in 1995 (*Stadt Lengerich v Helmig and others*) that it was not discriminatory for an employer to require all part-time employees to work the equivalent of full-time hours before they were entitled to overtime premiums.

A 1997 case showed clearly the dangers of not accommodating employees' requests to work flexibly. Zurich Insurance paid £20,000 to an ex-employee who was refused the chance to job-share. Janet Scholfield wanted to return from maternity leave to her post as marketing manager and share it with another manager, but this was refused: Janet claimed constructive dismissal at a tribunal. The settlement was made out of court.

The current position on pending European Directives on part-time working is detailed in Chapter 16.

Postcript

A final comment in this area comes from America, where temporal flexibility has been ingrained in the major tracts of the labour market for some decades. It is not often, however, that the plight of part-time employees hits the headlines, but a 15-day strike by 185,000 United Parcel Service (UPS) employees in 1997 proved successful in reversing the management decision to switch from full-time to part-time jobs. Early in the 1980s the Teamster Union had agreed to lower rates for part-time employees and the number employed by the organisation had grown steadily since that time. By early 1997, over 65 per cent of employees were part-time, earning around half the hourly rate of their full-time colleagues. The dispute was centred around the aim of the union to fight to 'stop large companies from shifting to throwaway jobs that do not support a family'. The outcome was a success for the union.

Statistics from the USA show that there are over 23 million part-time employees in total. Economists have argued that the healthy state of the US economy, where there is strong growth without inflation, is due in part to the flexibility that the large amount of part-time working brings to the labour market. It remains to be seen whether the UPS strike was a watershed and whether the drift towards an economy driven by part-time working goes into reverse (Walsh, 1997).

References and further reading

CAVE K. 'Zero hours contracts : a report into the incidence and implications of such contracts'. Huddersfield, University of Huddersfield, January 1997.

COLES M. 'Tune in to a life of career variety', *Sunday Times*, 31 August 1997, p. 24.

Flexible Working. 'Asda keeps it simple to keep its staff', September 1997, p. 15.

HANDY C. *The Empty Raincoat*. London, Hutchinson, 1994.

HUDDART G. 'Shifting to part-timers', *Personnel Today*, 26 January 1993, p. 14.

HUDDART G. 'Two heads', *Personnel Today*, 6 December 1994.

HUDDERT G. 'Zero hours give zero flexibility'. *Personnel Today*, 21 May 1998, p. 1.

IDS Study 548. London, February 1994.

OECD. *Employment Outlook*. Paris, Organisation for Economic Co-operation and Development, 1994.

OVERELL S. 'Banks attacked over zero-hours contracts', *People Management*, 11 September 1997, p. 16.

SYRETT M. *Employing Jobsharers, Part-time and Temporary Staff*. London, IPD, 1983.

WALSH J. 'UPS conceded defeat over part-time policy', *People Management*, 28 August 1997, p. 19.

End-notes

1 It would be wise for employers, in order to ensure avoidance of a contract of employment, to make the lack of obligation to offer and accept work quite explicit in their contracts.

2 Not all organisations have stayed with zero hours. Woolworths decided to scrap their scheme in 1998 owing to administrative arrangements' becoming increasingly difficult and to lower staff loyalty (Huddart, 1998).

4 PREDICTING THE UNPREDICTABLE: MEETING THE ORGANISATION'S NEED TO RESPOND FLEXIBLY

Introduction

Flexible practices in the workplace often reflect the calculated decision (but sometimes just the whim or impulse) of the consumer – one of that collection of complex decisions we make each day as to when and where to shop and what to buy at what price in what quantity. From a business viewpoint, unpredictability has sharply increased because the choice set before consumers has never been so great: we have an expanding ability to shop around through access to telephones, motorcars, and now teletext and the Internet, and there is increasing competition to provide convenient shopping opportunities through extended opening hours, telesales and sales recording systems.

In employment terms, such uncertainty in current and medium-term activities has caused many employers to extend the use of temporary employment policies. These have taken a variety of forms associated with the new concept of 'complementary workers'. The main ones are the more extensive use of short-term contracts, casual and temporary agency staff; a number of organisations have moved a stage further by setting up in-house, outsourcing contracts.

Organisations have also undertaken a number of other new initiatives, including annual hours (see Chapter 2) and changing shift and overtime patterns. A very recent development has been the introduction of call centres, which is dealt with in Chapter 8. This chapter starts with information about the current state of temporary and short-term employment; complementary employment is then explained and discussed, together with the use of agency labour and the legal implications; finally, there are sections on recent development in shiftworking. Within the text there are a number of short case-studies.

Temporary employment and short-term contracts
The current extent of temporary work

The proportion of the workforce employed on temporary contracts was very static within the band of 4 per cent to 6 per cent from the 1950s up to the early 1990s. It remained in a fixed pattern, falling at the onset of each recession and picking up again as the signs of confidence returned, and levelling off at the top of the business cycle. At this point, organisations started to convert some of the temporary jobs into permanent ones to keep those employees they wished to retain from accepting permanent positions elsewhere. At the same time, the expansion of the business often increased their need for immediate agency staff.

Table 8 shows, however, that a sea change occurred in the early 1990s when the proportion of temporary employees started to rise sharply, reaching 7 per cent in 1995 – a total of around 1.5 million employees. It is clear from this diagram

Table 8

TEMPORARY WORK IN GREAT BRITAIN 1985 TO 1997 (% OF ALL EMPLOYEES)

	male	female	total
	%	%	%
1985	3.8	7.3	5.2
1987	4.0	7.6	5.7
1989	3.8	7.2	5.3
1991	4.0	7.0	5.2
1993	5.0	6.8	5.9
1995	6.2	7.8	7.0
1997	6.2	8.5	7.5

Source: Labour Force Survey, spring quarters.

that although there is a small increase in the number of female temporary employees, it is the disproportionate increase in male temporary jobs, from under 4 per cent to over 6 per cent that has driven the overall increase, even while female temporary jobs at around 800,000 still outnumber male temporary jobs at 700,000.

Temporary employees can be divided into two main groups: those that work seasonally or casually, and those that work on fixed-term contracts (although there is some overlap between these in respect of those working on a fixed-term contract for, say, harvesting peas). The Labour Force Survey showed that the proportion of employees working seasonally and casually was steady at around 4 per cent from the mid-1980s and then fell to 3 per cent in the early 1990s. On the other hand, those employees on fixed-term contracts gradually declined during the 1980s from 1.5 per cent towards 1 per cent but then rose suddenly in the early 1990s to climb as high as 3.5 per cent by 1994.

Evidence collected in the 1995 Institute of Employment Studies (Atkinson et al, 1996) throws more light on where temporaries are employed. Again, as in much of the statistical information on flexible working, it is the service sector that has the highest percentage, at 12 per cent of all employees; hotels and distribution come next, at close to 10 per cent. The construction industry has a very small proportion (chiefly because a high proportion of their workers are self-employed), but there are skilled categories, technical and professional, who are employed on large contracts, such as on the Jubilee underground line, where 700 managerial and professional staff have been employed on fixed-term contracts. Here, substantial help is given to obtain the next job through outsourcing activities (Jager and Smith, 1997).

A 1996 report by outplacement consultants Sanders and Sydney found that the number of jobs offered on short-term contracts to managers and executives had greatly increased. Seventy-three per cent of organisations questioned had offered contracts on this basis over the previous year, compared to only 3 per cent in a similar survey five years earlier. Indeed, 70 per cent of employers thought that the use of fixed-term contracts would increase significantly (Sanders and

Sydney, 1996). A further report by the Reward Group in 1997 indicated that over half the companies had increased the number of their short-term contracts (*Personnel Today*, 1997).

Terms and conditions

The IDS survey *Jobs for All Seasons* (IDS Study 579, June 1995) reported that terms and conditions offered to temporary staff varied widely, depending on the kind of temporary contract and the tasks to be carried out. At one end of the scale, most lecturers and researchers on short-term contracts are offered the full range of terms and conditions open to permanent staff. Many other temporary jobs of short duration, however, exclude sick pay, holidays and other benefits. Qualifying service for holidays ranges from three months (Bass Breweries) to six months (Surrey County Council). Irrespective of service, all staff have the statutory right to maternity pay and leave.

Supply-side analysis

In terms of the characteristics of temporary employees, the largest percentages are in the age-groups 16 to 19 (17 per cent of that age-group) and 20 to 24 (11 per cent). A good proportion are well qualified: over 20 per cent have a degree, compared to 13 per cent who have no qualifications; 54 per cent work full-time and 46 per cent part-time (Labour Force Survey, 1995).

The increase in temporary work, particularly short-term contracts, can therefore be partly explained, by the vast expansion in higher-education take-up: a good proportion of these students will be actively searching for term-time contracts. According to a survey by 1996 GMB Union, 823,000 students (around 50 per cent) were working, of which half put in more than 9 hours a week. Not unexpectedly, the pay rates were low: the average was at £3.28 an hour (*People Management*, 14 August 1997).

A second increasing source is retired people – especially men aged 55 to 70, who may have been forced into early retirement by the recession at the end of the 1980s. A good proportion of these need the income, but there are also a

minority who are fitter than previous generations and welcome the activity, sociability and, frankly, the time taken up
by a temporary position. There has been such an increase in
early retirements in the public sector that the Audit
Commission has reported a strain on the government-funded
pension arrangements.

A further more recent development has been in the IT
sector, where employees have seen that working on a suc-
cession of well-paid, short-term contracts can have advantages over a permanent position. There has been a growing
number of reports of IT staff who have renegotiated their
employment contracts. Organisations find it difficult to
meet the demands for enhanced salaries because of the effect
on their pay structures and differentials, but they do not
want to lose the staff to a competitor or an agency. A deal is
struck whereby current employment is terminated and
replaced by a short-term contract with an attractive terminal
performance-related bonus. Before that contract ends, a new
one is negotiated for the next project. Other employees may
feel unhappy at seeing such bonuses, but few other positions
could be converted to the same arrangement and only a minority of employees have the courage to forgo the safety of
permanent employment, so the new contractual terms create
few ripples in the organisation.

The business level for temporary staff at employment
agencies has risen considerably in the last five years, matched
with a decline in the volume of permanent business, although
there were signs that the balance was altering in 1997.
Together with a higher volume of business come higher
demands from employers, especially on the quality front.
Agencies are setting up two sides to their business: a retail
side, dealing with traditional agency provision, and a wholesale side, in which mostly large employers require large volumes of temporary staff, often in warehousing or
shiftworking in manufacturing, and increasingly, at call centres. Employers here want a managed labour supply that they
can turn on and off like a tap, while retaining their core labour
force.

Do employees really want temporary work?

Information from the 1996 autumn Labour Force Survey, in which respondents were asked why they had taken a temporary job, are illuminating. Of part-time temporary employees (around 45 per cent of all temporary employees), only 28 per cent were looking for permanent employment. Of those working full-time (about 55 per cent of all temporary employees), around 50 per cent took the temporary work only because they could not find permanent work. Overall, then, around 40 per cent of temporary employees (around 600,000 employees or 2.5 per cent of the labour force) would prefer to have permanent positions. This may not be the whole picture, of course. Some employees may be on an initial short-term contract where the employer has indicated that it will become permanent, all things being equal, after six months, a year or two years.

Sander and Sydney have pointed out the disadvantages of short-term contracts:

- ☐ To enter into a commitment to the organisation, or to get involved in longer-term projects or social relationships, is difficult for employees.
- ☐ Financial planning becomes less easy for employees, especially on pensions, mortgages, children's education and holidays.
- ☐ Team-building in the organisation is affected as managers and permanent staff are less willing to provide key team posts for temporary employees or to give them the necessary training.
- ☐ Groups of employees on short-term contracts spread a culture of uncertainty in the organisation. Further bouts of redundancy may be expected and permanent employees may become uneasy as they wait for the axe to fall again. The culture is often associated with cynical viewpoints on the part of permanent staff.
- ☐ The benefits are considered, overall, to be heavily weighted towards the employer, which leads to an overall concept of unfairness, particularly where the use of short-term contracts is seen as a strategic and semi-permanent arrangement.

International comparison

Compared to the rest of Europe, however, the UK still has a very low percentage of temporary employees. For example, 32 per cent of all employment in Spain is temporary, and even in France, Germany and Japan it reaches 10 per cent. Only Belgium and Italy has a level around that of the UK (OECD, 1993). Most countries, except Japan, Belgium and the UK, have a roughly equal division between males and females in temporary employment.

The demand side: reasons for using temporary labour

A comparison of the reasons cited by employers in the Institute of Employment Studies 1995 with a similar IES survey in 1985 is shown in Table 9.

By 1995, when asked to choose the most important reason, 40 per cent chose 'Matching staffing levels to peaks in demand', which indicated a more strategic approach to the subject area. Covering holidays and sickness was quoted next on the list, at 27 per cent. It was interesting that very few employers quoted reduced wage or training costs. There was a strong correlation between the number of temporary staff employed and the rating of the strategic requirement as the key reason.

Other researchers in the late 1980s and early 1990s (Hunter *et al*, 1993; Hunter and McInnes, 1991) found that the newer strategies were strongest in the public sector and in distribution industries, but that the implementation of flexible labour strategies was more pragmatic than holistic.

As Atkinson *et al* (1996) sum up:

Table 9
COMPARISON OF EMPLOYERS' REASONS FOR USING TEMPORARY LABOUR.

	1985	1995
To cover holidays and sickness	(combined) 69%	59%
To cover maternity leave		38%
To match seasonal variations or peaks	40%	63%
To perform one-off tasks	33%	39%
To provide specialist expertise	19%	20%

Source: Institute of Employment Studies, 1996.

Broadly, the use of temporary labour seems to depend on the type of work and the tightness of the particular segment of the labour market concerned. Where the labour market is slack and tasks routine, casualisation is common. Where labour market conditions are tight and skill levels high, contract work with high levels of pay are more prevalent.

A new title: complementary worker

The label 'casual worker' or 'temp' conveys an image of employees of no great importance to the organisation – mostly unskilled, generally very short-term, and certainly of low status. There are signs that this is all changing. *Complementary workers* are employees who work in a non-permanent capacity for a host organisation to which they provide services either directly or through a third party, and who are already making a sizeable contribution to the business performance of their host organisation. In their study *Flexible Working Means Business* (1996), sponsored by Manpower, Kate Corfield and Alastair Wright set out the major changes that are taking place in this area:

□ Complementary working is spreading into sectors which traditionally employ people in permanent posts, such as banking, IT and the civil service.

□ Complementary working is extending into professional and managerial areas rather than just administration or casual labour. A typical *People Management* magazine in 1996 included around 40 positions advertised on a short-term basis, and the IPD's Locum personnel service has grown rapidly in recent years.

□ Complementary employees have increased in such numbers as to exceed the permanent staff in some organisations. For example, IBM's Service Plus division which services desktop computers and ancillary equipment employed 200 permanent staff and 900 complementary staff in 1996.

□ Complementary workers have made staggering inroads into areas regarded as core to businesses. For example, 50 per cent of the BBC's visual effects department – a key area of their operations – are complementary staff.

Table 10
DIFFERENT FORMS OF COMPLEMENTARY WORK SERVICES BY CHARACTERISTIC AND TYPE

	Characteristics					
	Who directs the work	Individual service or service contract	Knowledge/ skill level	Relationship to core workforce	Type of service contract	Relationship with supplier
Temporary Assignment	customer	individual	lo-hi (generalist)	substitute or supplement	individual contract	short-term simple
Contracting	customer	individual	hi (specialist)	complement	individual for services	short-term simple
Sub-contracting	supplier	service contract	lo-hi (specialist)	substitute or complement	contract for service	medium-/ long-term
Consulting	supplier	total service	very hi (specialist)	complement	negotiated outcomes	short-term operational/ strategic
In-plant	supplier	total service	lo-hi (generalist & specialist)	substitute or complement	total service	medium-/ long-term
Outsourcing	supplier	total service	lo-hi (generalist & specialist)	substitute or complement	total service including capital equip. premises etc	long-term operational/ strategic

(Row label on left margin: Complementary Work Services)

Adapted from: Corfield and Wright, p. 8.

The title 'complementary worker' encompasses a number of activities, and workers involved have varying characteristics, as shown in Table 10.

Location, work direction and relationship to core workforce

Employers will take different decisions concerning the location, the way the work is directed and the relationship of temporary employees to the permanent workforce. These decisions will principally be based on the nature of the contractual relationship. For example, in a contracting situation, such as software design, the work will mostly take place on the customer's premises, be directed by the customer, and complement the existing IT workforce. Payroll outsourcing, on the other hand, will take place off the premises, be directed by the supplier, and completely substitute for the original payroll staff.

Types of contracts

For individual workers, contracts are mostly temporary – but examples are now arising of agency providers who are treating their workers as employees and entering into long-term relationships with them. Manpower, with 170 UK offices and operations in 35 countries, is the largest example of an agency which directly and wholly employs all temporary staff, although the direction of day-to-day activities is handled by the customers. All staff enjoy 20 days of paid holidays after a qualifying period, and there are schemes for sickness and maternity pay, together with life and personal accident insurance.

The nature of the contract between the agency and customer also varies greatly. For an in-plant operation (see the case-study below) the responsibilities are to provide a total service involving all aspects of output, quality and time-managed service delivery within the customer's manufacturing or service environment.

Case-study

XEROX LIMITED, MITCHELDEAN

Xerox Limited, the European arm of Xerox Corporation, manufactures copiers and printers at Mitcheldean. Until 1980, 5,000 were employed at the plant. Intense competition from the Far East reduced that number to 1,000 by 1984, and it was then that the plant faced its most critical period. Investment in a high-performance production culture, with a sizeable proportion of complementary staff, was the outcome of various strategic HR designs.

The complementary staff, including management and supervisory staff, were hired through and managed by Manpower under an in-plant contract. This has proved so successful that the overall number employed has risen to over 2,000, of which 900 are currently employed by Manpower, mostly as semi-skilled operators.

Although the majority of the operatives still report to Xerox managers, Manpower are building up their internal management structure including a group of team-leaders and a small group of planners, designers and programmers. Interestingly, there is little differential in pay or terms and conditions – the benefit is in the commitment and productivity of these staff.

All Manpower staff are given thorough induction assessment and training, and the intention is always to encourage a spread of skills, especially on tool-based technology, during their employment on site. Nigel Stephenson, Manpower's manager at the Mitcheldean site, points out that this is not pure altruism on their part.

> We regard these employees as potentially flexible between a number of sites, so it is important that they collect as many skills as possible. Next year they could be at another client location which may be a food-processor or a pharmaceutical company or a brewer. As demand for copiers and printers varies, we are able to increase or decrease the labour force comparatively easily by switching them to our other sites where they can make an instant contribution. This saves Xerox severance pay at a downturn and recruitment costs when labour is needed, and it also provides a high degree of continuity of employment for our staff. I have even persuaded the local building societies to regard our staff with six months' service in the same bracket as if they were staff in any other organisation so they can obtain mortgages more easily.

Nigel's position is an interesting one for he combines a variety of roles that are not written on a job description. He is a recruitment consultant for the agency, dealing with re-deployment and other issues; he is a human resource manager on site, dealing with subjects such as manpower planning, performance management, training and pay; finally, he has a growing role as production co-ordinator, working with the Xerox management and his own small production management team. It is truly a position requiring considerable flexibility.

Consulting agreements are linked to negotiated outcomes, while the contract for a simple temporary assignment is based on providing a body in place over a period of time with a degree of quality and skills expectations.

Relationship with supplier

There are crucial differences here. Providing temporary staff can be a very simple and short-term relationship such as the contract for seasonal employees at Birds-Eye detailed in the case-study below. Contracting for a total in-plant or outsourcing operation will certainly be long-term, complex and, more importantly, *strategic*. The relationship will allow the company to respond quickly to changing market conditions without the ultimate responsibility for redeploying staff. A strategic relationship implies a close liaison on strategic resourcing plans arising out of the client company's long-term strategic plan.

Case-study

BIRDS-EYE WALLS

Birds-Eye has four processing plants — at Gloucester, Hull, Grimsby and Lowestoft — and uses temporary staff at all four sites. Seasonal staff, many of them students, are employed in the spring and summer, but staff are also employed on fixed-term contracts to allow for flexibility and to cope with the unpredictable nature of the demand for, and supply of, its products. The proportion of temporary employees has risen to as high as 50 per cent in certain plants when there is a changeover to new methods of working.

Sources of labour

- Advertisements are placed in the local job centre, where they are screened by job centre staff. Numeracy, dexterity and literacy tests are given.
- A database of formal seasonal staff is kept, and satisfactory past employees are contacted at the appropriate time.
- An employment agency is used.
- Speculative applications are dealt with by the personnel department.

Conditions of employment

Temporary staff work under the same terms and conditions as permanent employees, including pay, shift and overtime conditions, but there are exceptions for sickness payments (one year qualification) and there is no pension provision. The contract can last for a variety of periods, from six weeks to six months or longer.

Induction and training

Employees are given a two-day induction course which includes health and safety, communication and product awareness; most also attend food hygiene certificate courses. Induction is followed by on-the-job training.

Source: IDS Study 579, June 1995, pp. 14–15

Skills and knowledge

Contracting and consulting work almost inevitably means the supplier has to provide a high degree of skill and knowledge. There may, on the other hand, be very little skill involved in the labour provided for routine clerical work. Increasingly, however, the levels of skill required in complementary workforces is rising. This is particularly true with in-plant and outsourced operations where a collection of specialist skills (IT, engineering, technical, professional, etc) works alongside the more general skills of management and supervision.

Recognising this, a number of providers are concentrating on improving their skills bank. Manpower have developed a full set of office automation and IT skills training modules (Skillware and Techtrack) and encourage all their staff to accumulate these skills ranging from basic word-processing and spreadsheets to higher-level skills for IT professionals, such as in systems and database design. At the heart of the training is an effective skills assessment system which aims to guarantee the quality of the skills.

The motivation behind Manpower's investing substantially in a temporary labour force is:

□ A growing proportion of the labour force are no longer 'temporary' in the strict sense of the word. They can work on one assignment for an extended period, stretching to many years, or they can move regularly between assignments. The payback period on training is the same as for any 'permanent' employee in an organisation.

□ The more skilled the workforce, the greater the resources the organisation has to offer – it is, in fact, *all* they have to offer – so, in a world that respects quality, their assets have to be seen to be high-quality. (One of the generic training skills, incidentally, is customer care techniques, and Manpower aim for all their staff to achieve this module.)

□ The skills give the agency itself flexibility. When work

falls off at one organisation, employees with the right skills (or the right learning mindset) can be switched to another suitable assignment.

A final caveat is warranted at this point. Not all employers are moving to increase their temporary workforce. NPI, the pensions and savings group, who recruited a bank of their own temporary employees, have recently announced a decision to end temporary contracts (Whitely, 1997). Chief executive Alastair Lyons commented that giving advice and liaising with brokers were too important a part of good customer service to leave to temporaries. NPI created 100 additional permanent posts to replace a similar number of temporary ones.

Similarly, National Grid decided in 1997 to halve the number of temporary staff, following an internal attitude survey. Temporary staff regarded themselves as second-class citizens, a position emphasised by their exclusion from briefing groups, pension schemes and discounted share schemes. Geoff Kennedy, employee relations manager, commented: 'It is impossible to say that you value staff if you are not prepared to have them on the books' (Burke, 1997a)

Trade unions in the service sector also campaign, not unexpectedly, against temporary employees. BIFU, the banking and insurance union, has estimated that there are 10,000 temporary and casual workers in the financial sector, representing chronic underfunding, and is adopting a specific strategy to create new, cheaper and more secure forms of working (Cooper, 1997).

Interim management

Another new term in this field is interim management, which is estimated to have an annual turnover of £200 million and to be growing by 25 per cent annually. Around 10,000 managers work at a senior level, summoned at short notice to perform a specific task for anything from a few weeks to a year or more (Whitehead, 1997). As downsizing and de-layering have taken their toll, organisations remain unwilling to start increasing their permanent headcount and so look elsewhere for management skills to run short-term assignments.

Most managers involved are aged over 45, having had exposure to a number of managerial situations. Their willingness to take on these assignments is related to the difficulty at their age in obtaining a 'permanent' position.

Organisations use interim managers in four situations. Firstly, in project work where they have no in-house expertise – investigating a new marketplace, such as Scotland or Ireland, or helping to install a new budgetary control system. Secondly, when there is a truly temporary position – when, say, two companies are merging and one finance director leaves four months before the actual merger takes place. Thirdly, at a higher level, when a 'company doctor' may be required (together with a small team) to try to turn round an ailing business over a limited period of time. Finally, there are a growing number of cases of short-term senior vacancies due to maternity leave.

The advantages are clear. The managers are immediately effective (often actually over-qualified) and can make way when their assignment is finished for a less qualified and cheaper manager who will simply run the operation. An interim manager can be expensive – the cost lies in the range of £300 to £1,500 a day – but it is still generally cheaper and more controllable than a batch of consultants. Interim managers are also committed, for they work full-time on one assignment and need good results to be hired for the next one.

Operating with a complementary workforce

Organisations have two main choices in obtaining temporary employees. They can recruit them directly or through an agency. Table 11 (below) shows that organisations appear to do both in roughly equal amounts (Atkinson *et al*, 1996).

Table 11
MAIN METHODS USED TO RECRUIT TEMPORARY EMPLOYEES

Intermediate recruitment	General employment agencies	14.2%
	Specialist employment agencies	15.9%
	Job centres	14.2%
Direct recruitment	National media	3.0%
	Local media	7.2%
	Own bank of temps	16.5%
	Word of mouth	18.8%
	Unsolicited	5.5%

Source: Institute of Employment Studies, 1996.

Advantages of direct recruitment

☐ The costs are generally much lower, particularly if an organisation incurs no recruitment costs through using its own bank of temps, word of mouth or unsolicited applications.

☐ Selection can be more precise: the alternative is accepting or rejecting what is sent by the agency. (Agencies sometimes produce a set of CVs for short contracts at the skilled or professional end of the market, but will include this cost in their charges.)

☐ Employers are able to test the market rates rather than having to rely on the estimates of the agencies who have a vested interest in raising rates.

☐ Agencies do not always understand the full, precise requirements of the organisation. The staff provided may not have the right level of skill or qualifications, or the agencies may not have the volumes of personnel required at that point in time.

☐ Having two rates of pay operating on the same premises can be disruptive, particularly if the agency staff provided are better paid than the employees! Recruiting directly means that the pay system is preserved.

Advantages of using agencies

☐ Access on demand is a key advantage, as long as agency staff can be available at short notice.

☐ There is considerable saving of organisation time and cost in recruitment and selection, particularly if the staff are required for only a short period. Agencies are very experienced in recruiting temporary staff.

☐ Although the hourly rate appears to be high, there are no extras – whereas staff employed directly have added-on costs which are likely to amount to 30 per cent more as an absolute minimum, including National Insurance, probably stretching to 50 per cent when sick pay, holidays and a variety of standard company benefits are added on, depending on the length of the contract.

- Agencies may be very knowledgeable on the market for particular staff, especially specialist agencies (accounts, engineering). This expertise can be very useful to an organisation that has only limited, intermittent market contact.

- A number of agencies are now training staff themselves, especially in IT skills, so the quality of staff supplied can be enhanced.

- A longer-term relationship with an agency can mean that the agency recognises and understands the specific preferences of the organisation and its cultural uniqueness, so the needs of the organisation can be met with considerable accuracy.

- Agencies can deal with the employment paperwork.

- If a temporary employee does not match expectations for any reason, a call to the agency is all that is necessary, without the normal difficulties involved in terminating employment.

Sometimes organisations compromise between the two alternatives by creating their own in-house placement agency (see the case-study below).

Case-study
_____

CABLE AND WIRELESS

Organisations have always used a a minority of staff on a contract basis. In the 1960s and 1970s it was organised through a complex system of manpower planning by which careers were mapped out through a series of training and development assignments, masterminded by the personnel department. In the days of monopoly, this worked well because the inevitable overmanning was disguised. As soon as privatisation and competition arrived in the early 1980s, contract times were shortened and manpower slashed substantially, leaving few staff available for *ad-hoc* projects. Using skilled labour on short-term contracts through agencies became the norm instead across all telecommunications companies.

In 1995, having examined the costs and benefits of the existing system of using a selection of recruitment agencies, Cable and Wireless (C&W) decided to set up their own in-house placement group called Flexible Resource Ltd. The core of the operation is a database of 7,000 skilled people from support staff to high-level management and consultants: FRL has around 100 contractors working around the group at any one time. Although operating with a clear commercial focus, its objective is only to break even, and this was achieved in its first year, saving C&W around £500,000 in the process because it charges only half the normal agency rates. It has a full time staff of six, augmented by certain support staff on contract.

FRL differs from most other agencies in its understanding of the organisation and, crucially, of its security: it can be involved with projects even at a commercially sensitive stage.

A small percentage of the database come from permanent positions within Cable and Wireless, but all have made an informed choice to become self-employed – permanent employees would never be encouraged to make the move unless they had already decided to change their way of working. Once they have joined the ranks, FRL provides a strong support structure. This includes information booklets that cover networking, teleworking and setting up a limited company. Despite being self-employed, they are offered a special arrangement to allow them to participate in the C&W pension scheme as non-permanent members. They are, however, expected to take control of their own careers and to expect and plan for the unexpected – such as a project's coming to an abrupt stop for financial, contractual or even, in certain more unstable parts of the globe, political reasons.

Source: Walker L. 'Instant Staff for a Temporary Future', *People Management*, 25 January 1996, pp. 34–35

Legal issues in temporary employment
Drafting and using fixed-term contracts

An organisation has to take care when drafting fixed-term contracts, says Alan Fowler (1994). One of the key reasons for implementing such a contract is to ensure that there are no legal liabilities when the contract reaches its termination point. This is a notoriously complex part of the law, involving different rulings to exclude redundancy claims and unfair dismissal claims, so the policy and wording has to be quite clear on these and other points. Some key points are detailed below, but only in outline.

Readers are recommended to read a legal text carefully before entering into such contracts.

☐ If a fixed-term contract is going to be for longer than one year, there must be an agreed term in the contract for the employee to waive his or her rights to unfair dismissal. This means that no such claims can be made when the end of the contract is reached. The same applies for redundancy rights if the contract is going to extend beyond two years. The waiver clause could read: 'The employee agrees to waive any unfair dismissal and redundancy rights which may otherwise arise on the expiry and non-renewal of this contract.' Future legislation may ban such waiver clauses.

☐ The document action must either make the termination date quite clear (do not rely on word of mouth on this point) or, if it is a performance or task contract, pinpoint the end by including such a clause as: 'The contract will terminate on the date on which the project completion certificate is signed,' or: 'The contract will end automatically when the budgeted funds for the programme are exhausted.'

☐ If terminal bonuses are involved, the documentation must detail the conditions that are attached, such as the minimum productivity and quality levels and how they are measured, the cost parameters, and any other key features. Unless these are clearly laid down, the bonuses may well become a source of argument or even legal action.

☐ Renewal of a series of short-term contracts can give rise to redundancy and unfair dismissal rights if the overall result is to provide the relevant length of continuous service. At each renewal a new waiver must be obtained: the contract must be for more than a year, although, strangely, for redundancy purposes, the new contract does not need to be for a minimum of two years – it can be for any period.

☐ A series of short-term contracts is not necessarily a means of avoiding employees' claiming unfair dismissal or redundancy. In *Pfaffinger* v *the City of Liverpool*, where a college lecturer had worked under termtime-only contracts for some years and then left over a disputed change of pay, the court decided that he had accumulated service sufficiently to be able to claim redundancy.

☐ A clause must be inserted allowing either party to give notice of termination of the short-term contract, otherwise, should circumstances change and the employee no longer be needed, the employer will be saddled with the obligation to pay the salary for the whole of the outstanding period.

Are agency workers employees?

It was previously thought that workers who work through an agency but who are not employed by that agency were self-employed because there was no obligation to provide work (although agencies have, by law, to deduct tax and National Insurance). However, in *McMeechan* v *Secretary of State for Employment* (1995, EAT), the tribunal decided that McMeechan was an employee of the agency after considering all the terms and conditions of the contract – principally the degree of control exercised by the agency. This has made the situation less clear because the tribunal will have to look at the degree of control in each situation, before deciding the employment status. From an agency's viewpoint this is crucial because extended working through the agency runs the risk of temps obtaining full employment rights.

Employers' obligations

Employers do have obligations to agency temporary staff. Obviously the duty of care on health and safety grounds is identical for all staff on the premises, but there are also identical obligations on discrimination. An employer cannot specify the race or sex of the temps required, and cannot discriminate while they carry out work for the organisation. This even extended to a situation in which an agency temp wanted to return to the organisation where she had last worked before maternity but the employer only offered lower-value work. She successfully claimed for compensation against the organisation (BP) although she was not employed by that organisation (*BP Chemicals Ltd* v *Gillick*, EAT).

Qualifying period

At the time of writing, the two-year qualifying period is in doubt from two quarters. Firstly, the indications from the Labour government are that it may be reduced to one year (as set out in the *Fairness at Work* White Paper) at some time in the life of the parliament, thereby repeating its action of 1975. Secondly, a decision from the European Court of Justice is still awaited in the Seymour-Smith case in which two employees with less than two years' service are claiming that the two-year ruling amounts to indirect discrimination against female employees who are more likely to have shorter service.

Key factors in using complementary workers
Deciding the strategy

One point is clear from the beginning. To use complementary workers as a cost-cutting exercise alone is unlikely to succeed. As well as having a de-motivating and divisive effect upon both permanent and complementary staff, it would be regarded by all concerned as a short-term process. Strategy determines longer-term goals and an effective flexibility strategy is crucial.

At American Express, complementary workers are used to help the process of changing and consolidating services at a central site and in supporting new products. The company is able to see how successful a new product is in the early days without over-committing valuable and limited human resources. At NatWest, complementary employees have been used to help set up and run telephone banking and other operations that take place outside the traditional nine-to-five banking hours, instead of changing the culture and the terms and conditions of existing staff.

Another strategy has been to outsource to an agency the training for cheque-clearing operations so that staff hired through the agency are productive from day one. The overall strategy is to have a workforce that is 'just in time' rather than an overstaffed 'just in case' system.

Getting internal cultural attitudes right

Temporary employees have traditionally had a very low status in organisations and this stereotype needs to be removed. Managerial attitudes have to be altered so all employment options are considered. One or two organisations have given managers staffing budgets and the choice to employ permanent or complementary staff, which has helped them think carefully through the issues and their relation to organisational strategy. Another change is to understand that to control work services – people and technology – there is no need to own them. What is needed is to harness services from different quarters, co-ordinate them and ensure they are focused to achieve the required results.

The tensions between the two groups of employees can be a major difficulty, and one that is best solved by a careful, persistent and open communications process involving all parties to make the strategy quite clear and to give parity of treatment overall.

Assessing the training and learning implications

As the economy moves steadily towards a low unemployment base the issue of skills availability will become crucial. It is essential to agree informal contracts with temporary employees (whether directly or agency-employed) and with the agency over the training required to reach the skills levels and quality targets in the business plan. The division of training responsibility between the company and the agency is a key part of that contract.

A second feature is the creation of the learning environment. It is not easy to encourage employees to become interested and motivated in developing their formal and informal skills when their employment is on a limited basis, but many are now starting to realise that a variety of work experiences provide varied learning opportunities that can be valuable on their CV. (This is discussed further in Chapter 14, Flexibility and the Psychological Contract.)

Differentiate or integrate

Should temporary employees be distinguished from permanent employees in the workplace? In Boots' manufacturing plant at Airdrie, where 200 temporary workers are employed directly and through an agency, the agency employees work in a separate unit and have variations on the terms and conditions: this system works well administratively but there is a tendency for these workers to be regarded as second-class citizens. In IBM's Service Plus operation, where over 80 per cent are agency staff, a clear policy decision has been taken to integrate the two groups and remove the previous distinctions on car parking, social club, e-mail facilities and benefits. The integration is now broadly complete and employee briefing covers all workers in an identical fashion.

The IDS 1995 Study *Jobs For All Seasons* (IDS, 1995) indicated the variety of approaches towards benefits for complementary employees. At HTV, for example, fixed-term and freelance staff get paid enhanced salaries of between 5 and 25 per cent to compensate them for the lack of holidays, sick pay and pensions. Only 50 per cent of the organisations in the survey paid any form of sick pay, while around 70 per cent provided holiday pay, depending on service qualifications. Other benefits such as private health care and staff discounts were very rare, although Stena Sealink paid a profit-sharing bonus and unlimited standby travel.

Selecting the agency

Since the 1995 Deregulation and Contracting-out Act, agencies have no longer needed to be registered. There is self-regulation through the Federation of Recruitment and Employment Services (FRES), which has recently reviewed its code of practice and disciplinary procedure. With an estimated 15,000 agencies and an annual turnover exceeding £3 billion, it is important for it to work with a creditable organisation. FRES operate an arbitration service for clients and job-seekers. What is clearly necessary for employers is to choose an agency that has the experience that their organisation needs at the level it needs, and one that will share the same expectations of the development of the relationship between them. For example, the agency will need to be comfortably sure of accommodating the increased activities and responsibilities demanded by an organisation that is moving down the road of greater outsourcing and the use of complementary employees.

Where there are a large number of agency-employed staff, the role of the HR department may alter as it takes on the role of adviser and co-ordinator but is no longer responsible for delivering the day-to-day solutions.

Negotiating rates

There has been little mention so far of competitive rates. Most leading agencies take the 'Marks & Spencers' approach – to provide a premium-quality product with the long-term benefits that that brings. As with many other goods and services, low-cost items may fit in well with basic products but rarely in more complex long-term ones.

One important aspect here is that the arrangement will have to be agreed where an employer is unhappy with the quality of the labour supplied. Tate Appointments, for example, offer the Tate Watertight Guarantee, a 100-per-cent money-back guarantee for employers who are not completely satisfied with staff. Julia Robertson, managing director, hopes that this will highlight the need for agencies to take more responsibility for the quality of what may have been regarded as an orphan workforce.

Opportunities to transfer to permanent status

In Japan it is the long-term aim of complementary employees to be accepted into the core with all the benefits of lifelong employment. The differences in terms of employment are far less in Western economies but it is still an aspiration for a good proportion of temporary employees. The process whereby permanent vacancies are filled needs to be very clearly agreed. It seems completely logical that temporaries should have first consideration, but this needs to be formalised to avoid disappointment, disillusion and confusion.

Shiftworking

In the 1970s and 1980s, much of the flexibility initiative was directed at manufacturing processes in terms of multi-skilling and flexible shift systems. In this volume's predecessor, *Flexible Patterns of Work* (Curson, 1986), a whole chapter was set aside for the various shiftworking developments, especially those which allowed 24-hour, 365-day operations.

Details of three-, four-, five-, six- and even seven-shift working were laid out in their full complexity, explaining the benefits and disadvantages. As well as the general drivers towards improving flexibility detailed in Chapter 1, an additional factor was the movement to reduce the working week, especially in engineering. Taking an hour off the week throws most shift systems into disarray or into permanent overtime situations, so movements to re-jig patterns were very frequent.

Since the arrival of the recession from 1989 onwards, this driver has all but disappeared. Not only has the power of organised labour continued to decline but the support amongst members for a reduced week has subsided and been replaced by the need to negotiate a reasonable pay increase and some degree of job security. The growing popularity of outsourcing manufacturing abroad or to smaller suppliers has also put a brake on reducing hours.

Developments in manufacturing shiftworking have therefore been much slower. In a 1995 survey by IRS, fewer than 25 per cent of respondents had made any changes to their shift operations over the previous three years.

Types of shift systems

The Labour Force Survey 1996 showed the large variety of shift systems in operation (see Table 12).

The *two-shift system* remains the most popular shift operation, usually with a day shift and a night shift of around eight hours' duration and a gap between the end of the day

Table 12

NUMBER OF EMPLOYEES WORKING SHIFTS REGULARLY OR OCCASIONALLY: SPRING, 1996

Shift type	Number of employees		
	men	*women*	*total*
Morning shifts	37	36	73
Evening or twilight shift	68	106	174
Nightshift	226	147	373
Split shifts	109	81	190
Sometimes days or nights	159	422	581
Two-shift	741	530	1,271
Three-shift	452	222	674
Continental shifts	139	18	157
Weekend shifts	12	13	25
Other types	445	307	752
Total	2,388	1,882	4,270

Source: Labour Force Survey in Market Trends, December 1996.

and the beginning of the night. This is still common in the car industry, for example. However, 12-hour shifts are becoming more common, providing 24-hour cover for each day.

Continental shifts is a system in which employees rotate between day, evening and night shifts, usually changing weekly or monthly. They were introduced in many organisations in the early 1980s but are still not very widespread: only 157,000 employees work in those shifts. Their popularity has always been limited because employees change their shifts every two to three days, generating some disturbance to employees' biological rhythms.

A few organisations operate a weekend double shift in which employees work three 12-hour shifts, either days or nights, from Friday to Sunday. Perkins Engines at Shrewsbury began this system in 1996, and the payment at that point was a premium of time-and-a-half for Friday and Saturday and double time on Sunday (IDS, 1996).

Where shiftworking has grown is in the service sector. Around 70 per cent of organisations in this sector now operate some form of shiftworking. Between 1993 and 1995 the number of employees working a Sunday shift had increased by 155,000 to 2.5 million (LFS, spring 1995), most of which was attributable to the change in the Sunday trading laws. This report indicated that there were a total of around 4.1 million who worked on some form of shift work either on a permanent or occasional basis.

Examples of this development are in the IT sector, where 24-hour coverage is increasingly normal. Sun Life Assurance and Girobank are examples in which IT staff support 24-hour banking and insurance operations. Girobank employees work 13 shifts of 12 hours' duration over a four-week period, an average of 33 hours a week (IDS, 1996).

There have been a trickle of significant changes in manufacturing. Vauxhall's Luton plant in 1997 agreed a new 18-month rostering system by which employees moved to a three-shift system with hours averaged over 18 months. Employees work a basic 38-hour week plus or minus five hours, depending on demand. This movement towards increased flexibility is part of the company's package in its bid to build new models for the next century in the face of an overcrowded European marketplace.

For office staff there have been some introductions of nine-day fortnights. Oil giant Amoco brought this concept over from America, where most oil firms promote this practice as a move to 'green' commuting (Burke, 1997 (b)). Teams of staff in the 400-strong head office arrange work rotas between themselves to maintain a normal and effective service to customers. They record their own hours, overtime and sickness on the computer as part of the more trusting environment that Amoco are endeavouring to nurture.

Shift payments

Shift payments are as variable as the number of shift arrangements. Night-shift payments are made either as a fixed addition to day rates, a flat rate allowance per hour or shift, a weekly allowance, or an annual allowance incorporated into the annual hours scheme.

The 1996 IDS survey showed that premiums for working shifts vary:

Early shifts (mornings)	from 12.5% to 20%
Late shifts (afternoons)	from 17% to 25%
Night shifts	from 16% to 50%
Double day/two shifts	from 12% to 25%
Three-shift rotating	from 10% to 27%
Continuous shifts	from 17.5% to 60%

Shift payments have to be seen in the total context of the shift patterns, total hours, whether job and finish operates, and the level of basic pay and bonuses. Increasingly, there is a trade-off between these various aspects of shiftworking which is part of the whole flexibility picture.

Part-year working

Aside from the conventional arrangements of summer seasonal holiday work, a few other more unusual examples have emerged in recent years of organisations whose seasonal requirements have been converted into a variable manning strategy. The Whitbread beer company has a comparatively slack period between January and March, and a pilot scheme was put into operation in 1996 by which a number of draymen were employed for nine months of the year only. They are paid a terminal payment when they leave and a bonus when they restart on the day required. Because it is intended as a regular arrangement, employees have the opportunity to obtain regular temporary work for the three-month period, knowing they have the guarantee of a restart in April.

Conclusion

There is a very wide variety of temporary and shiftworking systems which are set up to meet the specific requirements of organisations and which constantly change in line with the marketplace. More information on outsourcing contracts is to be found in Chapter 7 and there are specific details on call centres in Chapter 8.

References and further reading

ATKINSON J., RICK L., MORRIS S. and WILLIAMS M. *Temporary Work and the Labour Market*, Brighton, Institute of Employment Studies Report 311, 1996.

BURKE K. 'National Grid cuts temps on its books'. *Personnel Today*, 19 June 1997 (a), p. 3.

BURKE K. 'Oil staff put hours down on trust'. *Personnel Today*, 4 September 1997 (b), p. 4.

COOPER C. 'Casual approach puts banks in the firing line'. *Personnel Today*, 21 August 1997, p. 13.

CORFIELD, K. and WRIGHT, A. *Flexible Working Means Business*. London, 1996.

CURSON C. *Flexible Patterns of Work*. IPM, London, 1986.

FOWLER A. 'How to draft and use fixed-term contracts'. *Personnel Management Plus*, September, 1994, pp. 23–24.

HUNTER L. and MACINNES J. *Employers' Labour Use Strategies* – Case Studies, Employment Department Research Paper No. 87, London, 1991.

HUNTER L., MCGREGOR A., MACINNES J. and SPROULL A. 'The Flexible firm: strategy and segmentation', *British Journal of*

Industrial Relations, Vol. 31, No. 3, September 1993, pp. 383–407.

IDS. *Jobs for All Seasons*: Study 579, June 1995.

IDS. *Shift Work*: Study 615, December 1996.

IRS. 'A hard day's night'. *IRS Employment Trends*, 576, 1995, pp. 9–16.

JAGER S. and SMITH D. 'Light at the end of the tunnel'. *People Management*, 7 August 1997, pp. 28–29.

OECD. *Employment Outlook*. Paris, Organisation for Economic Co-operation and Development, 1993.

Personnel Today. 'Recruitment alarm sounds'. *Personnel Today*, 9 September 1997, p. 80.

SANDERS and SYDNEY. *On the Move: A report on the growing use of fixed-term contracts in the UK*. London, 1996.

WHITEHEAD M. 'Mind the gap'. *People Management*, 9 October 1997, pp. 40–42.

WHITELY P. 'NPI shake-up puts an end to the use of temps'. *Personnel Today*, 18 September 1997, p. 1.

More information on interim management is available from:

IPD Locum Service: telephone 0181 263 3348
Association of Temporary and Interim Services (ATIES), 36–38 Mortimer Street, London, W1N 7RB: telephone 0171 323 4300

5   TELEWORKING AND VIRTUAL BUSINESS TEAMS

Introduction: Flexing the organisation through teleworking – what is going on?

The concept of teleworking – working at a remote location, using technology to ease communications – serves as a useful proxy for studying the effects of flexible working. Some organisations studied in this research have introduced this version of flexibility with great success, often in a limited way or in small pockets of the organisation. Very few organisations have been able or willing to broaden the practice of teleworking to its full, predicted, technological potential. The difficulties experienced by many in expanding teleworking go to the heart of many change management and practical flexible working issues. Problems of control, consistency of service and direction are all inevitably associated with teleworking, and are all potential stumbling-blocks – more so in organisations which rely upon traditional control systems and an inflexible management style.

A realistic estimate of how many teleworkers are currently operating in the UK is around 2 million. Some are part-time teleworkers while others are fully committed to the lifestyle and workstyle of a 'telecommuter'. Typically, the service industry has been the centre of most developments whereas employees in production or manufacturing remain largely tied to fixed locations. Although very few organisations can yet sustain a completely teleworked structure, it is becoming increasingly possible for sections of departments or even entire functions to be given the opportunity to capitalise on the opportunities of remote or distance working.

A leading-edge example of current practice, as one might expect, is Microsoft UK. The company employs around 700 permanent staff and a whole range of outside contract companies and consultants for special projects, such as technical support and software tailoring. Add to these indirect employees and the Microsoft UK payroll is probably nearer to 10,000. The demand for staff to work on many of Microsoft's projects is high from competitor or even partner organisations. This has led the company to use teleworking as an option, allowing it to capture a wider sweep of potential employees.

Even though teleworking has been around for some years now, many of the managers questioned in the survey undertaken for this book were unsure of how the term should be interpreted, and many had their own version to refer to. The increasingly widespread use of technology and subsequent mobility of information, coupled with the widely reported increased pressure of workloads at management or supervisory level in recent times, has forced a degree of *de facto* teleworking into organisations as something of a pressure-release valve, allowing more to be achieved in less time. The evidence suggests that this type of remote working at home and outside 'normal' work hours has largely become an additional, not alternative, feature of work for many in this category. Taking work home for the weekend or late evenings, while increasing the level of flexibility in working practices, is not true teleworking, but it could be the thin end of the wedge. Once employees realise that they can work, often more effectively, at remote locations, the ball will start to roll. Officially, according to a more detailed definition (Huws, 1992), a teleworker is someone who:

☐ has worked for the employer in question for at least ten days, or the equivalent number of hours in the four weeks immediately prior to the survey
☐ has been based at home for at least 50 per cent of this time
☐ has a direct contract with the employer which may or may not confer employee status
☐ uses both a telecommuting device and a computing device in the course of his or her work

□ would not be able to work remotely without the use of this technology.

The rise of teleworking

Teleworking is a version of flexible working that has captured the imagination of many writers and researchers and has encouraged the view that the future of work must include the teleworking option. Although teleworking accounts still for only a tiny fraction of the total employment, the numbers involved and the literature surrounding it is growing. *The Times* of 5 September 1997 reported that the number of UK employees working from home had increased between 1992 and 1995 by some 50 per cent.

The first publications on the subject emerged in the early 1970s, when the concept of taking work to the workers via telecommunications had an important part to play in the first modern energy-conscious era. The next wave of writers took a more futurist viewpoint. Typically, Toffler (1981) promoted the appealing concept of a return to some earlier rural idyll which became known as the 'electronic cottage'. These optimistic notes of the futurists are countered by writers who highlight the negative possibilities of teleworking – the potential for worker isolation, and exploitation. Popular press articles feature a similar dichotomy of views on the possible advantages of teleworking for work organisation, while large-scale business interests such as British Telecom and Mercury from the telecommunications industry continue to market the concept strongly. The final stage of development in the literature deals with the implementation of teleworking: a plethora of 'how to do it' guides aimed at giving advice to managers and to organisation leaders seeking to introduce or implement teleworking.

Huws (1992) claims that one in ten UK employers has at least one home-based worker, and one in twenty has true teleworkers relying on IT to work from home. A survey of 1,000 employers by the UK Employment Department identified the reasons for the growth in teleworking, suggesting that the main benefits to employers of using teleworkers were lower costs, more convenience and flexibility. The disadvantages of teleworking were thought by the same survey to focus directly on management control of the teleworkers.

In some cases the desire for introducing or trialling tele-working comes from the employees' side of the organisation, although it is more common for the employers' side to become keen to increase their numbers of teleworkers. The motivation for promoting teleworking nonetheless varies depending on which side of the employer/employee divide one looks. For the employer, teleworking schemes are merely one tool amongst many available, often designed to meet temporary shortages or to enable retention of certain valuable skills. The use of teleworking will need to be supported by other flexible working phenomena, such as 'hot-desking' (where employees share office facilities on their scheduled days in), 'hoteling' another temporary work facility hired as required, or even wholesale function or service outsourcing. From the employees's perspective, the introduction of tele-working is a big departure from normality and requires greater adjustment of work and non-work life. Perhaps this feature of teleworking is at least part of the answer to why the more optimistic estimates of projected growth of teleworking have not yet been fulfilled. (The Henley Centre for Forecasting predicted 2.5 million UK 'homeworkers' by 1995.)

While teleworkers may be self-employed, the number of employees who choose to work from home is on the increase, offering advantages to both employed and employer. Just by reducing travel-to-work time, teleworking can cut stress levels and help workers make better use of their time. Examples of companies who claim to have achieved the suc-cessful introduction of teleworking schemes include Rank Xerox, NatWest and BT, where the new working practices have brought not only cost advantages over traditional employment forms but also made it easier to retain and recruit staff unwilling or unable to travel. Working from home as a teleworker can easily be construed as a family-friendly employment practice, allowing the homeworker to schedule his or her work around family or community com-mitments.

Further evidence that the teleworking revolution is now

gaining pace can be found in the setting up of the Telecottage Association in April 1993, with sponsorship from BT and Apple Computers, to promote and support the concept of tele-cottages.

Costs and benefits of teleworking

Case-study

TELEWORKING ASSISTS RELOCATION AT MOBIL OIL

The relocation of the Mobil Oil Company Limited (MOCL) headquarters from London to Milton Keynes in the summer of 1995, involving over 350 employees, gave an added impetus to the company's desire to exploit the commercial benefits of more flexible working practices. The need for such a change came from an organisational policy to retain key staff who were unable to relocate and a realisation that business needs required some of the sales-force team to be located much closer to the customer than had previously been possible.

Secondary objectives were also identified that were much more wide-ranging, including overall office cost reduction, (estimated at approximately £7,300 per employee per year) increased family-friendliness, increased diversity in recruitment, increased empowerment, and general organisational process improvement.

The HR input to the process

Ideally the company would have wished to carry out pilot trials in order to anticipate more fully the working problems stemming from the move to more flexibility, but time constraints militated against this. The company used a variety of traditional HR techniques and practices to ease the way, including:

☐ interviews with all staff affected by the relocation with the relevant manager and employee relations adviser

☐ post-interview selection of positions and candidates for teleworking support

☐ identification of individual training and support needs for the teleworkers

☐ re-evaluation of the contractual basis of employment.

Teleworking was defined by the company as 'any measure that allows employees to be effective at remote [ie non-office] locations'. The company had experience of a number of sales teams who were effectively car-based, and used this experience to introduce more technological support to move further towards a 'virtual office' environment.

Selection of employees for teleworking

The selection decision was based on two factors – the identification of key employees who were unable or unwilling to relocate, and the identification of positions whose location closer to customers would be likely to improve business performance. Where these two classifications coincided, the process was then relatively straightforward – although the company assessed all employees eventually selected for teleworking to ensure they had the work discipline, organisation and ability to work in an environment that would not provide the traditional office support. A comprehensive package of training and development (including career management issues) was then implemented for those assessed as likely candidates for teleworking.

Managing the teleworkers

The training needs and concerns of the teleworkers' managers were also reviewed. Uncertainty on the part of managers about the loss of control over subordinates and the added challenge of 'remote management' led to the development of a package of training and skills development for this group in the areas of communications, goal-setting, and managing remote teams.

Employee reactions

The two stated objectives of the process led to quite different reactions. Those employees involved in the objective of 'locating closer to customers' – primarily sales employees – tended to view the move as an undesirable (though employment-saving) imposition. Those employees identified as key and offered teleworking to facilitate their retention were generally more positive about the development.

Areas of common concern included career development issues, work intrusion into home life, and matters of the adequacy of technical support available. Although no employees were forced into teleworking against their will (those who were unsuited or unwilling were found alternative positions), the view that teleworking was being 'imposed' without adequate consultation gave a negative spin to the

employees' view of teleworking, making further development of teleworking within the organisation more difficult.

Management reactions

Concerns over lack of control were common, as was the concern that
the degree of teamworking – which the company had previously valued
highly – would not be possible with a remote workforce. The integration of new teleworkers into teams was highlighted as a particular
problem. Sales-force managers believed that the concept was merely a
reworking of many existing practices and found the adoption relatively
straightforward. Other managerial concerns tended to focus primarily
on remuneration and compensation; the changes in style and methods
of appraisal called for by teleworkers were seen as less significant.

Lessons learned/conclusions

The company prepared written guidelines on the 'hard aspects' of teleworking or home-based working, covering all relevant legal and contractual information. As a result of this exercise the company found
that these guides should pay equal attention to the 'softer aspects' of
teleworking, such as performance management/improvement, career
management and communications.

In keeping with other similar organisational arrangements, the
company places considerable significance on the correct selection of
teleworkers, using clear criteria (for both the job and the person) to
determine suitability for teleworking. This practice will hopefully minimise the need for extensive and costly support mechanisms required
to maintain and develop the organisation's teleworking resource.

Introducing teleworking as an element of flexible working practices
will serve to reduce further the usefulness of standardised applications
of traditional HRM practices and policies, calling as it does for a package of HR policies some of which can be adapted from previous
regimes while others must emerge to meet the needs of a new and
demanding constituency.

There are undoubtedly well documented benefits to both
employer and employee of introducing teleworking. From the
employees' side these benefits will be far more than purely
financial. Young (1992) highlights the freedom to take control
over working patterns that teleworking affords the employee,
saying,

Teleworking, or working at home, allows individuals to have more control over their working day and environment. It supports a more responsible attitude toward work where workers are trusted rather than watched over, and allows a person to be closer to family and the local community.

Statements by the organisations consulted in the production of this book lead to the conclusion that the non-financial employee benefits are often largely ignored by businesses considering introduction or expansion of this type of flexibility. The calculation behind the decision whether to introduce teleworking or not is entirely a financial one, considering bottom-line impact above all else.

As a consequence managers who seek to increase flexibility through teleworking must be able to demonstrate that teleworking will either save money or increase productivity, and preferably both. Surveys from BT and the Employment Department claim to demonstrate increases in productivity of over 40 per cent in specific cases, but there is as yet little long-term hard data to back any attempt to generalise such claims. Much of the potential for increased productivity is situational and contingent upon the job or work tasks being considered and the abilities of the individual worker concerned. Perhaps a stronger argument is the view that inherent, automatic benefit to employers exists in having an effective teleworking function – that benefit being flexibility. Companies such as Freelance International (FI), which registered record profits in 1997, have found that the use of teleworking allows rapid response to demand without extra investment in fixed assets. FI has become a key player in a wide variety of industries through being the recipient of a number of outsourcing contracts in the flexibilisation of many other organisations. Using teleworking as a source of flexibility has created a distinct competitive advantage both for the companies doing the outsourcing and for FI.

In addition, teleworking consistently outperforms most conventional working patterns in another major organisational cost area – that of absenteeism. Whether this is due to the lack of commuting or to a more highly motivated and de-stressed workforce is neither here nor there: the benefits of reduced absenteeism are clear and quantifiable.

Like other corporate initiatives, demonstration of return on investment will be critical if teleworking arrangements are to expand in the future. The cost of setting up a single teleworker in terms of equipment alone is estimated by BT at around £17,000. High office rentals and difficulties in retaining staff for low-level positions provided a strong incentive for organisations to consider the flexibility through teleworking option. A BT survey entitled *The Economics of Teleworking*, reproduced in *Which Computer* (July 1993), identified a number of benefits to be gained from the use of remote workers:

□ productivity
□ reduced costs
□ retained specialists
□ recruitment of specialists
□ recruitment and retention generally
□ transport benefits
□ reduced stress.

It also noted several advantages to be enjoyed by the individual remote worker:

□ autonomy and increased job satisfaction
□ freedom from time constraints
□ a bridge in the career gap
□ a better balance between work and home life
□ cutting or eliminating commuting costs and time.

Principal disadvantages to the individual were identified as:

□ loss of face-to-face contact
□ less motivation
□ equipment issues.

And for the organisation, the main problems and difficulties were:

□ assessment of staff
□ assessment of jobs
□ convincing staff

☐ increased costs.

In a similar attempt to categorise pros and cons, Stanworth and Stanworth (1991) summarise the advantages to organisations of introducing teleworking as:

☐ productivity gains
☐ reduction of overheads
☐ retention of rare skills
☐ penetration of unusual labour market sources.

The principal potential disadvantages to the organisation are identified as:

☐ lack of commitment to organisational goals and culture
☐ problems of communication and supervision.

Future developments in teleworking

Kleiman (1995) projected that the number of telecommuters worldwide would rise to 13 million during 1998, based on the on-going march of technology and the increasing amount of knowledge- or service-based work that organisations will have to complete. The next step in the development of teleworking is likely to be international. UK firms are already investigating data links with the Philippines, where labour costs are likely to be one-fifth of those experienced in the UK. This potential threat to UK employment has led, not surprisingly, to trade union interest in teleworking. Remote working offers little chance for labour to be effectively organised, but some big unions are seeing the growth of teleworking as a potential niche market for new members. Unions with experience of teleworking, such as BIFU (the banking union) and the Manufacturing, Science and Finance (MSF) union, see that they may have a role to play in the negotiation of contracts and flexible working agreements between the organisation seeking to introduce flexibility through teleworking and the potential teleworker. An important part of negotiations, for teleworking clerical staff from the unions' perspective, is ensuring that they stay on the payroll, in order to maintain the same pension, leave and other benefit rights as office-based employees. Managers who are accustomed to operating in a highly unionised environment cannot expect the introduction of teleworking to remove completely the role of employee associations. Many negotiators would like to secure the right to choose to revert to conventional employment patterns without penalty or loss of promotion prospects if they begin to feel cut off and isolated from the parent company. Such a concession might be a major selling-point in such negotiations. Digital Corporation, a pioneer of many teleworking agreements, issues employees with a handbook on flexible working and training for all employees prior to the commencement of teleworking. Mercury Communications approaches the challenge of maintaining the integration and involvement of teleworkers by providing a help desk for remote staff to solve or alleviate many of the problems encountered.

Some legal aspects of teleworking

Case-study

CO-OPERATIVE BANK'S TELEWORKING AGREEMENT

The Co-operative Bank introduced a teleworking/homeworking agreement in October 1996 which has created much interest in the HR arena. The agreement was brokered between the main banking union BIFU and the Bank, and codifies a workable framework in areas such as equipment provision, special allowances, training and insurance. Closer investigation of this agreement and the issues it raises is a worthwhile addition to the debate, at a time when other organisations are looking for models of best practice to indicate how they might move ahead into teleworking.

Details of the agreement

The agreement defines teleworking as 'that which involves any job performed at or from home instead of at or from Co-operative banking premises'. The contractual place of work is therefore specified as the home address. In large part the terms and conditions of teleworkers in the employ of the Bank are identical to those employed in the traditional manner, and any conditions under the new agreement are intended to be as favourable as those of other permanent Bank staff.

The Bank places great emphasis on trust and communications between the teleworker and the relevant manager, and is concerned to ensure that those employed under this agreement are given every opportunity to become part of and contribute to a larger team of employees.

The Bank carried out two pilot exercises to test the feasibility of a number of operations for a distance-working model. The results of these pilots allowed the Bank to agree to use teleworking as one option amongst many to improve flexibility. The organisation is willing to consider other areas of the business that wish to introduce teleworking. The first stage in moving towards further teleworking in this way is via the HR function, who will assess the proposal for suitability against the Bank's own criteria. Line managers also have a role in the crucial task of assessing the suitability and the selection of staff with the potential for teleworking in conjunction with the HR department. Again, objective criteria cover the suitability of premises, the experience of the employee, and the characteristics and competencies which the Bank has identified as indicative of the ability of an employee to work effectively and productively in the home environment.

Any staff who wish to move into the teleworking programme but are refused on the basis of the line manager's assessment have the right to appeal against the decision in keeping with the Bank's standard grievance procedures. Prior to the appointment of a teleworker, the Bank intends to provide training and guidance on the requirements of teleworking, backed up by comprehensive support once appointed. No Bank staff will be forced to work as teleworkers against their wishes.

The hours of work for each teleworker are specified in the main terms and conditions of employment for office-based staff, although where practicable, current working practices and patterns will be reviewed with a view to increasing flexibility and achieving a balance between working hours that suit the personal circumstances of the employee and the business needs of the Bank.

The place of work is the teleworker's current home address. If a teleworker wishes to move to a different location, the suitability of the new location will be assessed by the Bank, and teleworking will only continue with the Bank's express agreement. The Bank will undertake to remove and refit equipment at the new address. Teleworkers are expected to attend office meetings, briefings and training, etc, in line with other office-based staff, this requirement is specified at the time that staff are notified about the opportunities for teleworking. Holiday entitlement is in line with the main statement of terms and conditions applicable at the Bank. Payment and allowances for teleworkers are in line with the evaluated grade for the job undertaken, although no territorial allowance will be payable to employees while working at home. The removal of this benefit has been phased in over a 12-month period. All other bank benefits will be available to teleworkers in the same way and under the same criteria as for traditional employees.

A teleworking allowance has been agreed between the Bank and the Inland Revenue, via the employee's PAYE code, to cover reasonable household expenses, such as heating, and lighting resulting from working at home. Tax relief will therefore be received at the following rates:

Full-time staff   £300 per annum

Part-time staff   (less than 21 hours per week) £150 per annum

The teleworker may claim further allowances for household expenses in excess of the above amounts if the claim can be supported by the Inland Revenue. Teleworkers who are workstation-based and work permanently at home will receive an extra allowance of £100 per annum in recognition of any possible additional costs incurred as a direct result of teleworking.

The Bank provides agreed equipment and is responsible for installation, maintenance and repair: the items remain the property of the Bank. A business telephone line is installed purely for business usage: all charges relating to its use will be invoiced to the Bank. In order to guard against the isolation of teleworkers the Bank ensures that regular team meetings with line manager and colleagues are held. In addition, daily contact is made between the office-based team and the teleworker. Teleworkers are represented on any charts or other documentation intended to demonstrate the structure or constituents of teams and groups within the Bank. Trade union representation, health and welfare benefits, and access to organisational support services are identical to those of office-based staff of the same or similar grade.

The Bank maintains its duty under Health and Safety legislation, and ensures (as far as is reasonably possible) the health, safety and welfare at work of all employees. Equally, all teleworkers (and other employees) are required to take reasonable care at work for their own health and safety, and for that of others who might be affected by their actions. All equipment supplied by the Bank meets the appropriate health and safety requirements; maintenance services are provided to ensure that standards are maintained and regular reviews are undertaken. The teleworker is responsible for maintaining his or her work environment to agreed standards so that Bank information and equipment is not put at risk. The teleworker is responsible for confidentiality and system security. The Bank is responsible for insuring the equipment that is placed in the teleworker's home.

If any employees wish to withdraw from teleworking they can formally apply to do so: the Bank intends to facilitate voluntary exit from the scheme – although the Bank sees the introduction of teleworking as a long-term commitment for both the Bank and its staff. The Bank and BIFU monitor and review the agreement on teleworking on a six-monthly basis to ensure that the terms of the agreement are operating effectively.

Conclusions

The Co-operative Bank's teleworking agreement detailed above represents many aspects of best practice in such situations and provides an excellent starting-point for other organisations seeking to introduce the advantages of teleworking to their business. The Bank has attempted to introduce teleworking as part of a desire to increase flexibility, and as such it should be seen as an element of a package which includes a number of other initiatives, such as job sharing. While the Bank has no desire to extend teleworking across the whole organisation, it believes that the option is a clear response to the changing business needs of its market, and as such is an appropriate HR intervention to improve customer service, employee satisfaction and overall organisation performance.

Charles Handy (1989) sees the teleworker as an extension of his idea of the 'Shamrock organisation', affording greater flexibility in hiring and firing and pushing ever more people into self-employment or temporary short-term contracts. Developments such as these alter significantly the legal relationship between employer and employee. Even where most aspects of the employment contract remain unchanged, relocating employees from traditional, regulated and controlled environments to remote, often home-based situations poses some potential legal difficulties. The aspect that is usually considered first is that of equipment insurance. Employees who are to be set up with thousands of pounds' worth of technological equipment in their home are unlikely to be covered for theft or damage on a standard home contents insurance policy. In addition, the health and safety aspects of homeworking are another shady area. In a traditional employment situation the employer has the duty to provide a safe and reasonably healthy environment. Teleworkers in effect have to undertake this duty themselves, and an employer would be wise to take expert advice on the implications of this change. Some organisational contracts such as service agreements might have to be renegotiated if they currently specify that all servicing will be carried out on the employer's main site. This will obviously not be appropriate, and a variation of such terms, including the concomitant increase in costs, will be required if the servicing is required to be at the remote location. Security of information is another possible problem: once files and documents leave the relative security of the office, the danger of losses resulting from missing or lost data is increased.

All of the factors in the preceding paragraph concern legal considerations from the perspective of the organisation. There is also a case for looking into the potential legal difficulties from the perspective of the employee. Teleworkers may run into difficulties if claiming certain expenses, such as power, lighting etc, against any tax liability, because from the Inland Revenue's viewpoint they remain employees, and any such expenses should be borne by the employer. Legal restrictions may also apply as to the use and performance of certain duties in a building designated as a place of residence. Although little objection is likely to be raised over a teleworker's using a spare room for office or computer-based work, if the teleworker causes disturbances to the locality through deliveries, or through other working arrangements that were not previously experienced, objections are to be expected.

The status of the teleworker as employee or self-employed, and consequently all kinds of employment rights and benefits issues, has been the subject of many arguments in companies and in the courts, prompting the question 'When is a tele-worker an employee, and when is he/she not?' At present it is possible for an employer to use teleworking to alter the status of an employee – but it is not easy. Case law based in the 1980s undermined the position of the teleworker as a non-employee, especially in *Nethermere (St Neots) Ltd* v *Gardiner and Taverna* (1984 IRLR 240; CA). The homeworkers (not teleworkers) in this case sewed trouser pockets. They determined their own hours of work and rate of production, but they were given instructions on how to complete the work, payment was fixed and not negotiable, and all machinery was provided and owned by the company. In this case the workers were held to be employees.

Workers can claim and be found by a court to be self-employed only if they can prove that they are in business on their own account. This condition is usually satisfied by the parading of several different clients, as in *Hall* v *Lorimer* (1994 IRLR 171; CA), or personal ownership of equipment, and the freedom to negotiate contracts, fees or even turn work down, as in *Harris* v *Reed Employment* (1985 IRLIB 281; EAT). However, the use of practices and terminology usually associated with the traditional contract of employment – eg disciplinary procedures, duty of fidelity, and a tight control over the work itself – endangers the desire to be declared self-employed, as in *Lane* v *Shire Roofing Co. (Oxford) Ltd* (1995 IRLR 493; CA) and *McMeechan* v *Secretary of State for Employment* (1995 IRLR 461; EAT), where workers were shown to be employees.

Self-employed status requires the careful drafting of contracts and the genuine scope for individuals to be their own boss, if it is not to be seen by the courts, and more significantly the Inland Revenue, as a dodge to avoid taxes, duties or other statutory employee/employer obligations. Considerations such as illness and sickness reporting need to be carefully thought through. Whereas homeworkers do generally demonstrate a lower tendency towards illness than those in traditional work relationships, this could merely be due to the failure to report sickness effectively, and employers cannot neglect their liabilities under the Health and Safety legislation. All employers should have policies in place for ensuring that the site of work (off premises or on) is safe and free of undue risk. Any equipment used must also be subjected to a risk assessment – eg the Display Screen Equipment Regulations 1992 still apply. It would seem to be a wise precaution to investigate the possibilities of offering training in safe working practices for homeworkers in order to avoid both the risks themselves and any claims of contributory negligence that might follow if a homeworker was injured.

When drawing up new contracts for employed homeworkers, it is preferable to build in the flexibility to allow for changes to the location of employment in case the situation arises where the organisation wishes to transfer people back to on-site operation. It may be, for example, that a performance or delivery problem cannot be solved in any other way. Other potential pitfalls include the EU working time Directive whereby the 48-hour working-week clause will restrict some of the flexibility available.

Resistance to teleworking

Despite the expected, if not easily quantified, cost and competitive advantages of new technology-driven changes such as teleworking, and the desire of organisations to introduce the concept more widely, there are some restraining forces holding back its advancement. One of these (possibly even the primary one) appears to be worker resistance. Throughout history the introduction of new technology into the workplace has thrust decisive increases in the control over work organisation and the pay-effort bargain into the hands of managers of the organisation. Teleworking potentially marks a distinct change in this trend, affording control of work quality and pace to the employee. Nonetheless, employees who have witnessed or suffered from the shift of power to employers as a result of technological change in the past may see the introduction of further technology as a threat.

A survey conducted by Crossan and Burton (1993) into the stereotype teleworker produced revealing indications as to what other factors might dissuade individual employees from fully adopting the idea of remote working. They found that 'The majority of teleworkers were female, married, with

child-care responsibilities, who were not interested in promotion.'

In addition their survey found isolation was not a major
problem for teleworkers.

The psychological aspects of teleworking studies indicate
that workers have adjusted more easily to teleworking than
their managers. Under teleworking schemes, workers based at
home or in telecottages linked only by fax, phone, and computer to their supervisors and colleagues can easily appreciate
the freedoms offered. Managers, however, do not always view
this set-up favourably since their position is often redesignated
from controller to facilitator. Many organisational information technology policies, of which teleworking forms only
a part, do not have a good track record – often because their
implementation suffers from the mistake of being heavily
biased towards getting the technology right at the expense of
getting the human side of systems structures and culture right.

The empowerment potential of teleworking

The implementation of teleworking programmes differs significantly from other change initiatives but can be both a
great leveller of knowledge and a great tool for empowerment,
given the correct organisational structure.

Information workers working at remote locations can have
all the data they need to make decisions and take action.
Computerisation of clerical work offers new opportunities to
learn and assume new responsibilities to previously unchal-
lenged employees, and offers access to on-line information
allowing first-line supervisors to make decisions once reserved
for upper management and staff. Information technology (IT) is
undoubtedly creating a whole new business environment for
corporations. The challenge is for managers of those corporations to see IT as a strategic and competitive resource.

Introducing teleworking and managing the teleworkers: practical considerations

Managers thinking about this form of flexible working must
consider the following factors and issues – in a way that
applies particularly to them – prior to developing the policies

and support mechanisms that enable the introduction of the type and extent of teleworking required.

1   Be clear about your reasons for introducing teleworking: they will undoubtedly influence the model used. Possible objectives might include cost/space saving, retention of key staff, easing of communications, etc. An alternative could be to increase speed of response times or to build updating procedures into established organisational practices. Teleworking gives organisations the opportunity to introduce some 'future proofing' to their policies and procedures, because technology can be re-specified as the teleworker's competence increases and as the teleworking function is developed.

2   Investigate the hard- and software required to support the process. Companies such as BT and Cabletel supply information and consultancy on the various systems available and their capabilities. An appropriate place to look into more detailed specifications of alternative work environments is the web page *http://www.haworth-furn.com*. Information can be found here on telecommuting, office hoteling, technology-based teamwork environments and facilities planning.

3   Take care in deciding on the criteria for the selection of staff for teleworking. Most studies recommend trial periods to test if staff members can achieve objectives under the new conditions, and regular reviews of performance and support requirements. Practical consideration must be given to how current performance can be taken to reflect potential for teleworking. Typically, those employees who have shown initiative, developed and implemented process solutions or managed projects independently can be found to have the required skills and attributes of a teleworker. Effective teleworking requires a higher degree of mutual trust between employer and employee than is necessary (or commonly found) in more traditional working environments. This by itself leads most organisations to trial teleworking with existing and reliability-proven employees.

4   Develop a code of practice for teleworking in your organ-
    isation. The code should cover things such as conditions
    and terms, insurance and legal implications, target set-
    ting and monitoring, reporting structures and procedures,
    career management for teleworkers, on-line or off-line
    support mechanisms, communications processes, etc.

5   Consider the option of putting out to in-house tender any
    functions or services that could be delivered effectively
    via teleworking. Departments, sections, or even individ-
    ual employees can be invited to contribute to the agreed
    specification that could be offered, and the business case
    for doing the work in this way. Volunteers for telework-
    ing programmes unearthed like this are apt to be keen to
    prove that the new delivery method is superior to the tra-
    ditional way. Meanwhile, negotiations over the specifica-
    tion of the service to be tendered give the organisation
    control over quality and delivery times – often a fear of
    those new to the teleworking concept.

6   Develop policies and procedures that allow for the recog-
    nition and integration of the teleworking teams in order
    that they remain (or become) part of the organisation
    both culturally and practically. The teleworker must be
    tied in to organisational communications processes, elec-
    tronically where possible, and given opportunities to con-
    tribute outside of his or her normal contract if applicable.
    Typically, a teleworking support group or help line
    facility might be used.

7   If the teleworking pilots are effective, look to diffuse the
    practice throughout the organisation, learning from
    implementation problems and policy successes as you go.
    If appropriate, integrate the teleworking process with a
    system of hot-desking (see the Herts County Council
    case-study below) to ensure that the accommodation sav-
    ings are made and to reinforce the new system of oper-
    ation (Ball, 1996). There are a number of imaginative
    ideas in this area, such as the purpose-built 70-foot-long
    table at media consultancy Michaelides & Bednash, cost-
    ing £5,000, installed as part of a refurbishing programme
    in 1994. All 11 staff work from the table, including the

managing partners, and there are no permanent places. Minimal personal storage is kept at the side of the room. 'No secrets, no politics, transparent operation' are the key features, according to partner George Michaelides (Wustemann, 1997).

Case-study

TELEWORKING AND HOT-DESKING AT HERTS COUNTY COUNCIL

There can be few business initiatives which combine the business case for flexible working practices, advance equal opportunities, have wider benefits for employees, and also manage to claim to have a 'green' pedigree. The Workwise initiative by Herts County Council (Herts CC) can lay claim to all of these, and is starting to prove to be a key to unlocking the potential of the organisation and its assets, especially its land, buildings and human resources.

What is Workwise?

Workwise is Herts CC's brand-name for its 'New ways of working' initiative: advice and support is given to departments, teams, managers and employees for projects arising from the scheme. It links the employment policies and practices with environmental and transport service delivery strategies. It actively encourages rethinking traditional ways of working – eg challenging working at fixed places for fixed times. And it provides the corporate infrastructure to facilitate individual projects – eg relevant strategies for accommodation, IT/telecommunications and employment policies and procedures.

What are the driving forces?

There were a number of factors which in the early 1990s prompted Herts CC to examine thoroughly its ways of working.

First, Herts CC has a budget exceeding £800 million involving 26,000 employees working at over 1,000 sites, but in the last 20 years it has had very little opportunity to expand. On the contrary, governments have on an annual basis successively reduced its funding leading the authority with no alternative but to cut costs or services. Cutting small slices (the salami approach) from staff costs and services, hoping that the public would not notice, was no longer a real option. More efficient use of sites and buildings was vital in the cost-reduction equation.

Second, the Council has responsibility for transportation and environmental issues across the county. It had become clear for some time that a fundamental rethink of transportation policies was essential to avoid permanent gridlock of the county's roads. Building new roads was out of the question, so it was vital to encourage people to use their cars less, especially at peak times. Because the authority is by far the largest employer in the county, it felt the need to lead from the front and design policies that would give an impetus to reducing employees' car travelling.

Finally, working towards the Opportunity 2000 action plan meant that the Council needed carefully to consider the working-time preferences of its female employees.

The major Workwise initiatives

A conference was held at County Hall in 1994 to generate discussion and involvement. Management, unions and staff from all departments were invited and presentations were made by leading organisations in the field, including Digital, New Ways to Work and Oxford County Council. This set the scene for actually changing work patterns.

The first pilot scheme was set up within the trading standards department, which is responsible for providing advice and enforcing the law on consumer and fair trading issues. In 1995 the department relocated around 70 staff from two sites into one, and also incorporated a number of new flexible features in the way the staff were to operate. The central office was equipped with new IT and telecommunications intrastructure which did away with dedicated desks but provided all the services that staff required. Staff were also encouraged to formulate a working style that incorporated working at home and from home, reducing the time spent at the office, and, significantly, reducing the time and cost of travelling. Improvements were made in the managerial and support systems for staff working externally to ensure that customer service did not suffer in any way. Agreement was reached with the trade unions to rationalise office relocation payments and on methods of defining business mileage which would keep to the right side of the law as defined by the Inland Revenue.

Oases and performance management

Two key features gave additional support to the scheme. First was the creation of Oases, the name given to the authority's nine drop-in centres which had some IT and telecommunications services. These were fully operational by early 1996, and allowed staff to find a workplace convenient to their home or on their business route where they could create reports, make and receive calls, and access required information. A further 20 Oases sites are planned to be in operation by the end of the decade.

The second feature was a cultural switch in performance management focus. The emphasis was slowly but steadily moved towards measuring achievement. Managing 'remote' employees has to be geared to how well they perform, not to where or when they perform. This change in perception produced a requirement for training managers and staff to become competent in the process of target-setting and monitoring the inevitable empowerment that arises from remote working. People were no longer to be judged by their visibility but by their success.

The immediate result was a saving of 10 per cent in travel time together with increases in staff productivity and customer satisfaction. The actual cost savings in business travel were of the order of 5 to 8 per cent, while employees themselves saved a chunk of their travel costs from home to work. Furthermore, a year or more into the scheme, very few employees wanted to revert to their old ways of working.

Further developments

Encouraged by this success, further initiatives got under way in 1997 and 1998. The largest is in the social services department, which has 4,500 staff, a third of whom are based at over 30 sites around the county. There had been plans to create two new office sites costing £1 million, but budget cuts prevented this and focused minds on creating a more flexible working arrangement.

After extensive project group consultation, it was agreed to start the process by reducing the number of sites at which central social services staff operated from five to two, and to open one purpose-fitted site. This would allow at least one building to be sold immediately and a further two at a later date to help fund the scheme. The new site was a floor of a converted 1960s warehouse in Hatfield which accommodated 130 staff sharing 100 workstations, and also provided meetings rooms, coffee areas and an Oasis area with ten workstations for other Council drop-in staff. It is planned for personal storage areas to be very limited in order to make maximum use of the space. Each member of staff therefore has a pedestal to be moved to whichever desk he or she is using. There will be library facilities on the intranet for all Council publications (procedure manuals, legal handbooks, etc) to avoid issuing sets to everybody. The new technology includes e-mail, voicemail, document-scanning and call-forwarding.

Staff teams had been asked to divide themselves into home-based, office-based and mobile employees. The latter would spend half their time working away from their bases either at home or using a variety of Council offices. Each group is entitled to the appropriate technology. Employees working from home have been wired up to the intranet; those mobile may have laptops or mobile phones, depending on the requirements of each situation. Each team has a budget within which to work. This gives them a sense of ownership and responsibility as well as one of reality.

The scheme went live in November 1997, and moves have been taking place steadily since, with continuous evaluation. The same process is planned for 1998 in respect of the district social services teams, totalling around 1,000 employees. It will be piloted in two districts first, headed up by two managers who believe strongly in the flexible working concept. It is estimated that the payback period on capital equipment purchase is only six months, assuming a productivity saving of 5 per cent and a reduction in the need for support staff consistent with the reduction in the number of sites.

In a message to social services staff in October 1997, Sarah Pickup, assistant director of resources, said:

> Workwise is not about degrading office accommodation or forcing people to work in ways or conditions that are unsatisfactory. Far from it. It is about looking for opportunities to increase our effectiveness through redesigning and getting the best use out of office space, and sharing and making the best use of scarce resources.
>
> Everyone in the department will understand that our prime objective is to safeguard essential services to vulnerable people ... Workwise will help us to make such savings and give us the chance to increase effectiveness through technology and changes to the ways we operate and communicate.

For Gill Rothwell, deputy director of personnel, there are a number of issues to be examined so that future schemes can continue to be successful:

> We need to look at the way managers approach the changes. For them the adaptation can be quite difficult as staff become more distant and less visible. We need to work with managers who find the changes immediately advantageous and which ones take to it with more difficulty. This will help us to design the required training and other support programmes. We also need to constantly review the way Workwise is operating, and see if the initial staff enthusiasm is maintained over the longer period. There are a number of other departments where this method of working could be introduced, and our experience to date will be extremely useful in identifying those areas and implementing new schemes.

Source: Wustemann L. 'Moving up a gear – Workwise at Hertfordshire County Council'. *Flexible Working*, September 1997, pp. 18–22.

Managing the teleworker

The largest area of concern for employers who are considering the potential of teleworking is that of managing the teleworker. A number of methods are used in those organisations with successful telework operations to counter the fear of loss of control. Payment by results gives the organisation direct control over outcomes of the teleworking process, and ties in effort to performance and reward in a highly traditional way. Incentive rewards and target-setting by managers can be applied just as easily to teleworkers as they can with in-house employees. The negotiation of targets might be more complex and more individualised, but one could argue that this provides the manager with an opportunity to focus the teleworkers' effort much more tightly on the objectives and goals of the organisation. Monitoring of achievement against targets via regular electronic or telephone contact can be supplemented by regular group or individual progress meetings.

Less common – but more in keeping with the principle of an empowered teleworking team – is the use of team meetings, electronically or otherwise, to discuss progress on a variety of project issues. Where the work being completed is capable of being monitored electronically for quantity of output (eg some forms of data entry or data preparation), telework output can easily be monitored on-line. Managerial action can then be directed to those workers who do not appear to be able to conform to the quantities achieved by other teleworkers, or to the agreed standards.

There is no reason to exclude teleworkers from other forms of performance monitoring, such as client feedback or detailed spot checks on work for quality and fitness for purpose. The use of time-sheets for controlling the activity of teleworkers would seem to be inappropriate – the whole point of the teleworking exercise is often to remove such forms of control. Time-sheets or some alternative form of recording working time may still be required, however, for purposes such as client billing, or health and safety checks.

Teleworking, motivation and virtual business teams

Case-study

LOCATION INDEPENDENT WORKING (LIW) AT ROYAL MAIL

In 1994 the Consultancy Services Group (CSG) of Royal Mail set up a pilot programme to trial the opportunities and challenges to be faced by the introduction of virtual business teams. The pilot involved a small number of selected staff from the existing group at various Royal Mail client premises around the country, who had some experience of remote working.

The project identified the following hardware/technological requirements for each individual member of the virtual team:

☐ a portable PC with fax/modem
☐ access to Postline (WAN/LAN) from other Royal Mail sites and non-Royal-Mail locations, eg at home
☐ colour monitor
☐ printer
☐ mobile telephone with hands-off car installation
☐ home telephone line and answering machine
☐ furniture (where necessary at home to meet Health and Safety requirements).

The objectives of the scheme

The objectives of the pilot were twofold. The first aim was to increase effectiveness in the delivery of Consultancy Services Group services. Improved effectiveness would enable CSG to make the best use of its resources through the introduction of changed work patterns, and work practices, so addressing the people issues of location independent working.

The second goal was to find a means to contribute towards reducing overheads and accommodation. The better utilisation of space and buildings would surely assist in achieving the overall target of reducing charge-out rates (internal fees) by 25 per cent by 1996/97.

A lesser objective was to use the pilot group from within CSG, if it proved to be successful, as a model for other areas within Royal Mail, which might at a future date wish to implement aspects of LIW and virtual teamworking. In this way the lessons learned and mistakes made by the pilot group could be used to inform further developments in virtual teamworking.

Although information on the results of the pilot is not available and remains too sensitive to be widely released, there are a number of learning-points and issues from the case that are worthy of scrutiny by anyone who is considering the introduction of virtual business teams in an organisation. In researching and evaluating the project, Royal Mail identified a number of crucial factors which to a large extent determined the level of success achievable. These factors related more to the organisation that was introducing LIW than to the individuals who were part of the project, often reflecting aspects of the established culture and management style of the organisation.

Conclusion: Royal Mail's identified success factors for the introduction of virtual teams

Management commitment

Moving from traditional work patterns to a virtual team set-up is a significant move for employees not familiar with the new expectations placed upon them. Reassurance from senior managers that the changes are supported and valued is crucial. Without this, employees might begin to think that the scheme was a ruse to simply save costs and would eventually lead to their complete removal from the organisation.

Monetary issues

The organisation found that cost savings resulting from LIW were a crucial consideration. They had to be monitored closely to accurately identify those savings which directly resulted from the project, and at least some of these savings had to be channelled back to the team in the form of other resources to provide an incentive for the people involved. More importantly, the organisation was able to encourage other managers in different sections to buy into the concept, by demonstrating that the cost savings achieved would provide a team or section benefit, not just an organisational one.

Administration

The dispersal of virtual teams engenders an increased role for the teams' administration function as the communications lynchpin. The chief administrative role rapidly becomes that of ensuring that communication channels are effective and open in order that the LIW environment is allowed to operate smoothly and efficiently. At the start of the project, in the light of concerns that LIW may mean administrative job losses, it is important that those managing the introduction of LIW emphasise the vital role that administration plays in making the project a success.

Selecting and motivating employees

Experience of the introduction of virtual teams has taught Royal Mail that a careful selection process is essential if the team and the individual are to operate effectively. To identify criteria that could be used by managers in selecting the personnel who might be suitable for LIW was a vital requirement. In addition the pilot determined that the chance to be part of a virtual team might be offered on a short-term basis, subject to withdrawal if individual performance or team effectiveness was below standard. Clear and regularly reviewed objectives for the virtual team member were also deemed essential, especially where a team manager was not going to be in regular (traditional) contact with the team members.

Touchdown centres

The concept of LIW is that any individual should be able to work at any location suited to the job in hand. This could mean at home, at a business centre, while travelling or at any location owned by Royal Mail. For this system to operate effectively, the organisational policy of restricted access to certain areas or sites will have to be reviewed. The project recommended the nomination of a number of designated 'touchdown centres' at selected sites in the UK for those involved in LIW. These centres should be easily accessible and have facilities available for the virtual team member to work with.

The motivational aspects of teleworking holds much potential for success because the workers themselves can be expected to be less stressed, more satisfied and more productive: those who voluntarily opt for this form of working have much to gain from making a success of the development. For many teleworkers, self-motivation becomes the main, if not sole, focus of drive and desire for achievement. On the side of the teleworker, many theoretical constructions of motivation support the view that self-motivation is really the only effective way of stimulating and sustaining excellent personal performance.

Fred Herzberg expressed the view, for example, that organisational motivation schemes can only serve to temporarily 'charge a worker's battery', but that if the worker doesn't have his or her own generator (ie is not self-motivated), sustained motivated performance is simply not achievable.

There is clearly considerable potential for self-motivation in the teleworking concept. In addition, many organisations are seeking to capitalise on such potential by putting together teams of teleworkers. The term 'virtual business team' has been used by BT, amongst others, to describe the phenomenon of remote individuals' working as mutually supportive teams to back up or develop business endeavours. The virtual business team is not a team in the traditional sense of the word: the team members may never actually meet face to face or even be in the same country, the connections between them are electronic not human and a virtual team meeting happens in cyberspace, not the team-leader's office. This form of teleworking poses a challenge to the view that many of the benefits of cohesive teamworking stem from personal interaction and human contact – a feature against which remote working, by its very nature, militates.

The answer to this apparent contradiction may lie, at least in part, in revisiting the traditional concepts of business teams and teamworking, many of which focus on developing team-wide working relationships by matching effective combinations of personality and team roles (eg Belbin, MBTI and the Team Management System recently developed by Margerison and McCan). Traditionally, teams have been thought to develop through predetermined stages in the typical sequence put forward by the Tuckman model of 'Forming, Storming, Norming and Performing'. The world of the virtual business team is far more unstable and owes more to techniques of networking, constructing temporary alliances, and an ability to operate effectively as a part of a number of teams.

The lack of physical contact implied by the concept of the virtual team may well restrict team development as it is currently interpreted, but the pace of change in our shifting business world, it could be argued, is such that teams no longer have the luxury of time available to them to go through prolonged stages of development, or to undergo the allocation of team roles according to the Belbin or TMS prescription. The virtual business team has the advantage of restricting the efforts of its members to a purely business focus: the efforts of team members can be efficiently channelled towards team objectives. Social or interactional aspects of traditional teams are no longer able to act as a drain on the time or energy of the team members or cause conflicting deflection from purpose.

According to Angela Eden (1995), many of the motivating and management issues behind virtual business teams are not that dissimilar to those of conventional teams. Nonetheless, managing a dispersed network of self-managed individuals has to take into account the needs of such autonomous workers. Eden believes that the virtual team must have clear, well-defined expectations of its members, and an accurate view of the skills (both quantitatively and qualitatively) that each virtual team requires. The implication of this approach is that much attention must be paid to the process for selecting virtual business teams. In addition, the terms and conditions offered to those selected for working in virtual teams will differ significantly from those traditionally offered.

Contactability is often a key determinant of the virtual team's achievements. Examples of approaches to this include the zoning of specific periods of contact time, when all team members can be available to communicate and discuss (electronically) team or organisational issues. Alternatively, periodic electronic conferencing may bring some interaction to the team, but will have to be supported and carefully planned if the team is operating across international time zones.

Conclusion

Management of teleworking or a virtual team still focuses on team targets, team maintenance and team supervision, all of which require the development of techniques that can be carried out remotely.

The use of teleworking as an aid to flexibility is also something of a hostage to fortune, because values can be 'designed in' to computer technologies (Mumford, 1981) – that is, hardware and software can be designed either to increase user flexibility or to limit it, to enlarge operator decision-making or to constrain it. It is therefore incumbent upon systems designers, vendors, purchasers and in-house design and development personnel to diagnose and discuss what a technology will do to people's work and their working lives.

The management of teleworkers calls for skills and techniques distinct and separate from those used by managers on a day-to-day basis. Significantly, consideration of the technological aspects of the change at the expense of cultural and organisational aspects is seen as a recipe for failure. IT-enhanced organisations which have captured the benefits of teleworking can also be seen as fertile breeding-grounds for empowerment philosophies, by widening access to knowledge-bases and giving lower-level employees decision-making capability. One of the inevitable difficulties raised by increasing use of IT facilities is likely to be an information overload, whereby employees may need to employ strategies or techniques for limiting the expansion of data they have to deal with to that which adds value to their function.

The impact of teleworking on organisational structures of the future is likely to be significant as the flexible, informal networks of computers increasingly replace formal hierarchies of bureaucratic organisation. Traditional approaches to using and seeking to control teleworkers may cause too much management activity to be aimed at both the restriction and monitoring of access to information. The price of such approaches will be a restriction of an organisation's ability to reach the full productive capacity of the teleworking function.

The strength of business interest in such events as the *Computer Weekly* seminars on teleworking or Henley Management College's Future Work Forum encourages the conclusion first announced by Francis Kinsman (1987) over 10 years ago, that teleworking is an idea whose time has come. Unfortunately it seems to have come too early in the development of many organisational management and development systems to be introduced effectively. The widespread use of teleworking for many business applications, across a range of organisations, remains more a matter of 'when' not 'if'.

References and further reading

BALL S. 'Hot-desking: revolution or evolution'. *Flexible Working*, November 1996, pp. 18–19.

BUCHANON D. and BODY D. 'Advanced technology and the quality of working life: the effect of word-processing on videotypists'. *Journal of Occupational Psychology*, No. 55, 1982, pp. 1–11.

CROSSAN G. and BURTON P. 'Teleworking stereotypes: a case-study'. *Journal of Information Science*, Vol. 19, No. 5, 1993, pp. 349–362.

CURRAN K. and WILLIAMS G. *Manual of Remote Working*. Aldershot, Gower, 1997.

EDEN A. Talk given to post-graduate students at Putteridge Bury Management Centre, Luton, England, 1995.

GEAKE E. 'Managers struggle to adapt to teleworking'. *New Scientist*, Vol. 138, No. 1876, 1993, pp. 22–25.

GRAY M., HODSON N. and GORDON G. *Teleworking Explained*. Chichester, Wiley, 1993.

GRIFFIN S. 'Out of site, not out of mind – managing remote workers'. September 1997, pp. 27–29.

HANDY C. *Understanding Organisations*. London, Penguin, 1989.

HUWS U. *The New Homeworkers*. London Low Pay Unit, 1983.

Huws U. *Teleworking in Britain*. London, Dept of Employment, 1992.

Kinsman F. *The Telecommuters*. London, Wiley, 1987.

Kleiman C. 'Telecommuting makes virtual office a reality'. *Chicago Tribune*, 29 October 1995.

Korte W. and Wynne R. *Telework: Penetration, Potential and Practices in Europe*. London, IOS Press, 1996.

Meall L. 'Homework as a growth industry'. *Accountancy*, Vol. 111, No. 1195, 1993, pp. 53–59.

Mehleman M. *Commuting by Cable, Chipping away at Society*, London, Prentice Hall, 1985.

Mumford B. *Designing Organisations*. London, Gower, 1981.

Murray B. and Comford D. 'Teleworking in the UK'. *Flexible Working*, May 1996, pp. 4–7.

Murray B. 'Members only – a guide to teleworking groups'. *Flexible Working*, May 1997, pp. 8–11.

Panucci D. 'The teleworking revolution is gaining pace'. *Computing*, March 1994, pp. 17–20.

Schumacker F. *Small is Beautiful*. London, Vantage, 1973.

Seigal L. and Markoff J. *The High Cost of High Tech*. London, Harper & Rowe, 1983.

Stanworth J. and Stanworth C. *Teleworking: the HR Implications*. London, Institute of Personnel Management, 1991.

Toffler A. *Future Shock*. New York, Pan, 1981.

Tregaskis O. 'Succeeding with teleworking'. *Flexible Working*, November 1996, pp. 10–12

Wustemann L. 'A not-so-occasional table'. *Flexible Working*, May 1977, p. 7.

Young K. 'Teleworking – Home Alone'. *Telecom World*, August 1992, p. 27.

6 MULTI-SKILLING AND FLEXIBLE WORKING

Introduction: 'It's work Jim – but not as we know it'

There is no longer any such thing as a normal pattern of work. Less than half of the UK workforce is in full-time employment, and less than one third adheres to a traditional nine-to-five daily pattern. A Cranfield School of Management research project recently pointed out that across the EU the proportion of employees in full-time permanent work is no more than half. On top of this, recent surveys estimate that on average US employees now complete so many hours per year that they are working one month more per year than they did 20 years ago.

Charles Handy (1994) identified a major paradox in working relationships that could easily become an indicator of the current age when he speculated that, both globally and locally, those who have time to spare outside work have no money with which to enjoy their freedom, while those with the ability and opportunity to earn are too busy doing so to enjoy their wealth. Flexible working offers something for those at both ends of the spectrum. At one end, the introduction of more flexibility offers the opportunity for some employees to reshape their working life, balancing more comfortably the pressures of work, family and community. At the other extreme, the use of flexible working practices might increase the imbalance pointed out by Handy, as those with the skills that employers value highly work themselves to a standstill, while those outside the labour market have no role to play and no income to depend on.

Mark Twain famously declared that if work were so great, the rich would have hogged it long ago. The evidence from many of our most successful organisations, and their managers, suggests that they have. The demands placed on employees in the rapidly changing business world that we now witness mean that one or two even highly valued skills are unlikely to be sufficient to sustain effectiveness in employment for more than a relatively short time period. So great is the competitive need to build a change capability into our organisations that the option of recruiting, developing and maintaining an increasingly multi-skilled workforce is an option no more. As job roles blur, organisation structures flex, and traditional functional boundaries continually realign, debate consistently centres on changes to the traditional view of what a job is and how it should be described.

Flexing the employee contribution through multi-skilling

Case-study

BREAKING DOWN SKILL BARRIERS AT SMITHKLINE BEECHAM

Often the breakthrough in introducing multi-skilled work procedures can be achieved only when barriers that hold back potential employee and organisational development are removed or replaced. Introducing multi-skilling in a manufacturing environment with entrenched working practices presents many of the toughest challenges imaginable. SmithKline Beecham attempted to do just that at their Irvine factory.

Background situation

The site was set up in 1971 and produces mainly semi-synthetic penicillins and other drugs. The multi-skilling project was inaugurated in 1992 with the objective of increasing the efficiency and effectiveness of working practices – and of dislodging some, if not all, of the restrictive demarcation agreements that had grown with the factory itself. Multi-skilling, though not a revolutionary concept, was interpreted fairly adventurously by SmithKline Beecham, who sought to introduce cross-skilling not just on a horizontal plane – ie between different crafts – but also on the vertical plane – ie between levels within their production teams – by equipping operators with basic engineering, materials movement and analytical skills.

The plant was heavily unionised, and management quickly realised that any attempt to introduce such a programme would fail without strong union support, necessitating a partnership approach to implementation. The threat of job losses and the lack of workers of skilled status was also a major concern for the organisation's union members, so considerable effort went in to negotiations at the earliest possible stage in order to build the levels of trust and teamwork required.

The practical steps taken

The first management task was to identify examples of areas in which increased organisational flexibility, achieved through multi-skilled operations, could make a direct impact on efficiency, and to focus effort on these areas. A number of joint white- and blue-collar working parties were then set up to map situations where it made sense for operators to carry out basic engineering tasks. One consequence of this approach was the development by these teams of the concept of the 'best person', whereby the idea that jobs were owned by particular groups or trades was replaced by the view that the most appropriate individual to carry out the task should be enabled, through training and on-going support, to do just that. This concept itself gave the company much more flexibility in the allocation of duties than was previously possible. It also provided support for craftsmen who feared the removal of their specialisms.

A further practical step taken was to invite outsiders and senior union officials from other multi-skilled sites to talk over their experiences of multi-skilling with union members. At all times the emphasis was put on establishing and supporting a team approach to work problems. Guarantees were called for and given by the company to secure union membership agreement, including an undertaking that no redundancies would be imposed as a result of the multi-skilling programme. Negotiations over benefits were also tied in to the process, and a pay deal worth 8 per cent spread over three years, coupled with a lump sum £200 payment, was placed on the table to swing the final membership ballot – which narrowly voted to accept the new arrangements.

The agreement reached recognises that multi-skilled working may not be universally applicable to all employees and all situations. Those employees who cannot achieve the required level of competence even after training will be allowed to remain within their core job boundaries. This clause did not, however, apply to new employees who, as a condition of employment, had to meet minimum standards across a range of skill areas.

Getting the unions on board was a crucial factor in allowing the company to apply for and win a 50,000-ecu grant from the European Commission Force (superseded by the Leonardo da Vinci scheme) programme. The grant helped the organisation to fund the spread of best-practice measures, including usefully bringing together groups who would otherwise still be working in relative isolation. A timetable of programmed quarterly meetings was established to allow the local TEC to help train 25 experienced shop-floor workers to act as assessors and trainers themselves to drive the multi-skilling programme from the shop floor. Coaching is a common method of learning for the operatives and much centres on building the confidence of employees to use their new skills though certification and accreditation. Where applicable, National Standards were applied by the company through NVQs; where no relevant standards could be identified, the organisation drew up its own internal ones, again in agreement with employee representatives.

Conclusions

This example constitutes an illustrative lesson to other organisations involved in introducing multi-skilling, and indicates what can be achieved with considered effort to bring a successful outcome from a bargain between two parties with widely differing agendas. The organisation's management was clear about using multi-skilling to increase efficiency and effectiveness through greater scope for flexible working practices. The programme was introduced with the express aim not of reducing the number of employees but of improving on their utilisation. The aim of the development was not to turn skilled electricians into fitters or *vice versa*, but to make sure that the person doing each task was the right person with the right skills. Union officials sought reassurance that the multi-skilling initiative was not simply being used as a stick with which to beat their members. Both sides knew that they faced tough competition from other similar producers who had already imposed or were moving quickly towards multi-skilled operation, and that without each other's co-operation the project would fail. As with many developmental interventions by organisations in highly unionised environments, the rhetoric became reality only after much negotiation and trust-building; only then could genuine partnership agreements be struck, which is after all the basis of all good and effective teamworking.

Once the decision to use multi-skilling as a form of flexibility is taken, consequences for the organisation and its employees must be considered and capitalised on. When employees become multi-skilled, either through a planned in-company programme or by their own efforts, the organisation has to be able to utilise these skills before they become redundant and surpassed by others. This means reorganising processes to bring the advantages of multi-skilled operations on-stream and managing employees in a different way. The development, in some organisations, of the empowered employee concept has slowly made tightly specified job descriptions less useful. If we add to this the fact that the multi-skilled employee can now perform a much more diverse set of tasks, it is clear that the traditional controlling approach to employee management is unlikely to get the best results.

Managers face different challenges in seeking to get more out of multi-skilled employees: challenges that in turn have more to do with employee attitude and motivation to deliver beyond the job specification. Because less of what organisations really want from employees can be accurately specified in written job descriptions, improvements in employee performance resulting from changes in attitude and behaviour are unlikely to be achieved through changes in these job descriptions. The potential improvements available from changes in employee behaviour form the basis of the gains available from multi-skilling work practices. Traditionally, the unwritten understanding between employee and employer included a duty on the employer to inform the employee accurately of duties, structures and responsibilities, whereas the employee's side of the bargain was to carry out such duties to an acceptable standard, within the structure and framework provided by the organisation. On this basis jobs were largely stable, repeated parcels of work, reporting relationships were stable, and outcomes were readily measurable and easy to monitor. The widespread introduction of multi-skilling makes this employment relationship far less clear and predictable, often throwing the emphasis on employees to do something about recognising, updating and maintaining skill levels if they are themselves to remain effective and flexible contributors to the organisation.

It is clear that stable employer–employee relationships exist in far fewer organisations than ever before and are likely to diminish even further in the future. The issue of what people do when in employment, when they do it, and more importantly, how they are expected to do it, lies at the very centre of the flexibility debate. The fundamental changes witnessed in many aspects of the employment relationship – which is already creaking with the strains of age – often centre on issues of performance and how it might be improved, measured and rewarded.

Valuing and rewarding a multi-skilled workforce

Measuring the quality of work and looking to maximise the value contributed by all employees has never been easy – despite wide-ranging research into time-and-motion approaches to gauging work value – and is still the root cause of much workplace dissatisfaction. In many ways time as the basis for the payment and structuring of work has developed into what is widely accepted as a compromise answer to the intractable difficulties of providing equal pay for approximately equal value. Employment contracts, even for what might be called 'knowledge workers', still regularly emphasise hours per day, hours per week, or hours per year, and very rarely focus on the real key employee contribution: quantity, quality and value of output. Managers faced with introducing and monitoring multi-skilled operations must face up to the difficulties of quantifying and rewarding an employee who contributes not just one or two skills but a diverse bundle of old, new, simple and complex skills.

Organisational development programmes that require the introduction of flexibility through multi-skilling are likely to fall foul of any over-emphasis on time at the expense of quality of employee input or achievement. Paying people for inflexible working periods while simultaneously demanding flexibility from the employee contains a contradiction that will only get in the way of managing performance. Flexible working undoubtedly needs to be accompanied by a new approach to measurement and reward of effort and performance: time-clock-based systems, entirely appropriate for the early stages of the Industrial Revolution as they may have been, have increasingly less to offer an organisation and its managers who are seeking responsive, flexible and innovative reactions and attitudes from its workforce.

Some would argue that we are merely returning to a situation that was prevalent prior to industrialisation – in which workers worked irregularly when and where they could find an employer willing to hire, although skill requirements were usually less demanding than today and unlikely to change much over time. Industrialisation, amongst other social changes, required a revolution in the work mind-set of employees. Organisations needed loyalty and commitment, demonstrable by strict timekeeping, from its workers if they were to justify the massive investment in capital from shareholders. In return, industrial companies offered long-term contractual relationships and careers for those willing and able to contribute to the development of the organisation. Now that far fewer employers are able to offer stable long-term employment, employees may soon revert back to a way of life without jobs as we know them.

Multi-skilling and multiple career paths

Many of the accepted conventions of employment have already changed and the modern world is on the verge of another huge technology-driven leap in creativity and productivity. But the 'job', as it is commonly understood, is not going to be part of tomorrow's economic reality. There still is and will always be enormous amounts of work to do, but it is not going to be contained in the familiar envelopes we call jobs. Many organisations are today well along the path to being 'de-jobbed'.

One employee response to this enforced flexibility is to review career aspirations and recognise that one of the benefits of multi-skilling will be a passport towards having greater employability, with whatever organisation needs your skills. This book is by no means the first to claim that work and the relationships that surround it have fundamentally changed, and that a move closer towards 'portfolio working' describes in part the flexible career-path situation we now see. Stability of employment with one, or at most two, employers from school to securely pensioned retirement is rapidly being replaced by portfolio careers made up of a patch-work containing advances, sideways moves, periods of unemployment or inactivity, and even retrograde steps along the way. In the future more than today, the typical lifetime of work will consist of relationships that are characteristically short-term, and uncertain. Multi-skilling provides one way for employees to come to terms with this new situation. Managers need to encourage and support, more than ever before, the efforts of employees to update skills and continually retrain, as job roles and competencies that were once sufficient to sustain a long-term working relationship become obsolete much more readily. For many, this means revising the conventional view that training and developing for individuals within organisations shall be treated as a cost and not, as is more appropriate, an investment in flexibility and future competitiveness.

The increasingly short horizons of employment agreements (the NatWest IT division routinely offers employment contracts that last no longer than three months) and the greater movement of employees between organisations raise a difficult issue with regard to the question of long-term employee development. When an organisation's HR function had the task of compiling career-long development plans (which often included issuing new starters with company retirement pension details) in the full expectation of reaping long-term benefits from expenditure, resources devoted to employee development could easily be considered an investment in future potential. Now that the chances that the workforce will stay around long enough to repay even only part of the investment are becoming increasingly less likely, and now that the pay-off periods are greatly reduced, the ability of HR directors to secure major funding for employee development is inevitably going to be reduced.

Whether updating of skills and ability is a cost borne by the employer or by the employee is generally determined by

the usual balance of costs and benefits. High-tech organisations who need to be at the leading edge of developments in,
say, software or programming languages can be expected to
place a high priority – and therefore a substantial budget – on
keeping employees actively involved in learning and self-
development. In contrast, if an organisation can meet any
new skill requirements from the general labour market, one
might expect the cost of updating to be borne more by the
employee through formal retraining in between periods of
employment. The shortening shelf-life of skills and the
increasing level of redundancy of the knowledge held by all of
us as a result of the pace of change in modern society serves
only to exacerbate this problem.

Wherever the eventual cost of developing tomorrow's
workforce lies (and some would argue for a more interven-
tionist governmental role than has been in evidence in recent
times), it must be the case that the traditional time-served
methods of apprenticeship, lasting three or even five years,
are long gone. The prevalent view amongst most employers is
that minimum competence levels or standards – rather than a
minimum period of time spent under tutelage – are the key to
skill acquisition. The introduction and continued persever-
ance by many organisations with NVQ-style competence-
based training is a clear reflection of this approach. NVQs
place no value on the time taken to learn a trade or skill: once
competence can be assessed and proven, the trainee can be
accredited with the relevant qualification regardless of how
long or short was the training time-scale.

Whatever training is undertaken, it cannot be future-proof,
and the belief that learning and upskilling, for the individual
or the organisation, can ever come to an end is a pretty forlorn
hope. The reduced shelf-life of individual skill sets brings
both benefits and challenges to those charged with training
and development within organisations. On the one hand the
resurgence of knowledge, learning and technical ability as a
source of competitive advantage means that the training and
development function could have a louder voice in the board-
room. The downside is that the time, effort and money
expended in introducing new skills and updating existing
programmes needs to be tightly targeted, evaluated and

monitored. Training budgets which have traditionally been hard-fought and hard-won in organisations are coming under ever-increasing scrutiny, and justifications relying on value for money and the effectiveness of training programmes aimed at securing short-term advantage now feature as priority items on many senior executives' agendas.

Achieving multi-skilling through teamworking, real or virtual

Some organisations have approached the challenge of achieving flexibility through multi-skilling very effectively by incorporating team-based solutions, whereby the need for a wide variety of skills is met collectively by the team or group. In this model individual team members can develop, extend and retain specialisms which in isolation may not meet organisational requirements, but which put together with the skills of the remaining team members may create a resource available to the organisation that is both expansive and complementary.

Case-study

A FLATTER STRUCTURE AT THE NATIONWIDE BUILDING SOCIETY

In the early 1990s the Nationwide began to abandon traditional management hierarchies in the non-retail part of its business and tried to develop a more multi-skilled approach with a much flatter structure. The use of self-managed teamworking was also thought to be a way of addressing the difficult task of improving and maintaining morale and job satisfaction. The Nationwide's development was something of a ground-breaking case, for although industrial producers and manufacturers have been growing increasingly accustomed to the use of self-managed teams, it was a relatively new concept for both the Nationwide and the banking industry in general.

The project

In 1995 the Nationwide's administrative centre in Northampton began to revolutionise the way it was organised. The centre has 12 teams dealing with mortgage and insurance customers, and the reorganisation project started by increasing training inputs on decision-making, conflict management and teambuilding skills. Each team comprised nine to eighteen members and had an appointed leader who was to operate in a coaching, not directing, capacity. The new team-based approach allowed the teams to make decisions, allocate tasks and make resource bids. The organisation also allowed for a degree of competition between the teams – but not to the detriment of the organisation, for the centre is judged as a whole by the performance of the worst-performing team.

The experience

The company found some resistance in the initial stages of the project: some members saw the project as a way of getting them to do the work of the managers with no extra pay. In addition, the existing leaders feared loss of control from the new regime. These factors taken together resulted in a temporary dip in performance as the new relationships and working practices were trialled and embedded. However evidence of improved performance after this preliminary drop is provided in the table below, which shows the Nationwide's attempts to measure team performance. The resulting improvements cannot be attributed solely to the introduction of teamworking, because numerous other initiatives cloud the picture, but the company believes that there are a number of instances where the new approach has led to improved performance.

Some team performance issues are comparable between the teams, such as sickness absenteeism, creating a spirit of rivalry which never existed before. Other changes in working practices involved two of the teams setting up better lines of communication with the branch network, the final effect of which was a reduction in the number of problem cases that came into the administrative centre. Staff morale in the new regime has increased, as judged by their own internal attitude survey, and at the same time there has been a marked increase in productivity and efficiency that has significantly reduced the amount of overtime working.

Further developments

Other sections of Nationwide business are now being encouraged to take on the self-managed team concept, and many of the lessons learned in Northampton are being introduced at other departments across the country. Even the HR function has not escaped the team-

Table 13
PERFORMANCE OF MORTGAGE AND INSURANCE
CUSTOMER SERVICE TEAMS

	Feb 1996	Feb 1997	Apr 1997
Productivity (items handled per day)	126	176	196
Staff numbers	184	157	154
Work items received per week	21,909	19,192	18,151
Work outstanding	4,565	2,653	2,305
Sickness (days per month)	114	24	27
Overtime (hours per month)	524	–	–
Turnaround (time to complete work item)	4 days	2 days	2 days
Complaints	361	216	60

Source: *People Management*, October 1997.

working approach: previously independent HR specialists are now coming together as a group of 18 to share the benefits of a multi-skilled team. The Nationwide is also now considering altering other HR and business practices (such as appraisal and reward and recognition strategies) to allow for the further development of the team approach.

Conclusions

The Nationwide experience of introducing self-managed multi-skilled teamworking is largely positive, but several aspects of its introduction led the organisation to conclude that key implementation factors must be addressed. Firstly, as with all new business initiatives, there must be a sound business case for its introduction, coupled with a clear understanding of the direction in which its development will take the business. The second vital factor is to have a way of evaluating progress towards this goal and an effective mechanism for correcting for any deviations. Thirdly, the introduction of self-managed teams cannot be seen as a quick fix: it will take an investment of time and effort to install and prevent lapses back into the old way of working when things go wrong. Employee and manager commitment to the new system is also seen as vital, and a plan for communicating the philosophy of teamworking plays a key role in ensuring this.

Traditional teamworking solutions can provide answers to such basic staffing problems as covering for absent colleagues or providing temporary stopgaps while organisations think out a restructuring process or replace employees. In addition, there is much evidence to support the view that effective and supportive teams and groups can provide fertile education and training situations for new members or those seeking to change their job role. Introducing new developments in communications and information technology now allows organisations to capitalise on a new departure for teamworking: the concept of the virtual team. Members of such teams rarely meet face to face; their workspace is infinite and not unrestricted; the team communicates via such methods as video conferencing, e-mail and shared software programs.

Trying to build team relationships with people who are not meeting is inevitably problematic, but the advantages of such arrangements in terms of flexibility, speed and diversity of membership go some way towards justifying their further development. In addition to the isolation factor, virtual teams who operate across cultural and geographical boundaries may also run into difficulties in interpretation of language and, more crucially, meaning. A further example of the move to virtual teamworking is at oil giant BP, where hierarchical structures have been replaced by a flatter, federated model, combining around 80 cross-national business units. BP has invested in the technology of e-mail, satellite links and video-conferencing to allow virtual teamworking, and the company aim is that all employees will have access to virtual team technology to use as and when appropriate. The company claims that savings in terms of shared knowledge have already run into millions since it started working on virtual teambuilding in early 1995.

A major advantage of using virtual teams comes where businesses need to select and develop numerous short-term project teams. For the project team members to be located at a variety of remote locations (a true virtual team is not restricted by time or geographical boundaries) means that they do not incur high travel costs and can achieve objectives at incredible speeds whereas the slower communication processes of a traditional team approach might hold back progress.

As with many other areas of new communications technology, some writers have warned against the dangers of over-communicating just because we have the technology to do it. Certainly, for employees to have to spend hours wading through hundreds of e-mail messages each day that are largely irrelevant to their job roles could quickly eat into the potential time and speed savings. Such as information-overload effect is often a consequence of over-compensation for the lack of face-to-face contact experienced in traditional team-working, by which useless information can be effectively filtered out.

The alternative to attempting to achieve multi-skilling via teams is for organisations to look to multi-skill employees on an individual basis, allowing for greater ease of transfer between organisational functions and therefore greater overall flexibility.

Case-study

RESTRUCTURING AT BAYER DIAGNOSTICS

Bayer, the well known German pharmaceutical giant, has since 1977 been the parent of a plant known as Miles Ltd, situated in Bridgend. With a headcount of around 270, the plant concentrates on the manufacture of dip-and-read testing strips and other self-medication products such as Alka Seltzer. In a review of its global operations Bayer looked closely at the possibility of closing down the plant. Fortunately the Miles Ltd management was able to develop and achieve a new structure which satisfied the parent company's desire for increased flexibility and responsiveness.

Developing the multi-skilling policy

In the early 1990s Miles Ltd in Bridgend undertook a detailed review of its manufacturing operations which concluded that fundamental reorganisation of working practices was required to win the continued support of its German parent company, Bayer. This reorganisation included a rethink on pay grading and structures, and caused the company to question its skill requirements both current and future.

A traditionally-organised workforce had to be convinced of the benefits of any changes, and the major communications channel to achieve this was the works committee, formed in 1990. This committee comprised the plant director, five direct-reporting managers, the IR manager and two representatives from each of the three recognised unions.

Multi-skilling became a pivotal point of the restructuring. The supervisory layer of managers was removed and the process workers were organised into self-managed teams. Each team is now responsible for production and maintenance of a designated area of the process, and can call for support from the engineering section, but is expected (and able) to solve most problems by itself. Prior to the introduction of multi-skilling, employees were divided into three bargaining groups along craft lines, making three distinct grades each with a series of possible increments, so totalling some 30 possible salary points. The new structure comprised only one pay spine with a total of nine grades; movement between grades was tied to the successful acquisition of new skills.

Not all employees were expected to become fully multi-skilled. The Bayer model (Miles Ltd adopted the Bayer name in 1995) allows employees to move through skill levels to become multi-skilled over an 18-month period. The company expects around a third of the current employees to reach the top level of multi-skilling but hopes that this proportion will increase in the future. In recognition that unused skills can easily become stale and outdated, the company does not waste time and effort on training employees in skill areas that they do not use regularly. This needs-driven approach has been found to maximise commitment on the part of employees and does not involve the company in paying for skills that are not required.

Conclusions

The benefits gained by Bayer Diagnostics from multi-skilling (apart from survival!) are reported to include:

☐ greater commitment by the workforce to the success of the plant

☐ improved trade union relationships

☐ a general view of skills-based pay as fair, and the recognition by employees that rates compare favourably with other local pay levels

☐ increased efficiency, such that front-line employees feel they have hands-on involvement in the success

☐ closer ties between those who plan the products and the engineers who service the machines.

The case illustrates clearly how multi-skilling can succeed as an element of a more general restructuring programme that includes a rethink of organisation policies in areas such as reward, promotion, and management reporting. Companies that seek to introduce multi-skilling in isolation without regard to accommodating changes in policy are likely to face major implementation difficulties and will be unable to reap the full potential rewards from the change.

Practical considerations for introducing multi-skilling

Many of the arguments in favour of multi-skilling focus on the potential flexibility benefits that true multi-skilling offers. A multi-skilled workforce can more easily adapt to peaks and troughs in the organisation's workloads, cover the absences of colleagues, and even allow the release of team members for further development activities. Nonetheless, any multi-skilling programme must be carefully planned to effectively capture the full benefits available. Four specific steps provide a model for managers who seek to introduce multi-skilling.

Step 1: Link the process of multi-skilling to business priorities

The concept of multi-skilling, by which employees are expected (and equipped) to operate in a number of areas, often underpins the degree of flexibility achievable by an organisation. As with all training initiatives, the success or otherwise of the exercise is often judged by some estimate of the contribution to outputs, and consequent income flows, that result. Precise links between specific training events and organisational performance are tenuous and difficult to quantify, and multi-skilling is likely to be no exception to this. As a consequence, organisational flexibility – like motherhood and apple pie – can all too easily be regarded as good for its own sake. But commercial organisations obviously cannot in general afford the luxury of implementing policy purely because things are 'good' in themselves. HR managers interviewed for a survey on empowerment by Ellis and Minnett (1997) made it clear, as one would expect, that the introduction of multi-skilling in their organisations was the result of cool calculations of business benefits.[1]

Step 2: Prioritise the business areas in which multi-skilling can make an impact

Before embarking upon a multi-skilling training programme,

the organisation must identify and examine areas in which the need for flexibility is uppermost, and then devise the training strategy to deliver the capability for flexibility where it is required. Having made the decision to go for multi-skilling, the HR priority is then to prepare the ground for the introduction and to provide practical support for this more flexible approach. Job rotation may kick-start the process, but implementation must take into account compatibility of functions and job roles. Taking people out of distinct, special-ist roles and moving them into others – ie multi-skilling them requires a major leap of faith that those who are effective in one specialist area can effectively transfer that ability to another, fundamentally different discipline. The implemen-tation manager must be sure that there is a genuine business case for the change, and be prepared to allow for the time it will take before the newly-skilled employees get up to speed in the new area. In many of today's highly competitive organ-isations employees are often expected to contribute, and add value, from day one in a new department.

Step 3: Plan for the release of the employees to be multi-skilled

Moving employees into different functions to exploit flexi-bility through multi-skilling requires a plan to fill the gap left behind, unless the old functions are to be disbanded. If tight labour budgets do not allow this, the multi-skilled employee may be forced to work in multiple roles. Employee-friendly learning methods – such as open learning materials, on-line learning support, or development workshops in-company – will be needed to provide opportunities for learning and skill acquisition. Introducing a newly-skilled employee could be eased with the usual mentoring or coaching arrangements using employees who are comfortable with the multi-skilling concept.

Step 4: Negotiate acceptance with labour representatives

This may involve negotiating agreement on objectives with sections or departments, and devising a policy on how moves towards multi-skilling are to be planned, monitored, deliv-ered and rewarded. Technological support systems and employee equipment issues will have to be clarified. If multi-

skilling will require substantial investment in tools or equipment, budgets and monitoring systems for the new plant will
need to be established. Multi-skilling is likely to be resisted
where traditional craft-based union agreements are in place
that set out demarcation agreements and agreed skill levels.
Removing or renegotiating these agreements will be vital if
multi-skilling is to yield the potential benefits. Union or
worker representative agreement to the new arrangements
may have to be secured through revising reward systems for
employees who achieve multi-skilling, whereas safeguards
for the non-multi-skilled employees will be of concern to the
unions. Skilled part-time short-term workers will constitute
a valuable multi-skilled resource, and effort must be put into
building and maintaining relationships with them or their
representatives if they are not to take their expensively
acquired skills to other employing organisations. Attempts
must be made to involve and communicate effectively with
such workers, and policies that have to do with reward, recognition and retention must recognise the value of building or
establishing their loyalty.

Conclusion

Multi-skilling is increasingly coming to the fore as a means of
answering many HR challenges. It provides organisations
with tremendous opportunities for increasing flexibility and
increasing efficiency. For the employee, multi-skilling offers
the prospect of greater job satisfaction and, more crucially,
greater employability to counter the increased risks and insecurity within the new employment relationship. Multi-
skilling represents a major step on the journey towards
increasing organisational flexibility: employees may even
receive pay benefits to accompany the increased opportunities available through multi-skilling. Organisations may
also find that multi-skilled employees are more likely to have
the confidence and desire to take on additional responsibility.
The costs of multi-skilling are very similar to those associated with other kinds of organisational training and development – eg loss of output during the training period, in
addition to the cost of the training itself. On the benefit side,
the HR practitioner should be able to construct a case for con-

sidering the costs of the multi-skilling programme to be an investment not only in improved skills for individuals but in the development of a flexible organisational capability.

References

ELLIS S. and MINNETT S. 'Using empowerment to turn employees into entrepreneurs: an internalisation too far?' *Training for Quality*, Vol. 5, No. 2, 1997.
HANDY C. *The Empty Raincoat*. UK, Hutchinson, 1994.
MULLER J. 'Rail operator snubs union over multi-skilled drivers'. *People Management*, 5 February 1998, p. 14.

End-note

1 Not all unions will accept this link. Train operator Heathrow Express clashed with unions over plans to multi-skill their drivers and change their job title to 'customer service stewards'. The link to customer service was not initially accepted by ASLEF, who saw their members as train drivers only (Muller, 1998).

7 OUTSOURCING

Introduction

A young consultant from a reputable company was once giving an enthusiastic and earnest talk to the board of a medium-sized engineering company about the enormous benefits to be achieved by the new concept of 'outsourcing'. Companies all over the Midlands were taking up this innovation at an increasing rate, and unless this company climbed on the bandwagon, it would be left behind.

At the end of the talk one of the older directors thanked him and then proceeded to give him a short history lesson on the organisation, starting in the 1780s when two of his distant ancestors had set up the company. Their method of working for the first 25 years had been to outsource most of their operations, themselves acting as only final assembler and marketeer. They even outsourced the bookkeeping and accounts. They did not call it 'outsourcing', however – it was sub-contracting. He did not disagree that the concept was a very valid one, to be carefully and continuously considered, but only disagreed that it was new!

That, of course, is the irony of this aspect of flexibility, and a source of criticism. It is a step back in time to an age when labour supply was plentiful, to be used and dispensed with as required. It is a reversal of the standard process over the last 100 years by which companies, as they grow organically, have taken in-house nearly all the operations and services that they previously bought in. It reached its pinnacle in Henry Ford's Detroit works, where iron control was exercised in a completely integrated structure over every aspect of activity through the employment contract. Now, the movement is towards vertical disintegration together with flexible contractual relationships.

Today's definition of outsourcing could be best summed up as: 'where an organisation passes the provision of a service or execution of a task previously undertaken in-house to a third party to perform on its behalf' (Reilly and Tamkin, 1996).

This distinguishes it from sub-contracting, which generally refers to work that has not customarily been carried on in-house. However, it can be stretched to include franchising arrangements and 'linked' sub-contracting, by which an organisation helps a group of employees to set themselves up as independent or semi-independent contractors. In France, for example, the practice of *essimage* or 'spin-off' outsourcing allows employees to create their own independent business activities linked to their former firm, which in turn, supports them by training or establishing preferential customer/supplier agreements.

In the Institute of Management's guide on outsourcing, Mike Johnson (Johnson, 1997) lists four top strategic reasons to go down this route:

☐ *to improve business focus* – Outsourcing lets a company focus on broader issues while having operational details assumed by an outside expert. It avoids siphoning off huge amounts of management resources and attention on non-core activities.

☐ *to gain access to world-class capabilities* – Outsourcing providers, especially in the IT field, can bring extensive worldwide knowledge and experience, giving access to new technology, career opportunities to employees who may transfer to the provider and competitive advantage through expanded skills.

☐ *to benefit from accelerated re-engineering* – This lets the provider, especially one that has already re-engineered to world-class standards, take over the process.

☐ *to share risks* – A co-operative venture with a provider can halve the risks.

There are two distinct strands in the current direction of outsourcing. Firstly, there is the move by organisations in the private sector to use outsourcing as a means to achieve cost savings and competitive advantages. Secondly, there were political moves by the last Conservative government to compel market testing (and thereby a degree of outsourcing) through legislation which brought in compulsory competitive tendering (CCT). The aim behind these political moves was to introduce competition into the public sector, especially the mostly Labour-controlled local authorities, and so to replicate the benefits reputedly achieved in the private sector. Although there is a link between the two – for some Conservative-controlled local authorities began to take out-sourcing seriously in the 1970s, long before any legal compulsion – we will look at these themes separately before assessing the current and future directions.

The drive to outsource in the private sector

The competitive environment described in Chapter 1 caused many organisations to look carefully at their cost and employment base to try to eliminate activities in which they should not have been involved. The general justification for strategic decisions in this area have chiefly been:

- □ greater ability to focus on the core activities that bring competitive advantage
- □ cost saving
- □ improved service and flexibility in business activities
- □ security aspects.

Focus on core activities

'Our managers have enough to do without having to worry about managing cleaning, maintenance or the drains,' reported an executive of a medium-sized engineering company in our survey. There has been a clear movement, beginning in the mid-1980s and picking up speed during the recession of the early 1990s, for organisations to restructure and de-layer, sharply reducing their managerial and supervisory staff numbers. Although tied up with cost reduction, the strategic direction has been to concentrate on mainstream activities and by eliminating marginal areas become 'focused'.

British Airways has taken this policy to the extreme in the 1990s, looking at every activity to see if it can be outsourced.

The airline's core activity is regarded as flying passengers, not as providing their meals, moving their baggage or seeing to their security. All of these are ancillary activities and can be put out to tender if suitable contracts can be negotiated. In 1997 BA transferred 85 per cent of its ground fleet services staff (415 employees) to outsource provider Ryder under a five year deal. The airline believes it can now concentrate on building its flight network, increasing its reliability and serving its customers. A further contract has recently been awarded to the Astron Group for printing and other services: Astron is featured in the case-study below.

Case-study

OUTSOURCING TO THE ASTRON GROUP

The Astron Group is a rapidly growing organisation that used to be called a jobbing printers – but this scarcely describes the variety of outsourced contracts that they are now operating from four sites in the Hertfordshire/Huntingdon/Cambridge area. They currently employ around 300 permanent employees, but added to this number are around 300–400 'associates' who work a variety of hours when required.

British Airways have recently awarded the company a five-year contract to produce all their printed literature. This activity, like so many of British Airways' operations, used to be in-house, but a review of their core businesses in the 1990s persuaded the organisation that printing was not at the core. This is despite the fact that planes cannot take off unless the correct flight documentation is delivered for each plane on time by Astron staff.

Working hours

At Letchworth, the flight documentation and many other sets of printed literature are produced by teams of employees split roughly 60:40 permanent to associate. The amount of work is unpredictable, for British Airways and other customers often give the organisation only 24 hours to complete. For this reason the working hours are quoted as between 6 am and 10 pm plus a full Saturday. Permanent employees work 150 hours over a four week period but their times of work are not fixed. A week in advance the amount of work available is indicated and the teams with their team-leaders organise themselves to be available to cover the work. Any additional manning needed is made up from the associates who are called in to fill the gaps. Overtime is worked only rarely when there is a severe bottle-neck of work emanating from a series of contracts or if there is a sick-ness epidemic. It is not uncommon for employees to complete their 150 hours in three weeks and then to take the fourth week off. By the same token, a change in plan from one of the customers can mean that some of the permanent staff will not be working for three or four days at the start of the month.

The associates

The associates are a mixture of people who, for a variety of reasons, make themselves available only for a limited number of hours. They may have caring responsibilities for children or older relatives which brings regular and special time commitments, or they may be students who are available in the evenings after school or on certain days while they are at the local college. Many of them have family connections at the site, for many extended families work there at different times. For personnel manager Katherine Woodward it is important to recruit associates for whom the variety of hours is not a disadvantage. They firstly need to be quite clear on both the nature of the contract – that they will usually be given little warning and that the hours of work for which they will be invited can vary – and the importance of the work they will carry out. No matter what their background may be, they are key employees who understand the importance of the deadlines and the need to satisfy the customers.

The skill levels required, except for certain specialist printing oper-ations, are not high, but a careful, responsible attitude is vital to ensure that the work is completed at the right quality levels. Associates are firmly told from their first day that their work can be a 'show-stopper': if it isn't completed right, the plane will not take off.

Teamworking and training

Teamworking is a vital ingredient in the success of the operation. The employees genuinely are empowered to organise the work them-selves, to share the hours in a constructive and co-operative way and to share also the responsibility to get the work completed on time.

Training is competence-driven. Associates are taught a selection of jobs so that they can slot into whichever position is required that day or week. When they become competent at the set of jobs enough to carry them out without supervision, they move onto a higher rate of pay. The final stage is to promote permanent staff onto the higher grade when they are capable of training other staff. If any permanent positions become available, they are offered to associates.

Conclusions

The chief executive, David Mitchell, has encouraged this way of working from an early stage of the company's expansion. 'I want committed people to work for me and I really do not mind how many hours they work. There has to be this mutual trust associated with the empowered workforce. I know they will make mistakes they might not make if they were under tight supervision, but I also know they would not use their initiative at vital times if somebody was standing over them. In the competitive world of outsourcing we cannot afford tight supervision: we need to reach the high standards demanded by British Airways and other companies through the intelligence and commitment of our employees who see what needs to be done and just do it.'

There has been a rapid increase in the last five years to outsource computer services, including payroll activities. Coopers & Lybrand estimate that 25 per cent of the payroll market is outsourced (*Management Today*, 1997). This has been a fascinating development to observe, for IT departments have often been the most difficult to manage, with change occurring constantly and knife-edge investment decisions needed rapidly. The staffing has also been fraught with high turnover and security implications. Lacity *et al* (1994) report the justification for outsourcing IT by one organisation as simply to eliminate a troublesome function and, by implication, relieve the senior executives of daily staffing and other crises.

Cost saving

The recent perceived growth in outsourcing began when large organisations examined the more traditional areas of cleaning, catering and office services and saw that smaller organisations with fewer overhead costs could provide a far cheaper service than the in-house service which had to carry high overheads and pay rates often locked into a job-evaluated system.

The contractor can put forward a more competitive price for a number of reasons:

- They become expert in their field and know how to achieve high levels of productivity.
- They operate with flexible staffing levels for whom part-time and temporary work is the convention to meet the needs of the many businesses for whom they work.
- Employees can be moved from one contract to another as required to meet swings in demand.
- The culture of the organisation is one that is customer-oriented so employees become used to short-term changes and variety in working hours.
- Service innovation arises naturally from an organisation geared to meeting the whims of a demanding customer, and such innovations can be transferred across many small contracts.
- Pay and rewards are much more likely to be performance-based.
- Benefits tend to be less generous, particularly in the areas of pension and private health insurance.

A further advantage of outsourcing which is attractive to the accountant is that all the costs are variable because the investment costs are borne by the contractor.

Improved service and flexibility

On a simple level, the providers of outsourced services for, say, cleaning or catering, know that they will lose business and reputation if they do not provide the level of service that the client wants and expects. Their job and the jobs of their employees depend on this. Contracts are generally constructed to allow a degree of flexibility to reflect changing business circumstances, such as an increase or decrease in warehousing facilities.

On another level, getting up to date in rapidly advancing technology can be an expensive business, so there is an argument to leave this to the specialist company and simply use their services. Such companies are likely to be small, highly skilled and nimble, this being the core activity on which they are focused. Should a better state-of-the-art service be offered by a competitor, the organisation can switch at the end of the contract period.

Where logistical aspects are involved, using a nationwide provider generally gives better methods of access than trying to achieve the result in-house.

Security aspects

Throughout the 1980s companies moved to outsource part or all of their logistical operations. The 1979–80 lorry-drivers' strike, when most lorry fleets were in-house, brought most companies rapidly to a halt, and the settlements reached caused considerable financial headaches. It was in the interests of both supplier and customer that deliveries would remain secure in any possible further strike situation. Organisations which were non-union or where unions were benign were especially successful in winning contracts. Political support was given to this movement by legislation outlawing secondary picketing.

Compulsory competitive tendering: the UK experience

One of the most controversial innovations of the 1980s was the introduction of CCT in the public sector – a process now called 'market testing'. In a openly ideological move to elim-inate 'municipal Socialism' – with its emphasis on public accountability, democratic ownership and mass provision and service for those in need – a batch of legislation was passed (Local Government Planning and Land Act, 1980; Local Government Acts of 1988 and 1992) to force local authorities to put their services out to tender in the marketplace. It began with routine highway and buildings maintenance, then went on to manual services such as refuse collection, street clean-ing and lighting. Finally, administrative services came into the firing line, including IT, personnel, facilities management and legal provision.

Overall, the evidence (chiefly from the Audit Commission) has been strongly in favour of success. Substantial savings, often in the order of 20 per cent or more, have been achieved and quality has been maintained or improved. These findings have been questioned within local authorities where issues of comparative quality and monitoring costs have been raised, but few argue against the fact that the public have benefited from the initiative.

Not that external providers have won all the contracts – far from it. The regular reports on contracts by the Local Government Management Board show that Direct Service Organisations (DSOs) have continued to win a majority, especially in areas such as sport and leisure management. However, winning has often been at the price of fundamentally changing their ways of working to match those organisations in the private sector who they are bidding against. In street lighting, for example, flexible shifts have replaced fixed starting and stopping times; operatives carry out all lighting repairs and installations, rather than just concentrating on one area; and payment systems have reflected individual and team effort rather than been composed of a straight hourly wage plus regular overtime. The effect has been a more efficient force, but at the expense of greatly reduced numbers: 20 per cent saving has often arisen from 30 per cent fewer employees.

An interesting development throughout CCT has been the monitoring of contracts, a factor which became included in the tender document from an early stage in its development. Complaints from the public have been counted and published, independent customer surveys commissioned and warnings issued to the contractor (including the DSO where relevant) where the service has been found wanting. Prior to CCT, the public had to grin and bear it or attempt to exert political pressure through a local councillor. It is now rare for the provider of a poor local authority service to survive for long: early termination of contracts is not unknown. An example here is at Enfield Council in North London, where three major contracts for cleaning and catering in schools and at the civic centre had to be retendered following news that the DSO was effectively facing bankruptcy. The problem arose from a tribunal decision that the Council had to reinstate national pay terms and conditions, which pushed up the costs by around £500,000 and made it impossible for the DSO to meet its financial targets under the contracts (*Enfield Advertiser*, 1997).

Examples of market testing

The largest outsourcing agreement in Europe was signed in 1993, when the Inland Revenue passed an estimated £41 billion worth of work over 10 years to EDS. It was expected that by the end of 1997 the total UK civil service outsourcing each year would exceed £10 billion and a further £2 billion in local authorities (Rothery and Robertson, 1995).

There are a number of organisations in the education field that have grown on the back of a form of market testing. Nord Anglia Education, for example, provides three main services to local authorities. It has career services contracts for 11 authorities; its schools inspections have risen from six in 1995 to 150 in 1997; and it also operates 15 schools in the UK and overseas. It expects to get a large slice of the 16,000 nursery inspections required over the next five years (Kavanagh, 1997).

Difficulties in the outsourcing process

Defining the contract

No contract is simple to formulate, but outsourcing services are more prone to difficulties, particularly where the level of service is defined. This is a key area because the contract is worthless unless there are opportunities to terminate it if quality is not sufficient. But how, for example, do you define a satisfactory level in a catering service or the ambulance service? Experience has provided measures that can be used, such as through user surveys, but these can be time-consuming and expensive.

Sub-contracting in the construction industry is strewn with examples where arguments over contract definition (in particular the issue of whether something is an 'extra' or an integral part of the contract) finish up in the courts or at costly arbitration. The same can apply in any outsourced activity.

Bureaucratic nightmare?

Under CCT, contracts can, almost literally, weigh a ton. Contracts for street cleaning or grass verge cutting, even in a small authority, can be 600 pages long and need to be carefully examined by prospective providers. They are this length for three reasons. Firstly, there is the need to carefully specify the work that has to be done, how it is to be done and the detailed quality measures. Secondly, the legal department will have recommended many additions to ensure that the contract is watertight. Thirdly, the massive size itself is important because it may discourage many outside providers, especially smaller ones, giving the in-house providers a better chance to win the contract.

Contracts in the private sector are less likely to face such problems – but legal difficulties mean that contracts are tending to become more complex each year.

Losing control

Many organisations would be very pleased to lose control of cleaning or catering, but in more strategic areas (IT comes immediately to mind) there has to be a degree of hesitation before passing over these activities to an outsider – not just because the security risks increase but because the organisation's body of knowledge becomes reduced. If there should in the future be a need to reverse the decision, it may not be quite so easy to take responsibilities back on board at the level of competence required. Organisations that have needed to do this have faced some severe management resourcing problems.

Such arguments are well rehearsed in relation to sub-contracting activities in manufacturing, where vital research and development skills, experience and career opportunities can be lost if it is decided to outsource a major component. A lean organisation may become anorexic and miss vital opportunities that arise, often unexpectedly, if those focused experts have been lost through outsourcing. Some argue that the problems get worse the longer the work is outsourced. This is because the provider progressively knows more about the organisation while the expertise within the organisation deteriorates.

Another area in which control is lost centres on the actual employees who work on the contract. Recruitment, discipline and termination is in the hands of the provider. The provider's employees may not share the values, commitment or enthusiasm that the organisation would ideally like, but possible action is limited unless controls in these areas are written into the contract.

Dealing with the provider

Employees may face some frustrations in dealing with an outside body in activities that concern them. This arises more in IT than in most other areas for the process of setting priorities in an external system development can be far more complex than in a situation where all the IT is managed in-house. It is also quite common for the outsourced service to be better focused – so employees can be disappointed when making peripheral demands that used to be quickly met under the previous less focused but user-friendly regime.

Maintaining the quality

Even if quality standards are agreed and measures are in place, it still remains a difficult situation if the provider does not meet those standards. When failures occur in-house, heads may roll and direct action can be taken, but this is more difficult to enforce with a contractor. Time-consuming negotiations take place, and if these fail to achieve results there is only recourse to expensive legal actions which may arise if the contract is terminated after due notice. A number of local authorities have insisted on a provider's putting up performance bonds which the provider loses if the performance does not meet the standard: 170 CCT contracts for building cleaning alone incurred financial penalties in the second half of 1996 (LGMB, 1996).

The viability of the provider

Providers may be flexible and nimble-footed in meeting the client's needs but sometimes they fall over or simply disappear. In the six months to December 1996, 21 CCT contracts in the leisure sector were terminated due to two leisure companies' going into receivership (LGMB, 1996), and contracts with a further six private companies were terminated on similar grounds.

Transferring employees

The rules for transferring employees come under the general banner of TUPE, the Transfer of Undertakings (Protection of Employment) regulations, passed in 1981, which arose under the 1977 European Union Acquired Rights Directive. Recent interpretations of this act both in the UK and in other EU countries have made this the most difficult to understand and have presented some extreme operational difficulties. These are too complex to deal with in detail in this publication, so readers are referred to sources at the end of this chapter. One must say, however, that the law in this area has the habit of changing drastically overnight. Recognising this, *People Management* introduced a 'TUPE update' column every month in 1997.

Difficulties can arise because employees often have to transfer without a choice (although they retain the same terms and conditions for an extended period, usually at least six months) or they are presented with the options of staying with the organisation but in a different role, or transferring or of taking redundancy. They need, and would expect, impartial advice – which may not be forthcoming from the organisation who will have its own agenda in terms of individual employees. There are ethical dilemmas for personnel staff where it may be in the organisation's interest to pursuade difficult or unsatisfactory employees to take redundancy or to transfer. As Judith Howlings (*People Management*, 6 March 1997, p. 55) said: 'TUPE is a complicated area. There are no golden rules, because each situation will be different. Thus, employers should always consider taking proper legal advice before a transfer takes place.'

Issues to be considered when outsourcing

Deciding whether to outsource

Some of the questions that must put before initiating the process include:

☐ Are there any security points that would encourage or discourage outsourcing?

☐ What is the nature of the process to be outsourced? If it is

Table 14
TEN PIECES OF ADVICE FROM TEXACO

Texaco's corporate service department has a record for careful outsourcing pro-grammes. Here corporate services manager Colin Bannerman gives ten points of advice for would-be outsourcers to remember:

☐ Any area or activity can be outsourced. However, the company should have a clear direction and strategy to follow before committing to move functions outside its direct control.

☐ The most successful outsourcing projects have moved indirect functions for the host company to an outsourced supplier whose *main* business it is.

☐ If the vendor is using the services he is providing as an add-on to attract clients, there will be little focus on the success of the new structure.

☐ One of the largest barriers is the cultural acceptance of a supplier relationship rather than an internal service, largely because the hierarchy and power-base of many managers is built on direct control or position authority. The conflict between these dimensions creates instability with external providers. Recognition and reward systems must be re-tuned to support new management practices.

☐ Good communication and shared values are important, both formally in a contract and informally in the culture of the two organisations. If services or quality is important, a method of managing through the contractor must be found.

☐ A measurement system should be used to determine direction and success for the outsourcing programme. However, there are no universal measures with which to grade all services.

☐ Don't follow the US examples just because they exist. Any outsourcing must be justified as a good course of action in your own situation each and every time.

☐ The drivers for sourcing/outsourcing come from technological change and resource management. If these factors evolve differently due to location and/or timing, then the sourcing questions should be answered differently.

☐ Consultants are valuable in breaking the mind-set of managers and companies. However, changes introduced by consultants will not change companies unless the managers and employees work with the new system.

☐ If companies find that advantage can be gained by bringing services under direct management, why not? The drivers for insourcing or outsourcing should be considered – not the fashion!

Source: Johnson, 1997.

a core activity, then outsourcing should proceed with extreme caution even where the other factors are encouraging. Local authorities, for example, were concerned at the instructions from the 1996 Beresford Report, which determined that the percentage of white-collar work to be tendered would rise. For example, in finance areas, it would rise from 35 per cent to 65 per cent. This could well cut into the strategic core activities.

☐ Can performance measures be easily put in place to ensure that satisfactory progress is being made by the provider?

☐ What are the key objectives? Is it improved performance or cost saving or a combination of the two? Can they be quantified?

☐ Are there any viable alternatives to outsourcing, such as a joint operation or a further attempt at in-house improvement?

☐ What skills may be lost through the process? Will the overall training and development policy of the organisation be affected?

Setting the standards

Issues here include the more obvious areas relating to operations which have to be clear, unambiguous but not too complex, but also areas such as the quality of the staff involved. This may be measurable in terms of qualifications or experience (although many excellent IT staff can be unqualified and much experience is measured in weeks rather than years), but standards of behaviour and attitude are far more difficult to define. It is better to try to involve outsourced staff in company affairs relating to training or social activities so they become better integrated into the company culture.

Controlling the contract

There are two parts to this. Firstly, ensure that the process for agreeing a contract is carried out successfully. This involves drawing up the specification, including the duration of the contract and the nature of any penalties for non-performance, the way that a short-list of contractors will be selected, and how bids will be invited, evaluated and awarded. Under CCT, this process is circumscribed by law and common practice and needs considerable skill, experience and expertise to avoid claims from potential providers who have been excluded.

The second part of the process is to manage the contract itself. There have been a number of experiences under CCT where a contract has been awarded to a provider who has offered the lowest tender but the authority has been hostile to that provider for historical or personal reasons. (The authority may have wanted to keep the contract in-house.) Most of these contracts have ended in acrimony because the authority has acted to the letter of the contract rather than its spirit, and has invoked unfair penalties. It is clear from this experience that, generally, contracts will only work effectively if there is mutual understanding and a good degree of trust. There has to be some allowance at the start of the contract as the provider learns about the details of the contract and the organisation, recruits the staff and gets the work under way. There has likewise to be a judgement as to how long the 'probationary period' is – for catering it is very short indeed: staff expect an improved service from day one – and how reasonable it is to threaten any penalties, if they are part of the contract, and the nature of those penalties.

Terms and conditions of the provider's employees

It is always a difficult situation if employees of two different organisations are working side by side under different terms and conditions. Back in the 1970s, unions used to insist that sub-contractors who came onto an employer's premises must be paid the same rates, although complex bonus arrangements often clouded this point. Today, unions rarely have powers to influence this situation – but it can still affect the morale of employees if the provider's employees have far better terms. It is worth setting up a system of careful liaison to try to avoid areas of gross comparison.

Transferring employees

Apart for the complexities of TUPE, there is the major issue of how and when to tell the staff involved. Reilly and Tamkin (1996) set out the two views:

One view is to do it as late as possible, to minimise the risk of sabotage, and only through the incoming contractor, who then has an early opportunity to state his case. This means that staff hear directly from their potential future employer who can address their concerns. The alternative opinion is the diametric opposite. It argues that concerns over sabotage are exaggerated and precautions can be put in place to reduce the risk. The principal aims of the transition, it is felt, should be to gain employee support for the process and minimise fear of the unknown. This, it is believed, will be assisted by early information which avoids rumour developing.

Transferring back

An unusual situation arose when Lloyds Bank merged with the TSB. An evaluation of the IT facilities at the joint operation showed that outsourced work could be brought back in-house. A five-year contract with Sema entered into in 1996 was terminated by agreement, and the 100 staff involved were told at first that they would simply transfer back to Lloyds-TSB without any compensation. However, after negotiation with BIFU, it was agreed that they could remain with Sema, take voluntary redundancy at enhanced rates or transfer back with a 5 per cent pay rise and a £2,000 lump sum.

Conclusion

There is a view among some employee representatives that the whole area of outsourcing has been introduced with a different agenda. It is a way to frighten employees by threatening to outsource activities so that performance improves. There may be little or no real intention to actually transfer the work but the perceived threat is sufficient to drive through changes that would prove difficult to achieve otherwise. Employers thus manage to change working practices, hours of work, terms and conditions and whole sets of attitudes not through the threats of loss of business through competition but by an implied or actual threat of outsourcing. This issue is taken a little further in the chapter on the psychological contract (Chapter 14).

References and further reading

ENFIELD ADVERTISER. 'Council's own workforce face bankruptcy'. 27 April 1997, p. 10.

JOHNSON M. *Outsourcing ... In Brief*. Oxford, Butterworth Heinemann, 1997.

KAVANAGH P. 'Inside track', *Sunday Times*, 23 November 1997.

LACITY M., HIRSCHHEIM R. and WILLCOCKS L. 'Realizing outsourcing expectations'. *Information Systems Management*, Fall 1994, pp. 7–18.

LOCAL GOVERNMENT MANAGEMENT BOARD. *CCT Information Service Survey, 1996*. Report No. 14. London, December 1996.

MANAGEMENT TODAY. 'The payroll handover', August 1997, p. 13.

REILLY P. and TAMKIN P. *Outsourcing: A Flexible Option for the Future?* Brighton, Institute of Employment Studies Report 320, 1996.

ROTHERY B. and ROBERTSON I. *The Truth About Outsourcing*. London, Gower, 1995.

SKYTE P. 'Outsourcing – what about the workers?' *Flexible Working*, July 1997, pp. 24–30.

More information on outsourcing is available from:
THE OUTSOURCING INSTITUTE, 45 Rockefeller Plaza, New York, NY 10111. Telephone 800 421 6767.
KPMG IMPACT PROGAMME, 8 Salisbury Square, London, EC4Y 8BB. Telephone 0171 311 1000.
FACILITIES MANAGEMENT ASSOCIATION, ESCA House, 34 Palace Court, Bayswater, London, W2 4JG. Telephone 0171 727 5238.
ANDERSEN CONSULTING, 2 Arundel Street, London, WC2R 3LT. Telephone 0171 438 5000.

More information on TUPE is available from:
LEWIS D. *Essentials of Employment Law*. 5th edn. London, Institute of Personnel and Development, 1997.
LOCAL GOVERNMENT MANAGEMENT BOARD'S ADVICE UNIT ON CCT on (telephone) 0171 296 6736.
O'BRIEN C. and CHESHIRE C. 'Law and the flexible workforce'. *Flexible Working*, May 1996, pp. 29–31.

WILLIAMS R. 'The Suzen judgement – the TUPE world turned Upside Down?' *Flexible Working*, May 1997, pp. 27–28.

In 1997, *People Management* magazine carried a monthly definitive guide to developments in business transfer law, written by John McMullen.

8   CALL CENTRES

Introduction

Call centres sit uncomfortably in the pantheon of flexible working practices. They are not an HR system that determines conditions of operating, like annual hours or shift rotas. They are first and foremost a marketing device that improves the communications between customers and the organisation for a variety of purposes – selling insurance, processing money transactions, servicing an electricity account, operating a vehicle repair service, and pure public relations in share flotation operations.

The link with flexibility takes two forms. Firstly, there is the sheer novelty of flexibility for the customer for whom all aspects of the transaction can take place from the armchair. Secondly, the need for covering a wide spectrum of hours – sometimes 24 hours a day, seven days a week – has produced some flexibility initiatives. An associated factor of flexibility is that an organisation can set up its call centre anywhere in the UK.

London Electricity, for example, has set up its call centre in Sunderland, where there is greater availability of labour at lower pay rates. Research has indicated that callers prefer and trust staff with Northern or Scottish accents, so many centres have sprung up in Yorkshire (Leeds in particular is known as 'the call centre of the North' and has its own call centre employers' group), in the North-East and in Scotland, where Edinburgh and the Highlands are preferred locations.

There is also the fact that call centres are growing fast. Already by 1997 260,000 workers are employed on a full-time or part-time basis – which is over 1 per cent of the working population – and this is expected to double by 2001. Over 3,000 work at the First Direct call centre in Leeds, and 2,000 at Sky Subscriber Centre in Livingston, Scotland. There is even a Certificate in Call Centre Management, designed by the L&R Group, a call centre consultancy, and launched in 1997 by the Institute for Direct Marketing.

William Hill, the betting firm, began a telephone betting service in 1987 with a staff of 30 which gradually climbed to 50 by 1992. Since that time, however, the number of calls has expanded greatly, and there is now a staff of over 300. It is quite likely that the spread of mobile phones has a strong connection here.

Flexibility or the new Taylorism?

Call centres have been technology-driven. They are the product of a combination of complex computerised systems, which allow the trained call-operator access to every customer's account and to every relevant element of the company's operations, and the automated call distribution system (ACD), which does away with the need for a switchboard and allows management to fully monitor and analyse every call. The technology, however, has produced some of the worst features of mass communication. Simon Roncoroni of L&R reported at a 1997 IPD conference that he had seen 'offices where individuals sit in tiny pig-pens with high screens round them, or in a long line as though they were in a factory'.

There are call centres which resemble the industrial sweatshops of the past, involving very cramped conditions for staff who work on their computers throughout their shift under very tightly controlled conditions. Those on specialised sales areas even have a script written for them so that it is easy to believe that their individuality is being negated. In many ways this is identical to the assembly line created by Ford engineers from the theories of Frederick Taylor and parodied by Charlie Chaplin in the film *Modern Times*. It is as far removed from a flexible environment as you can get.

Lack of control over working time and methods is a great contributor to stress. It becomes, as Merilyn Armitage (1997) has called it, a 'psychic prison' from which inmates are tempted to use any device to escape, including continuing to speak to a caller who has long since hung up so no one else can get through. Absenteeism and sickness levels are notoriously high – one centre experienced a 20 per cent absence rate according to a survey carried out by Merchants Group.

A further ratchet of control is secured by tying the pay system to an individual's performance, measured (so accurately) by the number of successful calls per hour. To complete the picture, the disciplinary system comes into force when a print-out shows that the employee does not appear to be earning his or her keep. There is some evidence of a rapid 'burn-out' after only 12 to 20 months' service (Welch, 1997); Vodafone's personnel manager is quoted in this article as expecting only a year's service from the typical applicant. A study of 106 units by the Merchants Group (*Personnel Today*, 1997) found that absenteeism averaged 4.8 per cent, compared with the CBI average figure of 3.7 for all employees. The report implied that a rate over 4 per cent indicated some kind of problem with stress, morale or integrity.

Advantages of call centres

Despite the apparent difficulties, there are substantial financial and operational advantages:

☐ The high commission costs (30 per cent or so) in selling financial and other products are eliminated.

☐ At the end of a phone an operator could make as many as ten sales a day, while the door-to-door insurance salesman would be satisfied with two.

☐ There is a sizeable reduction in overheads where large numbers of costly high street premises are replaced by much cheaper office facilities tucked away in much cheaper geographical locations.

☐ Staff are easier to recruit in most areas where call centres are located, and accept lower pay rates than in areas from where the business comes.

☐ There is also considerable saving on service costs. Lever Brothers has set up a call centre to deal with customer complaints and requests for advice on its detergent brands. Supermarkets normally charge £25 for handling each complaint.

Operating a call centre

There are two basic types of call centre. There are the help-desks, which give out flight or train times, book cinema seats, or give technical advice and information, especially on IT products but also on areas of public concern, such as the centre run by the Environment Agency who run the Thames call centre with six operators. The second type are the inter-active processing centres where an operator may sell something to you or fulfil your requests, such as deducting money from your account. No forms need be completed: the use of a password is sufficient.

An IDS survey in 1997, which examined 60 call centres, showed a mixture of manning operations. In one fifth of the centres, part-time staff were in the majority: there was a small core of full-time staff to act as the basis for each shift and a variety of part-time shifts at different times of day – mornings, afternoons and evenings. Yorkshire Bank (Leeds) and Laura Ashley (mid-Wales) are examples of this style of manning. The sales call centres for Anglian Double Glazing have a part-time evening shift who spend 3–4 hours ringing up potential customers to try to arrange visits by sales representatives.

Other centres were more conventional, involving a majority of full-time employees and overtime worked where necessary – which is very much like a traditional manufacturing shiftworking arrangement. Northern Rock Direct (Newcastle), for example, has no part-time staff, while Halifax Direct (Leeds), Scottish Widows (Edinburgh) and London Electricity (Sunderland) all have more than 80 per cent of their staff on a full-time basis.

A call centre set up in 1994 on Rothesay, on the Scottish isle of Bute, by TSC has employees with an average age of 30. In an area of high unemployment it becomes easier to recruit mature workers.

Forty per cent of the call centres studied operated a 24-hour, 365-day service – but not all paid shift premia. Many staff the evening and night services with part-time employees on conventional payments, while some make shift payments below the industrial average, such as London Electricity (Sunderland) who pay a 10 per cent premium.

The use of temporary staff is much in evidence: 15 per cent in total, with over 60 per cent employing a proportion. IBM is an interesting case, for the operation is outsourced to an agency and all of the employees work under agency temporary conditions. The high proportion of temporary staff is not surprising because many of the call centres are new and need time to reach a conclusion on the ideal staffing levels. Females make up 70 per cent of the staff, occupying a higher proportion in the home-shopping call centres for companies such as Littlewoods and Laura Ashley.

Innovations

We have seen that most call centres have been set up by engineers and that the staff has been trained to fit in with the computerised environment to gain the highest level of productivity. Productivity may certainly rise at first but a block will develop until, as in all jobs at all levels, the employees' skills, inventiveness and commitment are fully utilised.

A number of organisations have recognised this and are taking action in the areas of recruitment, teamwork, staff development and pay.

Recruitment

Psychometric tests are being developed to identify those staff that work well within the system and who have a high boredom threshold, which is a crucial factor.

Getting the right staff was taken a stage further by the L&R Group who helped HMV set up a direct service call centre. They set out to recruit genuine music fans who would not only be able to research the music database but also had the knowledge to advise over the telephone. Adverts were placed in the *NME* and *Classical Music Magazine*, amongst other media, which generated 1,000 applications: 500 were interviewed by phone, 75 were put through psychometric and product knowledge tests, out of which 13 candidates were finally accepted. Staff turnover since the service started in 1996 has been minimal. Friends Provident concentrate on recruiting staff with people skills, as these are far more important than insurance knowledge (McLuhan, 1998).

Teamwork

It has been recognised that teams can act as remarkable motivating forces and can help staff use data positively rather than negatively, especially in the areas of problem-solving. First Direct have encouraged teamworking by introducing self-managed teams in 1996 at one of its three call centres. Part of the process is for peer-group monitoring to take place, which becomes far more supportive than the 'Big Brother' approach of a supervisor listening in without the operator's knowing.

Staff development

Taking calls which deal with a very limited range of subjects can quickly de-motivate call centre operatives. It is also inefficient, having to redirect callers to another number or another office or both. This is why most organisations enter into a fairly extensive skills-stretching exercise to ensure that operators can handle all calls on all subjects, and can achieve greater job satisfaction. Insurance companies, for example, used to have rigid divisions between offices that sold insurance, those that dealt with queries, and those that handled the claims. For the average broker this was a nightmare, having to remember who to deal with at the insurance office concerned. Royal Insurance was one of the first to change the system and create a multi-skilled force of insurance advisers who could take calls from brokers in all the areas and handle all of the activities. After a trial it was found that brokers are more likely to promote a particular insurance company if they find communications with it efficient and friendly – and one call to handle everything was a major step in this direction.

The AA have recently retrained their agents to take more than one type of call. Insurance sales staff can handle membership enquiries, while people who usually provide traffic and weather information can also handle emergency breakdown calls. In the IDM Certificate, developing the skills of employees is seen as a critical competence of call centre managers. One-to-one coaching is the subject of a complete module and deals with the importance of developing a coaching culture within the system where it is seen as genuinely supportive at all levels.

A further module is called *Staying sane in the call centre* and examines the sources and causes of personal and team stress in the call centre environment, and how to diffuse them.

Pay systems

Basic rates of pay are not high in general. The median salary range in 1997 was £9,500 to £11,500, with Scottish Hydro-Electric and Tesco (both at Perth) on that range. Vodafone's rates at centres across the country from Glasgow to Dartford are much higher (£12,000 to £15,000), as are the Prudential operations in the south of England with rates stretching up to £17,000. All of these may not be strictly comparable as they depend on the complexity of the product and the degree and significance of the advice given to customers, as opposed to providing information or dealing with simple complaints.

Bonus schemes operate in the vast majority of centres. Because an individual's performance can be measured so easily, it is tempting to make all payments on an individual basis – and most call centres started off on this basis. William Hill, for example, has a bonus scheme which takes effect when operators exceed a call threshold (1,250 calls for full-time staff, less for part-time and Saturday-only staff). An hourly payment is then made depending on an efficiency calculation based on the length of calls.

Schemes such as this are certainly popular with the high performer in a competitive environment, but it does tend to mean that teamworking becomes less important and to encourage a culture in which co-operation appears to be unimportant.

Mixtures of individual and team rewards are common. Barclaycall (Coventry) and Pearl (Peterborough) tie one half of bonus payments to individual performance and the other half to team performance. Most of the bonus payments are non-pensionable and made as a lump sum annually or six-monthly. A number of schemes have limits on the bonus payments – as low as 2.5 per cent at Co-op Banking (Skelmersdale) whereas Littlewoods bonus has a limit of 20 per cent.

Organisations have experimented with ways of reinforcing teamworking by awarding prizes to successful teams. AGF

Insurance, for example, set up a monthly prize of £250 to the most successful team in terms of team member availability for taking calls and a set of quality standards organised on a points basis. The prize was awarded in vouchers to be chosen by the team, which could include corporate entertainment events, or meals out. Customer Contact Company, which designs and manages call centres for direct businesses, encourages group bonuses as an important part of its operations.

A significant development is that *overtime pay* is operated only in a small minority of centres. This is to discourage an overtime culture and because the flexibility of hours and shifts is built into the overall scheme. There are some variations, such as at Barclaycall (Coventry), where overtime at time-and-a-half is paid if staff work in excess of 140 hours a month, while BT pays a premium of time-and-a-quarter for the first six hours worked each week, beyond a total of 41 hours gross (IDS, 1997).

Operate directly, or outsource?

The final innovation is to outsource the whole operation to a specialist supplier such as Sitel, Vertex or Cap Gemini. Vertex runs United Utilities' call centres in the north-west and also operates some call centre services for local authorities, such as in the debt-collecting field. Nor is geography important – the distribution of parking fines for London boroughs takes place at a call centre at Forres in the far north of Scotland. This will inevitably be a burgeoning development as the price of telephone calls and operations continues to decline.

Outsourcing provides the opportunity for small companies to put their toes in the water. Top Line, based in Gateshead Business Park, opened a facility in 1997 at which companies can run a two-week pilot scheme with limited costs and an estimated target. It is not uncommon for small companies to underestimate the cost and complications involved in operating a call centre, as David Smith, marketing manager, explained (Hoare, 1997): 'We are not a telemarketing agency where all you need is a phone, a seat and a desk. We are interacting with clients' office systems, often using very sophisticated reporting methods and specialised databases. What the client pays depends on the management we put in, not telephone minutes.'

A similar arrangement is offered by the L&R Group with their Call Studio, which provides dedicated staff and resources based on anticipated levels of call activity. They use the analogy of a 'broadcast' where staff are auditioned, go backstage and rehearse as part of their training, knowing that their message will go out to far more than the number of customers they actually talk to.

Different estimates are made on the entry costs of an efficient call centre but the consensus would appear to be that the minimum set-up costs are around £100,000.

References and further reading

ARMITAGE M. 'Give call centre staff a stake in their jobs'. *Personnel Today*, 31 July 1997, p. 8.

HOARE S. 'Call centre'. *Director* November 1997, pp. 76–79.

IDS *Pay and Conditions in Call Centres*. IDS Report No. 739, June 1997, pp. 27–35.

McLUHAN R. 'Feelgood factors'. *Personnel Today*, 12 February 1998, pp. 26–27.

MENDAY J. *Call Centre Management: A practical guide*. Newdigate, Callcraft, 1996.

Personnel Today, news item, 3 July 1997, p. 3.

WELCH J. 'Call centres in crisis over staff shortages'. *People Management*, 9 October 1997, p. 9.

9 FLEXIBLE REWARDS FOR INDIVIDUALS

Introduction

Angela works for one of the major insurance companies as an agent selling pensions and life assurance, working on commission only. She works from home, attending meetings once a month at the regional office, and she has leads communicated directly to her by e-mail. She fixes her own appointments, works many evenings and weekends, and completes most of the required paperwork. The payment system is essentially simple, giving her a proportion of the first year's premiums, but there are a number of complexities depending on the nature of each policy sold and whether policies have been cancelled in the 'cooling-off' period. She averages one deal a week, but this can vary greatly and her monthly payments have varied between zero and £6,000. She once went six weeks without a sale and was on the point of throwing the job in before achieving three successful deals in a week.

George works for a small printing company as a machine printer on a basic pay of £300 a week plus a bonus relating to his individual output. The bonus can pay, in theory, up to £200 a week, but he is dependent on the machine's output and on how long the printing runs are. His original apprenticeship skills have been augmented with training on new equipment, including basic maintenance and fault diagnosis. Because most of the printing contracts are regular and involve long runs, his bonus has settled at £80 a week, with a variation of only £10 or so on either side except on the very rare occasions when the machine has broken down and he has had to call in a specialist mechanic. He works a fixed-day shift of 8 am to 4.30 pm.

These two individual flexible pay schemes are at opposite ends of the spectrum. For Angela, her flexibility in hours, the initiative required and her willingness to risk a reliable salary, are rewarded with opportunities of a very high income directly related to her own efforts and skill developments. For George, the emphasis is on reliability and consistency, with payments on a fixed pattern rewarding continuous production and the use of acquired skills.

We have seen earlier that one of the key items of the strategy of successful organisations is flexibility in providing products and services. If this is to be put into practice, it will have to be aligned with the organisation's own cultural values. Individuals will need to be customer-focused, to respond quickly to changing customer requirements and to co-operate in changing patterns of production, sales and service. They will need to be more ready to take on board new skills and consistent quality standards and to increase their job role to encompass inspection, training and administration. They will need to be more ready to come up with improvements, sell them to their colleagues, and put them into effect. In short, they will need to be ready to demonstrate their commitment to the flexible needs of the organisation.

Systems of pay flexibility

Reward systems can help to reinforce this required change in the behaviour of employees in four main ways:

☐ by encouraging them to adopt the required behaviours or competencies that lead to improved performance: a system known as *competency-based pay*. Flexibility would be one of these competencies, and achieving a high mark on this measure would lead to a greater reward.

☐ by encouraging the learning and adoption of skills that aid flexibility which can be both technical and administrative. This is *skills-based pay*.

☐ by increasing the proportion of an employee's pay that is contingent upon his or her performance and the performance of the organisation. This increased variable pay element is often implemented as *performance-related pay*. Employees are rewarded for what they currently achieve, the goals they meet, the objectives they pass – not for their position or their past performance.

☐ by allowing more freedom for an employee's basic salary to rise through replacing the rigid, constricting job-evaluated salary structure with its fixed pay grades and scales with a much looser *broadbanded structure* in which salary determination itself is much looser and where more movement is possible, based chiefly on performance.

There is often an overlap in these four categories so that, for example, performance-related pay (PRP) frequently incorporates competencies and skills. Each area will be examined first and then the conclusion will show how many organisations draw the categories together into an integrated policy.

The use of these four initiatives varies. A 1995 survey of 216 organisations by Business Intelligence and *Personnel Today* found that PRP was by far the most popular at 70 per cent, while skills-based pay was operating in 18 per cent, competency-based pay in 12 per cent, and broadbanding in 10 per cent (Ashton, 1995).

Competency-based pay

George Milkovich (Milkovich and Newman, 1996, pp. 680–681) defined the subject thus:

> Competency-based pay links pay to the depth and scope of competencies that are relevant to doing the job. They are typically used in managerial and professional work where what is accomplished may be difficult to identify.

There is slowly growing interest in linking the competency movement with payment and reward systems. In America, a 1995 Towers Perrin study showed 20 per cent of larger companies included competency in their pay systems, while research by the Industrial Society found a combined figure of 18 per cent for the use of skills- or competency-based pay in their UK sample (Industrial Society, 1996).

There are three main steps in setting up a scheme: defining the competencies, measuring the levels of competence, and conversion into a reward system. None of these is straightforward, and the whole subject area is one of considerable controversy.

Defining the competencies

Consultants who first defined competencies for a few large organisations used psychological techniques, such as repertory grids or critical incidents, to capture the actions of employees regarded as 'expert performers' by both managers and their colleagues. These performers produced results that clearly helped the organisation to meet its defined goals. The essence of what they did to achieve success was codified into competencies. Some of these competencies apply to all staff in the organisation and are called 'core' or 'generic'. The more popular ones include creativity, effective communications, and problem-solving. Others are specific to particular roles or are specialised in particular departments. These could include individual competencies in a research centre (eg statistical data analysis) or in a market trading arena (eg speed of market movement analysis).

Significantly, no two organisational competency frameworks are identical because the needs and requirements of every organisation are different.

Measuring the levels of competence

Having defined a set of competencies for each job, the next stage is to define a set of measures by which an individual employee can be placed on a ladder of performance leading up to the top rung of 'fully competent'. An example of a simple competency-level structure at a telecommunications company is shown in Table 15.

Each level is clearly specified by assessments that are largely subjective but which can be supported by objective measures such as the number of customer complaints and any feedback from major customers. An advance at each level is intended to demonstrate the importance of adding value to the organisation. A few organisations, principally in the USA, have set up a certification scheme whereby employees' competencies are tested objectively and they move up to the next level when they are certificated as competent. This is certainly feasible in fields such as call centre work and retail

Table 15
'THE CUSTOMER COMES FIRST'

Level	Identifying Customer Needs	Customer Relationships	Responsiveness	Co-operation
5	Anticipates customer requirements / Works with the customer to develop the business relationship	Sets customer expectations at a high but achievable level / Win-win situations sought between self and customer	Seen by customer as a partner	Always listens to the customer and suggests improvements to customer's wants / An ambassador
4	Seeks to anticipate customer requirements / Listens to customers and influences customers' views	Asks customers for feedback and follows customer comments through	Sought by customers as an adviser	Performs in ways that enhance both personal and company image
3	Reacts to customer requirements / Understands customer's viewpoint	Accepts ownership of customer problems and complaints / Adds value to the business relationship	Customer is satisfied / Performs in line with reputation and image	
2	Performs own job without proper regard for customer opinion / Needs constant reminding about customer skills	Customers sometimes dissatisfied / Falls short of customer-first value		
1	Limited awareness of customer needs or the effect of own actions / Adds no value to the relationship			

sales but far more difficult for competencies relating to, say, purchasing or personnel.

Conversion into pay

In many ways, this is the easy bit! Assessments can be easily converted into points so that a total number of points determines the level of pay increase, usually through a grid system as often used in performance related-pay systems (see Table 17, page 188). In the telecommunications company scheme, the five competencies each carry a maximum of five points, making a total maximum of 25 points. Other schemes may have a variation in total marks for each competency, ranging from two for the less important ones to ten for the key competencies.

Advantages of paying for competencies

- ☐ Employees are left in no doubt as to the behaviours required in the organisation.
- ☐ Rewarding these behaviours focuses employees' attention on trying to match those competencies and to improve in areas in which they are judged wanting.
- ☐ Training and development activities have a clear positive target, which is to improve competence. Employees put effort into the scheme because they want to make progress and achieve a higher assessment which will lead to more pay.

Drawbacks to paying for competencies

- ☐ Although the assessment process is more robust than older-style appraisal schemes in which employees were rated on a scale of 1 to 5 for 'drive' or 'initiative', it still remains a highly subjective measure, open to criticism for bias, favouritism or ignorance.
- ☐ Competence requirements are different in most positions within the organisation. Leadership needs in the postroom, for example, differ greatly from leadership needs on the factory floor, so every position will need its own set of competencies.
- ☐ Drawing up the competency scheme can be a long, tortu-

ous and costly process if it is to be unique to an organisation. Even then it needs to be regularly updated as situations alter, which incurs further cost.

☐ Using competencies that are easily understood – such as teamwork, leadership or customer care – can lead to a cynical approach by employees who can regard it as a mere justification for giving differential pay increases.

☐ Helping employees to get better at their jobs is one thing – to base their pay on it is another. Managers who make the competence assessments may be too influenced by employees' pay needs rather than their true competence level.

☐ Employees may possess a high level of competence but not necessarily be good at achieving results. We have all come across the employee who is all too willing to satisfy a customer's needs (and therefore has a high level of customer-care competence) but who spends too much time with that customer and may incur too many costs in refunds or allowances. As Armstrong puts it (Armstrong, 1996, p. 295): 'It leads to over-emphasis on inputs rather than out puts; knowledge, skills and behaviour rather than results.'

Skills-based pay

Skills-based pay provides the direct link between the acquisition of particular skills or qualifications, which improve the level of an employee's flexibility, and pay supplements or increases. There is a very strong association in studies by Lawler (1993) in the USA and Cross (1992) in the UK with other features of human resource management, including employee involvement, restructuring and total quality management (TQM).

As Lawler (1993) puts it:

A high level of employee involvement may be necessary for companies to realize fully the benefits of skills-based pay. Increased employee flexibility and broadened employee perspectives may be wasted if employees are not given the power to use what they learn through participation groups and job designs that create greater self-management ... Rewards for learning multiple jobs may also facilitate job rotation and cross-training which are essential to self-managing team designs.

Providing a reward is a clear sign to employees of the value of accumulating needed skills and of taking part in the involvement process. For example, maintenance employees at Vauxhall have a skills-based pay scale which includes the job title 'advanced fitter/electrician' in respect of a person who is able to tackle assembly line breakdowns, whatever the cause. This replaced the traditional divide between the two skills – of fitter and of electrician – which had led to inevitable inefficiencies in running the line with either double manning or delays in waiting for the right craftsman. Employees with these job titles have taken the lead in initiating improved preventative maintenance schemes. A further set of skills lead to the job title of 'advanced technician' for a person who deals with control-room functions.

Closely associated are the TQM practices which include self-inspection, direct exposure to customers and just-in-time inventory systems. To operate these practices, employees need to develop skills such as diagnostic testing, customer-relations skills and effective planning.

In order to meet the competitive pressures, the manpower requirement often drops with the introduction of skills-based schemes because the levels of productivity, quality and efficiency rise. This may happen suddenly as part of resolving a crisis situation or through a voluntary system, leaving employees who are prepared to adapt to the multi-skilling culture. By the same token, a number of managerial and supervisory layers are often removed, leaving empowered employees who need to learn new skills. The enhanced pay arising from the process goes some way to alleviate the decrease in opportunities for promotion and the pay increases that they would have brought.

Aspects of skills-based pay
Accreditation

Measuring the attainment of enhanced skills can take two forms. Firstly, it is possible for a company to use an internal system of accreditation with tests constructed to its own requirements. BHS (formerly British Home Stores) started down the NVQ route but then switched in 1994 to its own training and development package called Spotlight on Success. All of the company's 14,000 employees were enrolled in the scheme which consisted of 18 components (or 'acts'). Employees had to complete nine acts to part-qualify and receive a £5.00 a week increase, and the remainder to complete the course and receive an additional £8.50 a week. Due to difficulties that employees found in completing all 18 components, the total was reduced to 12 in 1996, with seven as 'core acts' and the remaining five leading to qualified status (IRS, 1996).

The second system is to link the assessment to an external accreditation system. The most popular is NVQs. Rhone-Poulenc Agriculture in 1993 introduced a system for multi-skilling process employees based on NVQ modular training and education packages, with the object of creating multi-disciplined teams. Participation is voluntary although most employees have agreed to take part and to draw up training contracts. These detail the existing skill levels and specify which training modules will be taken over a specified time period, maximum three years. In recognition of their progress, they receive staged payments as they advance to craft technician status. The pay increase from start to the achievement of craftsman status can be up to £4,000 per year (IDS, 1996).

Skills rewards are not necessarily in monetary form. In Welcome Break motorway catering, employees enter into a programme of skills development under their Staff Winners Award programme. The awards they receive are essentially a certificate and a badge when they complete various modules.

Investment

As with any major training initiative, there are often high start-up costs. This is not just in training equipment and instruction but in the planning, skills analysis, testing and evaluation stages. By the time the periods spent off the job and the skills-based pay itself are taken into account, the scheme will need a very high pay-off in increased efficiency to warrant a successful conclusion.

Who obtains the skills?

The question arises as to which employees should have the opportunity to become multi-skilled. At Rhône-Poulenc, it is offered to everybody but remains voluntary. This should ensure that only the enthusiastic take part in the training, but it may leave a remnant of unskilled, unmotivated, unempowered employees who are not cost-effective. On the other hand, to make it compulsory is always a dangerous pathway in training where employees can be obstructive and de-motivating for the rest of the team.

Difficulties

Apart from the high start-up costs, another major difficulty is to ensure that the skills, once achieved, are utilised. If the planning has been accurate, this should only be a minor operational problem, but in reality the length of the training period (two to four years, usually) makes it very difficult to actually foresee the business requirements that far ahead. It can be a depressing process for all concerned if employees go to the effort to get multi-skilled and receive payment and then do not effectively use many of their skills.

The case-study below is an example of skills-based pay at SKF, an engineering company in Luton.

Case-study

SKILLS-BASED PAY AT SKF (UK)

In May 1996, SKF, the Swedish-owned bearing company, concluded a major review of the pay and conditions of shop-floor employees at its Luton plant. Production had recently been reorganised into 'channels' or cells where a wider range of skills were required, and it was vital that the concept of flexibility within the channels was emphasised and reinforced.

For its 240 *non-craft employees*, a skills-based pay structure was introduced, comprising a single basic hourly rate and a series of increments, paid for attaining each of six skills modules.

The six skills modules are:

Setting	Quality
Tooling	Materials flow
Total preventative maintenance	Team representation

The increments for these modules range from 25p to £1.65 an hour: employees nominated to a module but not yet fully qualified receive 30 per cent of the increment. Nominations to the skills modules are carried out by a sub-committee of the Joint Negotiating Committee which is comprised of two union and two management representatives.

The team representative is the highest grade of direct employee, and all non-craft employees get an opportunity to progress to that position. Skills modules may be taken in any order but certain combinations of modules are required in order to progress to the team representative position.

For the 40 *craft employees*, a new 'channel technician (maintenance)' grade has been created. Each technician will be assigned to work for a production channel to provide a full maintenance service. Three skills modules have been designed for craftsmen, which are:

Technological development

Manufacturing and operation process

Continuing professional development

Each increment is worth around £1,000 per annum.

As part of their responsibilities, craftsmen spend time training employees in their channel even while receiving full training themselves in mechanical and/or electrical skills.

These skills-based pay features are associated with other flexible working developments, including a pilot flexible week system by which employees may be stood down for periods of up to four hours a week when demand for the company's products is low and may have to make up these hours when demand picks up again. In return, the company has promised that any further compulsory redundancies will be contemplated only as a last resort.

Source: IDS Report 720, September 1996, pp. 29–31.

Performance-related pay

Paying differential rewards based on an individual employee's performance is a flexible pay system which is increasingly replacing the rigid pay-for-the-job or pay-for-seniority traditional systems.

How widespread is it?

A number of recent surveys have shown that performance-related pay (PRP) is operating formally in 40 to 60 per cent of organisations surveyed (IPM, 1992; Cannell and Wood, 1992; Industrial Society, 1996; IPD, 1998). Despite a considerable degree of scepticism surrounding the outcomes of PRP, the majority of organisations believe that there should be pay distinctions between those individuals that perform well and those that do not. This is the fundamental principle underpinning PRP, and one with which most employees agree in a number of attitude surveys that have been carried out (Thompson, 1993; Marsden and Richardson, 1992; Dowling and Richardson, 1997).

How does it operate?

The essential features are:

☐ At the beginning of each year, the organisational objectives are cascaded down to departments, and a framework of targets and measures is established for individuals. These are either determined by the line manager or, more commonly, agreed between the manager and the employee after discussion.

☐ The objectives are SMART – Specific, Measurable, Agreed, Realistic and Time-based.

☐ During the course of the year, several informal and formal meetings take place to discuss progress towards achieving the desired outcomes.

☐ Any required training and development required to assist achievement of the objectives is discussed and implemented during the year.

☐ At the end of the year a formal meeting takes place at which the level of achievement is discussed and a decision reached on performance. Each objective is examined and marks or points awarded which are then totalled up to produce a final mark.

☐ This mark is then converted into a performance rating. At this stage an employee can appeal against the rating.

☐ In turn, the rating is converted into pay either through a salary increase or, less commonly, an annual bonus.

Table 16
THE MECHANICS OF PERFORMANCE-RELATED PAY

There are six objectives for an employee to achieve, with the following weightings:

Objective 1	Weighting 30%	Objective 4	Weighting 10%
Objective 2	Weighting 20%	Objective 5	Weighting 10%
Objective 3	Weighting 20%	Objective 6	Weighting 10%

At the end of the period, a decision is reached that the level of performance on the objectives is :

Objective	Achievement level	Weighting	Outcome
1	80%	30%	24 points
2	100%	20%	20 points
3	90%	20%	18 points
4	50%	10%	5 points
5	100%	10%	10 points
6	60%	10%	6 points
		Total points	83 points

Conversion to salary increase
In a simple scheme it operates as follows:

Points	Salary increase	Points	Salary increase
0–49	nil	80–84	4%
50–59	1%	85–89	5%
60–69	2%	90–94	7%
70–79	3%	95–100	9%

Here, the Employee gets a 4 per cent increase.

Table 16 sets out an example of the mechanics of the scheme.

In a more complex scheme, the salary increase would also take into account the current position of the employee in the salary grade, so a salary-increase grid would be produced as shown in Table 17 (page 188).

In support of PRP schemes

- It is fair to distinguish between the high performer and those that are only average or below average.
- Making payments to high performers reinforces the message that the organisation recognises and encourages high performance, and establishes a clear culture throughout the organisation.
- The process of setting objectives clarifies what employees need to achieve and thereby focuses their attention and effort.

Table 17
AN EXAMPLE OF A PAY-INCREASE GRID

	Current position in pay band				
Performance score	70–85%	86–99%	100%	100–115%	116–130%
Outstanding	25	15	10	8	6
Excellent	15	11	8	6	4
Good	10	8	6	4	2
Satisfactory	6	4	2	0	0
Below required standard	2	0	0	0	0

Example

Pay band £14,000–£26,000
Midpoint = 100% = £20,000

Employee A on £15,000 (70–85% range)
Achieves excellent rating
Salary will rise by 15% from £15,000 to £17,250

Employee B on £24,000 (116–130% range)
Achieves good rating
Salary will rise by 2% to £24,480

☐ By being focused, employees act in a flexible way to achieve the required results rather than simply carrying out their job as defined by the job description. They become facilitators and problem-solvers and circumvent bureaucratic barriers.

☐ The opportunity for differential earnings is a recruitment aid, attracting ambitious, results-oriented applicants.

☐ Achieving results and obtaining good pay increases is a positive force for raising morale in the organisation.

Criticisms of PRP schemes

☐ The list of objectives is rarely larger than eight or ten to avoid a scheme's becoming too complex and unwieldy. This emphasis on a small and selective number of objectives means that employees tend to concentrate on these objectives only, to the detriment of many other factors in their job. Routine aspects can be deferred and objectives that don't make the main list are often forgotten.

□ An individual may make every effort to achieve his or her own objectives, but it may be at the expense of co-operation and teamwork. 'I'm too busy to help – I have to work on my objectives,' is an all too often repeated remark in practice.

□ Not all objectives can be easily converted into measurable targets. It can be straightforward for sales and production, but even here, targets need to take on board the quality, cost and time-based aspects. In other areas the actual definition of success can cause considerable controversy and, in practice, acrimony. For example, a personnel officer has the target of producing a report which sets out recommendations on improving equal opportunities. How is the result to be measured? Producing it on time is one thing, but what about the content? How good the report is becomes a purely subjective matter.

□ It is not clear how good a motivator PRP is. In most schemes, the pay difference between the average performer and the high performer is, at most, only 3 or 4 per cent. On an average salary of, say, £20,000, this represents an after-tax monthly difference of only £35 or so. Most evaluations find that employees do not regard PRP in financial terms as an effective motivator.

□ Managers may be tempted to pick out their favourites to award them higher PRP than the rest of the staff, creating a considerable sense of cynicism and unfairness.

□ Managers, on the other hand, may not want to go through the hassle of differentiation and the difficulties it causes, and may put all staff on the same level – which produces, ultimately, the same effect. Distributive justice, as it is called, has not been done or been seen to be done.

□ Individual PRP can work against teamworking. If individuals are assessed entirely on their own performance, they will want to shine, to claim all achievements as their own rather than a team's.

Making it work

Helen Murlis (1993) has set out a series of key criteria for the successful implementation of a PRP scheme. The criteria include:

- top management 'ownership' of the concept and commitment to its introduction as an integral part of the organisation's strategy, and personal involvement with its implementation
- strategic integration of the system with the organisational objectives and with its human resource and pay strategy and policies, which include a clear and shared vision of the organisation's future
- a robust performance management (PM) scheme on which pay increases are based, introduced in phases from the top downward at a pace that ensures that employees understand what is happening and why
- integration of the PM scheme with the way that employees are managed, rather than as an additional paper exercise, including regular reviews during the year and no surprises at the annual review date
- a review that encourages honest, positive and fair management of poor performance and affords time and resources to put the situation right
- rewards that should be capable of being 'significant' for the market sector, and be easy to understand and be publicly defensible
- avoidance of the use of PRP to compensate for recruitment problems, market pressure, inability to promote, taking on significant additional responsibilities, and other issues which risk confusing the messages implicit in the system
- substantial training and communication for all concerned to ensure that PRP is thoroughly understood
- regular reviews and flexible adaptation of the scheme as lessons are learned and a response to employee feedback that reflects the way an organisation needs to constantly develop and change

The case-study opposite is an example of performance-related pay in a retailing organisation.

Case-study

PERFORMANCE-RELATED PAY IN 'R. SMART', RETAILER

Smart's are a niche retailer with 300 shops across UK high streets, specialising in a selection of high-quality goods. In total they have 2,500 employees, including 350 at their head office in North London.

In 1993 they introduced a new system of performance-related pay to match changes in the business requirements towards a higher-quality service and to make the shops a more self-reliant, integrated force. Previously, the recruitment of staff, the window displays and much of the ordering systems were centrally controlled, but this had now been changed so that staff needed to be competent in more areas and prepared to assist in the three above activities.

The new scheme had four key measures of performance:

☐ *Personal commitment*, which looked at the employees' willingness to take on projects over and above their day-to-day job, their commitment to, and achievement of, deadlines, and their willingness to work flexible hours (but not necessarily long hours). Examples might include taking on the training of new employees or leading discussions at team meetings.

☐ *Job knowledge, qualifications and experience*, which examined how much employees had learnt of the company's operations and how they used this knowledge and experience in practice to the benefit of the organisation. An example might be becoming expert at one of the administrative systems.

☐ *Achieving objectives*, which dealt with how well employees achieved the personal objectives agreed at the beginning of the period concerned.

☐ *Capabilities*, which defined the behaviour, skills and qualities required of employees to carry out their role effectively. An example might be in customer care where an employee may receive letters of appreciation for special attention to a customer's needs.

Each of these attributes is measured once a year by means of a thorough discussion between job-holders and their supervisors or managers, all of whom have had training in the process of performance management.

There are four ratings possible under each heading which are:

Unsatisfactory	= 0
Satisfactory	= 1
Good	= 2
Excellent	= 3

The total ratings are then added: the maximum is 12 points. The expected proportionality of employee ratings is:

Unsatisfactory	= 0–3	points	0 per cent
Satisfactory	= 4–6	points	16 per cent
Good	= 7–9	points	68 per cent
Excellent	= 10–12	points	16 per cent

There is an appeal system (rarely used) which allows a further discussion between the employee and the manager of the unit or the general manager of the division.

Conversion into pay

A table is used to convert the rating into pay, which is affected by the position of the employee in the salary band. Those that are at the top of the band will need a high rating to stay at the top. Those at the bottom of their band could have a higher pay increase even though their rating is lower. This operates in a fashion similar to the salary grid in Table 17.

Note: R. Smart is not the real name of this organisation but has been used to preserve anonymity.

Broadbanding

Broadbanded structures are more likely to be introduced in flexible organisations which do not believe in extended hierarchies, are concerned about continuous development and employ a high proportion of knowledge workers

Armstrong M. (1996, p. 199)

How broadbanding has arisen

At the end of a conventional job evaluation exercise, all the jobs studied have been awarded a total of points for all the job factors that have been examined. The next phase is to lay out all those jobs in numerical points order and create a set of grades by fixing boundaries at particular points scores.

In the past it has been common to create at least six and sometimes as many as 20 grades. The aim has been to create equity by highlighting the differences between the sets of jobs, and to give greater rewards to those whose jobs are rated higher than others. The structure is seen to motivate by encouraging employees to bid for promotion to a higher job through a permanent, fair and transparent system. A higher job, a higher grade, a bigger salary: nothing could be simpler or fairer. The first major grading system like this was set up by the US government in 1923 and operated, with some amendments, for 60 years.

Today, the external environment has changed considerably. Promotions are now far fewer because organisations have de-layered, greatly reducing the number of management and supervisory positions. Employees need to be far more flexible, willing to change their roles and learn more skills to meet the needs of the quickly changing national and international marketplace. The stiff, hierarchical grading structure is far less likely to match the quick-moving responsive culture required in both manufacturing and service industries.

One further criticism of the multi-grade system is that it can encourage an employee to adopt a rigid approach to the job. 'My job has been described closely – it has been fixed at a particular grade – therefore that is the job I am paid for. I am not prepared to do anything new or extra outside of the job description unless I am paid more for it.'

In this situation, employees would apply for re-grading which, in itself, tends to be something of an adversarial contest. If the employee wins, it can well upset other colleagues and lead to further claims. This can in turn result in grade drift which causes salary drift and headaches for the remuneration specialist. If the employee loses, the extra work will be carried out grudgingly, if at all. Too often employees think of themselves, or describe others, in terms of their grades. In one large engineering company I asked what job a particular employee did. 'Oh, she's a grade 4,' was the reply – as if that explained everything! In this respect, the system has a dehumanising aspect.

Employees also can see themselves within a function-based hearth operating as 'vertical chimneys' with few transfer opportunities and considerable friction between the functions.

How broadbanding works

When the job evaluation has been completed, the artificial divisions which normally distinguish between grades are ignored. There are two ways of grouping the jobs together. What normally happens is that all the jobs that have the same generic titles – such as manager, supervisor, operative, clerk – are gathered into one large band. All the managers go into one band, all the clerical staff into another band. A second alternative is to have a band of job families such that most of the jobs relating to, say, purchasing or sales administration go into one band. This allows all of the employees in an organisation to fit into a salary structure which may have as few as five broad bands. The difference between this scheme and a conventional grading system is that the band salary range is much wider. An example of an organisation that has a broadbanding salary scheme with five overlapping bands is shown in Table 18.

Being broad, there is a large difference between the top of the band and the bottom. Sometimes the top of the band can be 250 per cent higher than the bottom (ie a range for the managers band may extend from £16,000 to £40,000).

Moving up the band is the key to the whole concept. First of all, the decision process is in the hands of the departmental manager to act within guidelines and in line with his or her budget. This replaces the formalised and personnel-controlled re-grading process. The criteria for authorising movement fall into four main areas:

Table 18
BROADBANDING SYSTEM SALARY BANDS

Senior management	£30,000 – £60,000
Management	£20,000 – £38,000
Professional/Technical	£13,000 – £25,000
Support 1	£10,000 – £15,500
Support 2	£7,000 – £12,500

- a *competence* approach by which clear guidelines are laid down on the acquisition of important competencies: measuring them is not easy and will be a mix of subjective analysis, the attainment of NVQs or equivalent, or through third-party judgements, such as in 360-degree appraisal
- an informal system of *job development* in which employees move from probationer through experienced employee to expert performer, with guidelines on how long that should usually take
- *the enlarging experience* approach by which employees move between jobs and between departments, gaining extra skills and generally becoming more useful and knowledgeable employees
- by *performance*, such that the outcomes of the performance management scheme indicate a movement up the band due to enhanced and proven performance.

The benefits of broadbanding

Advocates of the scheme put forward four major advantages:

- Employees have a much greater incentive to achieve results for the organisation. If they become more competent, have a higher performance or enlarge their skills and experience and become more flexible, then they can be paid more. This encourages the type of values that organisations want to promote. Employees do not have to wait to apply for grading or a promotion.
- Given the reduced number of managerial and supervisory jobs, employees can still make progress within the organisation. By employees improving and being motivated to improve, the job of the overstretched manager becomes easier.
- The system is far more flexible. New jobs and processes can be introduced easily without worrying about employees' narrowly-defined jobs.
- Because decisions are in the hands of the managers they will act realistically and responsibly towards their staff and their total salary bill.

The downside of broadbanding

It can be seen that broadbanding is not much more than a type of salary structure in a small, informal organisation that has not yet found the necessity for job evaluation. (In fact, broadbanding can be so flexible that there is actually no need for job evaluation at all.) This informality can lead to all the accusations of subjectivity and favouritism that led to job-evaluated wage structures in the first place. Unless the criteria for salary progress are robust, understood well and operated fairly, the system will not be seen as fair itself.

There can also be a tendency for it to be expensive. Under narrow grades, employees came to the top of their grade and realised they might have to stay there unless promoted. Under broad bands, most employees see an almost unlimited opportunity to make continuing progress, and managers may find difficulty in holding salary increases back – particularly if employees meet the required criteria.

Employees may be de-motivated if their efforts meet the criteria but the manager's budget restrictions prevent the increase. Under traditional job-evaluation schemes, budget restrictions could not stop a re-grading.

Making sure that managers act in a consistent fashion across the whole salary structure is not easy. Personnel's role here is crucial in acting as an auditor, an adviser, mentor and informal adjudicator. Without such fallback, the flexible pay structure is likely to fall into chaos. When operated imaginatively and effectively, however, it provides a flexible framework which can accommodate an organisation's quickly changing needs far better.

As Milkovich explains (Milkovich and Newman, 1996, pp. 285–286):

> Flexibility is one side of the coin; chaos and favouritism is the other. Broadbanding presumes that managers will manage employees' pay to accomplish the organisation's objectives (and not their own) and treat employees fairly. Historically, this is not the first time greater flexibility has been shifted to managers and leaders. Indeed, the rationale underlying the use of grades and ranges was to reduce the former inconsistencies and favouritism that were destructive to employee relations in the 1920s and 1930s. The challenge today is to take advantage of

flexibility without increasing labour costs or leaving the organisation vulnerable to charges of favouritism or inconsistency.

Conclusion

A final important element stresses the value of flexibility in pay for the organisation. By increasing the contingent element, the organisation shares part of the risk with the employee. Should employees fail to make the targeted contribution for whatever reason, internal or external, then their pay will decline in line with the income/profit of the organisation. If a traditional pay system was operating instead, employees would continue to receive the same pay regardless of their performance or the performance of the organisation. Many organisations are moving towards using a combination of these systems to support flexibility.

References and further reading

ARMSTRONG M. and BARON A. *A Guide to Broadbanding.* London, IPD, 1997.

ARMSTRONG M. and MURLIS H. *Reward Management.* London, Kogan Page, 1997.

ARMSTRONG M. *Employee Reward.* London, IPD, 1996.

ASHTON C. *Pay, Performance and Career Development.* London, Business Intelligence, 1995.

CANNELL M. and WOOD S. *Incentive Pay.* London, IPM, 1992.

CROSS M. *Skill-based Pay: A guide for practitioners.* London, IPM, 1992.

DOWLING B. and RICHARDSON R. 'Evaluating performance-related pay for managers in the National Health Service'. *International Journal of Human Resource Management,* Vol. 8, No. 3, June 1997, pp. 348–366.

IDS. *Skill-based Pay.* IDS Study No. 610. London, September 1996.

INDUSTRIAL SOCIETY. *Rewarding Performance. Managing Best Practice No. 20.* London, Industrial Society, February 1996.

IPD. *Performance Pay Survey.* London, IPD, 1998.

IPM. *Performance Management in the UK: An analysis of the issues.* London, IPM, 1992.

IRS. *Pay and Benefits Bulletin 414*. London, December 1996, pp. 2–3.

LAWLER E. *et al.* 'Who uses skill-based pay, and why'. *Compensation and Benefits Review*, March/April 1993, pp. 22–26.

MARSDEN D. and RICHARDSON R. *Motivation and Pay in the Public Sector: A case study of the Inland Revenue*, Discussion Paper No. 75. London, Centre for Economic Performance, London School of Economics, 1992.

MILKOVICH G. and NEWMAN J. *Compensation*, 5th edition. Chicago, Irwin, 1996.

MURLIS H. *Criteria for the Successful Implementation of Performance-Related Pay*. London, Hay Management Consultants, 1993.

THOMPSON M. *Pay and Performance – the Employee Experience*. Brighton, IMS Report No. 258, 1993.

10   PAYING FOR TEAM FLEXIBILITY

Introduction

We have seen in the previous chapter that paying for individual flexibility through performance-related pay, skills and competency-based pay can cut across the teamworking message that uniformly accompanies the raft of organisational improvement objectives. Teams are increasingly regarded as the driving force in high-performance organisations and need to be encouraged and sustained. Individual flexibility is part of the picture, but generating and supporting team flexibility gives the opportunity for far greater levels of performance improvement.

Teams have inherent advantages, according to Katzenbach and Smith (Katzenbach and Smith, 1992, pp. 18–19):

> They bring together complementary skills and experience that, by definition, exceed those of any individual on the team. This broader mix of skills and knowhow enables teams to respond to multifaceted challenges like innovation, quality and customer service ... Teams are flexible and responsive to changing events and demands and, as a result, can adjust their approach to new information and challenges with greater speed, accuracy and effectiveness than can individuals caught in the web of larger organisational connections ... By surmounting obstacles together, people in teams build trust and confidence in each other's capabilities ... Teams have more fun ... Teams are not as threatened by change as are individuals left to fend for themselves.

Given all these perceived advantages, it is no surprise that organisations have spent more effort in setting up and supporting teams in recent years. No surprise, indeed, given that those same organisations tend to be the ones that down-sized and de-layered during the late 1980s and early 1990s and can now only achieve their business goals if the teams have a degree of empowerment. It is then only one small step to reward success in teams – something that generally takes place through any of three different methods: profit-related pay, gainsharing and team-based pay.

Profit-related pay

Profit-related pay (with its variations called profit-sharing schemes) treats all employees in an organisation as a team and pays a bonus directly related to the profits of the organisation. Mostly, a large proportion is paid 'on account', with a final bonus when the actual profits for the year are announced. It has, until 1997, had substantial tax advantages, but these will be phased out by the year 2000.

Gainsharing

Gainsharing is an American concept which is just beginning to spread to the UK. It is similar to profit-related pay but it has two main differences. Firstly, the profit is not calculated by financial conventions but by predetermined aspects of the company's operations which are understandable to employees. They may include sales, production costs, quality measures, waste, and levels of debt. Gains made over the targets are shared among all the employees concerned, who are regarded as the team. Secondly, the calculation is made for an operational unit – a factory or a mine, for example, which has a geographically separate entity.

Team-based pay

Team-based pay can take many forms in different organisations but the common factor is that groups of employees receive a bonus or other rewards arising from the achievement of the team. It is often present in sales operations and is now beginning to spread to service-based organisations for which responsiveness to the customer is a vital ingredient of success.

In all these systems, the flexibility aspect is that the pay is contingent upon achieving the required targets – it is not a fixed cost, but a variable one.

Profit-related pay

Profit-related pay (PRP) was introduced in 1987 and had a slow start initially but has now become a victim of its own success. As late as in 1991 there were only 1,500 schemes covering 400,000 employees, but the figures for 1995–6 showed a rise to over 10,000 schemes covering over 2.6 million employees – and a cost in lost tax revenue to the government of over £1 billion. The last Conservative government's budget in 1996 announced that the tax relief on payments to employees would be reduced in 1998 and removed altogether in 2000.

Criticisms of profit related pay

Many of the schemes of the past three years have been introduced to benefit from the tax advantages rather than for organisational purposes of employee motivation. The schemes have been set up primarily so that tax saved in pay is shared between the organisation and the employees.

Paying 90 per cent of the PRP on account, as happens in most schemes, it is difficult to see the motivational element or the encouragement to adopt flexible practices to achieve results. In most cases, the results are too distant and unrelated to any one individual's performance. In any event, it could be argued that variations in the profits from one year to another would normally occur due to changes in the corporate environment or through poor investment decisions rather than because of human endeavours.

The units used as measures are too large in most cases for individuals to identify their contribution to the results achieved. This is especially true with large organisations such as The Burton Group or Tesco.

Of the three types of team payment, PRP is certainly the weakest in terms of supporting flexible working. It may attempt to offer a form of parity of reward for employees, to share the success in achieving profits and to act as a retention

incentive, but these are distant objectives in the whole picture of flexibility.

Gainsharing

Gainsharing arose from experiences in the USA of the 1930s
where organisations needed to make substantial operational
changes to survive in the depressions. The original scheme
was devised by Joseph Scanlon, a union negotiator with
accountancy training, who saw ways to overhaul productivity
and persuaded the owners that a co-operative venture with
the full participation of the employees was the only way to
succeed. It did succeed, and the model has been copied in a
variety of forms in America ever since. The recession in the
late 1970s and the arrival a little later of competition from the
Far East created a situation similar, although less extreme, to
the 1930s: interest has shown considerable growth during the
1980s and 1990s.

Schemes are based on sharing productivity gains made
through savings in labour and other costs. A simple example
is shown in Table 19.

Schemes have developed over the years to bring in
measures other than just labour costs. Savings on waste and
stock levels, reducing accidents, even getting debtors to pay
their bills, are incorporated into company targets with a

Table 19
AN EXAMPLE OF A GAINSHARING SCHEME

Historical annual data over past three years

Sales value of production (SVOP)	= £40,000,000
Total wages cost	= £12,000,000
Wages as a percentage of SVOP	= 30%

The gainsharing pool would start to operate when the wages percentage drops
below 30%.

Operating period: month of January 1998

SVOP	= £4,000,000
Total wages cost target (30%)	= £1,200,000
Total wage cost – actual	= £1,100,000
Gainsharing pool	= £100,000
Divided 50% to employees	= £50,000
Divided between 1,000 employees	= £50 per employee for the month

Table 20
OWENS CORNING: GAINSHARING POINTS EARNED IN APRIL 1995

Category measured		Points available for hitting or exceeding target	Actual points earned
Plant performance			
– HD: heavy density, rigid insulation products	Job efficiency	75	0
	Operating efficiency	75	75
– RS 2 & 3: rigid piping sections	Job efficiency	50	50
	Operating efficiency	50	0
– Filming unit: decorating suspended ceiling tiles	Job efficiency	50	0
	Operating efficiency	50	0
– RS 1: rigid piping sections	Job efficiency	25	25
	Operating efficiency	25	25
– Uncured: insulation material used in the automobile industry	Job efficiency	25	25
	Operating efficiency	25	25
– Supercrown: cavity wall insulation	Job efficiency	25	25
	Operating efficiency	25	25
Safety	Recordable accidents rate	50	50
	Lost workday rate	50	50
Housekeeping		100	0
Attendance		100	100
Customer satisfaction index		100	0
Credit control		100	100
Total points available in month: 1,000			
Actual points earned in month: 575			

Source: IRS Pay and Benefits Bulletin No. 418, February 1997.

mechanism by which the savings made are shared between the organisation and the employees.

Experience has shown that the key to making it work is the setting up of joint gainsharing committees in which managers, supervisors and employees work together to devise and implement improvements that can affect the figures.

There are only a few schemes currently working in the UK. BP Oil introduced a pilot scheme in 1992 and now operates a separate gainsharing plan at each of its North Sea assets. Each one has targets based on production, costs (especially labour costs), safety and environmental issues. The specific targets are all different, depending on the various requirements of the sites, although a serious attempt is made to create a 'level playing-field'. The outcome has varied but the payments to employees have averaged around 8 per cent. An evaluation of the scheme by employees has shown that they have a growing understanding of the business and cost environment that has made them consider the wider implications of their work, and especially where costly mistakes can be made.

At Owens Corning in St Helens, the 1995 scheme is based on the measurement of 11 categories, six of which measure the efficiency of production lines (labour and materials) while five are based on more general measures (safety, housekeeping, attendance, customer satisfaction and credit control) as shown in Table 20 (page 203).

Points are accrued under attendance, for example, if the absence level falls below the target of 2.9 per cent and customer satisfaction is calculated through an index which measures on-time deliveries, order fill rates and data accuracy. The total points are converted into pay, and the payment is made once a fortnight. It is important that employees receive a return as often as possible to stress the relationship between effort and reward.

A further example of a scheme in the public sector is shown in the case-study below.

Case-study

GAINSHARING AT THE ROYAL NAVAL ARMAMENT DEPOT, BEITH

RNAD Beith is a self-contained industrial complex in Ayrshire employing 500 engineering and support staff. Its main role is to store, maintain and distribute sophisticated missiles, torpedoes and sonar equipment on behalf of the Royal Navy. The nature of the task calls for output to be achieved while maintaining rigorous safety and quality standards. It is part of the Naval Bases and Supply Agency, created in October 1996 as part of the Next Steps programme, a government initiative designed to provide more delegated power to management. Such delegated power allows managers to develop policies supporting the continuous improvement of the units, including enhanced responsibility for deciding how money is to be spent, resources allocated and services delivered.

Another government policy that has had an impact upon the Depot is the initiative known as Competing for Quality, in which commercial practices are promoted by exposure to competitive pressures. This helped create a more commercial approach at Beith, resulting in their securing orders such as an £84 million sub-contract with GEC Marconi for the assembly and in-service support of certain guided weapons.

An interest in gainsharing as a concept began in the Agency's forebears in the late 1980s. From their headquarters in Bath they explored the possibility of realising a more participative approach to productivity improvements at support bases around the country. The aim was to deliver a co-operative approach to real step changes in productivity, breaking down the 'them and us' management/employee divide, and to replace tired and costly schemes developed in the 1960s and 1970s.

Reward schemes had been in place since the 1950s but had been individual piecework arrangements or group schemes based on output only. These schemes were seen to be reaching the end of their useful life, earnings and productivity had reached a plateau, and the focus on output alone meant that sufficient attention was not being given to quality and delivery times and other important features.

Headquarters personnel staffs arranged for steering groups to be set up in Beith and other depots to look for a more meaningful bonus system that would allow a greater degree of employee involvement, thereby utilising the knowledge and experience of the shop-floor workers in realising efficiencies.

From an early stage, a degree of security entered the discussion: an agreement was reached with the trade unions that there would be no compulsory redundancies arising from improvements that resulted from a new scheme. This was a vital element for it meant that employees' fears were assuaged that performance improvements would simply lead to job cuts.

A variety of proposals arose out of steering group discussions and a formal gainshare agreement was implemented in 1995. Although there have been minor adjustments, the main features of the original scheme at Beith are detailed below.

Scheme objectives

These are tied in with the business plan for the Depot and focus on three areas to generate actual cash savings from within operating costs:

Task objectives including quality-of-service targets
Management of change objectives
Cash reduction objectives

For the year 1995–6 there were a total of 17 objectives, some critical and others supportive. The *critical* ones included:

– accomplishing the activities in the Tasking Statement which meet customer service criteria for time, quality, costs and outputs (these are set out on a detailed statement of planned performance on individual contracts)
– achieving minimum savings on cash budget.

The *supportive* ones included:

– reducing the incidence and cost of accidents by 20 per cent
– reducing average absence to below 8 days per year
– achieving ISO 9002
– setting minimum discrepancy targets for the stocktaking cycle
– achieving 95 per cent of planned training
– complying with all legislation and regulations on health and safety, welfare, energy conservation and environmental matters.

To be successful, the objectives have to be reached *and* the cash savings achieved, the incentive being that any legitimate cash savings over and above the minimum target will be shared between the workforce and the Treasury.

Conversion into bonus

The performance is monitored during the year and communicated to employees. The bonus is paid in two six-monthly instalments. At the end of each six-month period, the Depot's board receives a set of accounts raised by the resident management accountants that report on how far objectives have been achieved and how much cash has been saved, together with a calculation of the consequent bonus proposed. Once verified, these accounts are passed to the Bath HQ, where they are subject to a robust audit and a final decision is made on the level of the productivity pay-out.

If the objectives have been achieved, some 50 per cent of the cash savings are available for distribution to the employees on an equal basis. A maximum payment is currently in place, amounting to 4 per cent of pensionable pay. The payments are non-pensionable. The remaining 50 per cent of savings return to the Exchequer or go towards capital investments in the Depot or elsewhere in the Agency.

Adjustments may be made if the objectives are not all fully achieved, to take into account over-achievement for key quality and delivery targets. For example, delivery of an important contract one month early might compensate for non-achievement of a training objective.

The tricky issue of allowances for external influences was tackled. It was made clear that savings resulting from 'windfalls' – such as a mild winter that allows cash to be saved on snow clearance – do not count towards the bonus calculation. On the other hand, political decisions that cause temporary difficulties also do not count towards the calculation.

Although all staff are eligible, those with a poor appraisal record or who have received warnings for poor work or attendance do not receive the bonus. The payment made in 1996–7 was approximately £650 per employee.

Employee involvement

Four initiatives, detailed below, have been taken since the early 1990s to support gainsharing and promote employee participation in the running of the organisation.

The Joint Performance Panel (JPP)

Established as part of the gainshare framework, the JPP consists of six management and 12 trade union representatives. Its key tasks are to identify, explore, agree, facilitate and monitor efficiency measures which improve performance and save cash, and to communicate thoroughly these measures to all the employees. The Panel sets up task-groups if necessary to look at particular proposals and problem areas. A monthly statement of progress to date is presented to the Panel.

Team briefing

Building on the existing well-developed Agency-wide scheme, progress on gainsharing has become a key part of team briefing at RNAD, Beith.

Task-groups

In order to support gainsharing and enhance the Depot's commercial output, a new initiative has taken place to set up cross-departmental task-groups who are to look at particular contracts or problem areas. Task-groups also act to bring together shop floor and management.

Staff Suggestions Scheme

As part of the MOD, Beith also works to the MOD Staff Suggestion Scheme. Individuals and groups of employees are encouraged to bring forward ideas to improve the way things are done in their work areas. A payment is made to those employees that make suggestions that lead to genuine improvements and cost savings. The payment is commensurate with the impact that implementation of each suggestion makes.

The introduction of gainsharing has focused the employees' minds on how their tasks are performed. In the first year of the Scheme's operation over 300 suggestions were made, and there have never been fewer than 100 under review. The pay-out under the scheme in 1995–6 amounted to over £5,000, and estimated total savings were in excess of £200,000 after three years.

Assessment of gainsharing at Beith

Gainsharing at Beith is cautiously seen as a great success. The workforce are happy to receive higher levels of bonus in their pay packet than under the previous scheme, and they also have direct involvement and transparency through such things as task-groups and team briefings. Management are happy because they have realised bottom-line savings while finding a vehicle for accessing the knowhow of the workforce and producing real synergy.

The economic and political environment has changed, and job security has declined since the end of the Cold War – with the inevitable reduction of the Defence budget as a consequence. The successful communication of this hard fact and the common sense of the employees concerned has helped the gainsharing scheme to be successful. This has had the result of enhancing the long-term future of the Depot and the workforce by continually improving the level of service to the customer.

While the trade union side still fiercely defend the rights of the workforce, the shared approach has reduced the potential for friction between management and the employees. In short, employees are far more concerned with improving performance and achieving results. There is no doubt that the guarantee of no compulsory redundancies helped facilitate the change even as the number of involvement initiatives continues to ensure that all employees both have the opportunity and are encouraged to take part in the improvement process.

It has not been easy to achieve: the mindsets of managers, shop stewards and the workforce have had to alter. The local trade unions have supported the whole process because it is based on consent, uses the ideas and talents of the employees, and helps to secure long-term employment in the area.

The unit is fortunate insofar as, with 500 employees, it is relatively small enough for all workers to identify with the business. The size of the bonus, at about £12 a week, may not sound large but it has acted as a reinforcing agent, encouraging the necessary change in attitude.

There remains one vital aspect to be developed and resolved: the ability of the Depot and Agency financial systems to support the costing and auditing of savings. This has been a major weakness in the first two years of the scheme, delaying payment of bonus and causing tension in a number of directions. The gainshare arrangement can be successfully integrated with financial systems, and the Agency is committed to achieving that objective.

Advantages of gainsharing

□ The employee involvement process, when it works effectively, ensures that employees fully understand the key goals of their unit.

□ By becoming more involved in their work, employees are more likely to make a greater contribution through 'smarter' working.

□ Rewarding all employees in the unit generates a sense of fair contribution and recognition.

□ Teamwork is encouraged by the same process. There is some evidence that it is very effective. A 1994 study showed overall performance increases in a sample of companies where gainsharing had been introduced (Cooke 1994).

Disadvantages of gainsharing

- The scheme may be very effective in its early years, but it then reaches a plateau from where improvements are difficult to achieve, so that pay-outs start to fall. Expectations then become disappointed and employees become disenchanted with the scheme.
- Continual improvements in a competitive industrial setting can lead to a continual process of job losses. If compulsory redundancies are to be avoided, incentives to encourage voluntary redundancy become more costly.
- External influences – such as a problem with a major contract – can have a short-term, but devastating, effect upon the scheme.
- A significant proportion of employees may not feel inclined to get involved with the key goals of the unit, regarding these as management matters, and simply want to get on with their routine job.
- There may be too much concentration on the few key objectives, to the detriment of other important areas which get insufficient attention. For example, the Health and Safety Executive (HSE) has been concerned at the operation of the gainsharing scheme at CoSteel in Sheerness, where one of the key targets is reducing reported accidents. Following up a complaint from the de-recognised union ISTC, the HSE have indicated their view that the scheme 'could be a disincentive to report injuries' although they have decided not to take any action against the company (Overell, 1997).

Advice on implementing gainsharing

There are three major elements to get right from the start:

- Ensure that the *unit concerned is identifiable* and not too large. In practice, this should mean a geographically discrete operation of not more than 600 employees.
- Decide on a set of between four and eight *performance measures* that are key to organisational goals. They should be simple to understand and be incorporated into the organisation's financial control system so that duplication in measurement is avoided.

☐ Set up an *employee involvement system that is inclusive* and not restricted to representative groups, such as unions. The involvement system must concentrate on understanding the measures and encouraging employees to contribute towards improving them as individuals and, particularly, in teams. Committees must have a major degree of empowerment and credibility. Success must be widely broadcast.

Team-based pay

Ten years ago, outside of sales operations, team pay usually meant factory group bonus schemes based on output. These schemes were often begun in the 1970s to circumvent government pay controls, and suffered a number of disadvantages:

☐ Because they were directed solely at output, other factors were forgotten, including quality, safety and on-time delivery.

☐ They were operated in a mechanical way through work-study measurement systems with constant disputes about allowances.

☐ The control factors were often the subject of negotiation between management and unions, so that there was poor communication directly with those taking part on the shop floor.

Many employers became determined never to get involved in such schemes that were complex, inflationary and de-motivating all in one. Organisations have therefore changed their approach in this area in three main ways.

Firstly, they have altered *factory schemes* to incorporate *far more performance measures that are aligned with the company's strategic plan.* Quality and customer service are the main players here: measures have become far more simple to understand using those that are commonly applied throughout the business; allowances have been reduced substantially or eliminated altogether to reduce arguments and to try to get the message across that anything that goes wrong in the business creates a problem that everybody has a responsibility to try to help solve. Ethicon moved in this direction in 1991, and four years later reported that team pay had helped to deliver a reduction in lead time from 30 to 12 days, and work in progress had fallen from 750K to 400K sales units, on top of lower production costs and a better-quality product (IRS, 1996).

More interestingly, the team pay concept has been introduced in a number of *areas outside of sales and production*. For example, the Benefits Agency scheme provides a mechanism to encourage and reward special achievements, and provides an opportunity for unit managers to be given more flexibility to tackle special local problems or difficulties – for example, to improve benefit clearance times or customer service (IRS, 1995). Other examples include:

☐ The small teams in Victoria Wine shops have regular contests based on a number of performance criteria, including shop displays and customer-satisfaction audits (IDS, 1996).

☐ Dartford Council pays a bonus to functional teams for achieving a set of targets agreed at the start of the year. These targets are extra to their normal operational roles (Stredwick, 1997).

☐ The Automobile Association gives rewards to teams that top league tables on performance measures such as speed of response and percentage successful roadside repairs.

☐ Pearl Assurance make payments to administrative teams at their Peterborough head office based on a collection of measures including cost, speed with which they turn insurance policies round, and the quality of service as judged by customer-satisfaction surveys (Arkin, 1994).

☐ Lloyds Bank has team incentives for all branch staff below junior management level, paid quarterly on the basis of performance measures including sales and service quality (Armstrong, 1996).

☐ SunExpress combines individual payments to its telesales teams with a team based commission system on a 70:30 ratio which encourages the operators to work with each other rather than adopt a totally competitive attitude (Carrington, 1995).

☐ Alliant Health System of Louisville, Kentucky, set up a system of teams which can achieve 'certification' by meeting a set of performance standards. These include complete flexibility in the team, a weekly communication meeting, budget operation and a stability measure. When a team meets all the certification requirements, each member receives a bonus of up to $1,200.

The third major development has been the increase in *variety in the method of payment*. Moving away from a weekly bonus pay-out, organisations now pay the rewards as an annual bonus, as a one-off non-pensionable award, or as an occasional award for special team performances. It can also be paid in non-cash forms, such as vouchers, holidays or group outings. Examples include:

☐ The best-performing after-sales-service team (as defined by a customer survey) at Citroën Cars flew off for a meal over the Atlantic on Concorde (Williams, 1994).

☐ London and County Bus Company have set up an arrangement for teams to be given feedback on the achievement of targets relating to driving and maintenance leading to an annual team bonus. This has resulted in an improvement in efficiency and a reduction in accidents (Williams, 1994).

☐ In the late 1980s, Everest Double Glazing ran an interfactory contest each year in which the best-performing factory team won a weekend in Majorca with their partners (Stredwick, 1997).

☐ American Airlines awards to teams that come up with successful ideas points that can be converted into vouchers, holidays or cash on an annual basis (Gross, 1995).

Common features of team-based pay success

Brown (1995) has set out three clear factors that correlate with team-based scheme successes:

☐ defining the team correctly, so that team membership is directly relevant to the task in hand: small teams where targets can be clear and immediate (such as in sales, scr-vice or credit control), larger teams for indirect activities where the performance cycle is longer and more difficult to measure

☐ a clear strategy, with objectives to engage employees in a collective effort to achieve business goals

☐ involving employees in the rewards, including designing and evaluating the measurement processes and taking decisions over the pay distribution – for example, a decision has to be taken over whether pay should be distributed according to salary, whether all rewards should be shared equally, or even whether there should be a combination of the two.

Conclusion

Paying groups and teams in relation to their performance is an area that is being closely examined by many organisations. The IPD survey (Armstrong, 1996) reported that almost half of its sample were considering introducing some form of team pay within the following 12 months. The later IPD survey (IPD, 1998) found that 8 per cent of organisations operated a form of team-based pay, with payments averaging 10 per cent. The perfect combination of flexible, empowered and motivated teams is an ideal that organisations are looking to achieve – and pay systems can be one of the key drivers that reinforces endeavours towards these objectives.

References and further reading

ARKIN A. 'An incentive to work together'. *Personnel Management Plus*, November 1994, pp. 2–23.

ARMSTRONG M. *IPD Guide on Team Reward*. London, IPD, 1996.

BROWN D. 'Team-based reward plans'. *Team Performance Management*, Vol. 1, No. 1, 1995, pp. 23–31.

CARRINGTON L. 'Rewards for all'. *Personnel Today*, 17 January 1995, pp. 37–38.

COOKE W. 'Employee participation programme: group-based incentives and company performance'. *Industrial and Labour Relations Review* 47, No. 4, 1994, pp. 594–610.

GROSS S. *Compensation for Teams*. New York. Amacon, 1995.

IDS Study 607, August 1996, pp. 19–21.

IPD. *Performance Pay Survey*. London, IPD, 1998.

IRS. 'Team performance bonuses at the Benefits Agency'. *Pay and Benefits Bulletin No. 368*, January 1995, pp. 6–9.

IRS. 'Team Reward: Part 2'. *Pay and Benefits Bulletin No. 400*, May 1996, pp. 2–8.

KATZENBACH J. and SMITH D. *The Wisdom of Teams*. Boston, Harvard Business School Press, 1992.

OVERALL S. 'Controversial injury policy given all clear'. *People Management*, 28 August 1997, p. 32.

STREDWICK J. *Cases in Reward Management*. London, Kogan Page, 1997.

WILLIAMS M. 'Incentives and bonuses'. *Personnel Today*, 3 May 1994, pp. 21–24.

11   FLEXIBLE BENEFITS

Introduction

There has always been a degree of flexibility in benefit pro-grammes. A minority of employees have been offered mar-ginal choices in cars, pensions, life assurance and private medical insurance since the 1960. But it was in the USA in the 1980s that a system of formal choices was put together to become a flexible benefit system, sometimes called 'cafeteria benefits'. Between 1980 and 1988, the number of such schemes rose from 8 to 800 (Hewitt Associates, 1988).

In the UK, the development has been much less swift. Today, there are fewer than 100 fully-fledged schemes, having risen from a handful at the beginning of the 1990s. The main reasons for the slow growth compared with the USA are that the tax regime has been far less kind and that medical insur-ance plays a much less important role in the UK. Those schemes that have been introduced, however, have had a very high profile – such as the pioneering Mercury scheme. Just as interesting is the staff reaction where schemes have been introduced, which has been very positive indeed.

There have been a number of factors in the last few years that have led to a growing interest in the subject.

☐ Organisations are increasingly moving away from rigid, collectively determined pay and benefits agreements towards individual contracts which allow for much greater flexibility in working practices and rewards.

☐ The convergence of employment practices in transnational companies have encouraged the spread of such concepts. What happens in Virginia today will spread to Virginia Water within a couple of years.

☐ Computer technology is now available that is capable of handling the complex decision-making processes involved in flexible benefits, and at reasonable cost (Johnson, 1996).

□ There are a number of consultancies which are actively researching and developing the idea.

□ Although the UK tax regime has not been particularly helpful, the 1986 Social Security Act enabling employees to opt out of pension schemes and take out personal pensions instead inaugurated the process of instilling in the minds of employees the fact that decisions on benefits were not solely in the hands of employers.

□ The nature of the employment scene has been changing substantially since the early 1980s: there is now a far higher proportion of women in the workplace. The type of benefits that they would like does not necessarily mirror the traditional male-oriented package on offer.

□ A number of corporate newcomers in swiftly growing industries – notably in the financial and communications sector – have wanted to stress their innovative role and have seen flexible benefits as a means to recruit and retain skilled employees. It reflects their policy of differential competitive positioning in the marketplace. Birmingham Midshires Building Society, for example, recognised that they offered a variety of attractive mortgage products to customers but simply said to employees 'Here are our benefits – take it or leave it!' Their motivation was to build on the success they had achieved with customer service awards (the 1996 Management Today/Unisys service excellence award was one example) and transfer this to excellence in dealing with staff.

What flexible benefits mean

A useful definition is that it is 'a formalised system that permits individual employees to influence the make-up of their pay and benefits package, so that they may select certain items and reject others to match their personal requirements.'

In an organisation where such a system is working, various stages usually take place:

□ The organisation decides the nature of its benefits programme. Some benefits will go on being provided to all

Table 21
DIFFERENT FLEXIBLE BENEFIT PACKAGES

John		Debbie	
Cash	£34,750	Cash	£28,850
Security	£1,100	Childcare	£4,300
Medical	£250	Security	£850
Computer	£1,500	Medical	£150
Pension	£2,400	Car	£3,800
		Pension	£1,450
		Extra holiday	£600
	£40,000		£40,000

Source: Hewitt Associates.

staff; some benefits will be provided at a basic or core level, although employees can choose to enhance them; and some benefits will be completely optional.

□ Each employee is informed of the range of benefits that can be chosen, usually through a menu indicating the cost in points or cash terms

□ The employees will then be told the value of their own individual benefits 'plan' – ie so many points or so much cash, depending on their position in the salary or grade structure.

□ Once a year, employees make their choice from the menu. If their choice exceeds the value of their individual plan, they have to make up the difference out of their salary. If their choice is valued at less than their plan value, the remainder is paid as additional salary. An example is shown in Table 21.

□ If exceptional circumstances arise during the year – such as promotion or divorce – employees may be able to change their programme choice.

Practical issues
What are the core benefits?

Most organisations regard it as essential for employees to retain certain crucial benefits. For Price Waterhouse Consultants, these are:

□ life assurance at salary × 2

□ personal accident insurance
□ permanent health insurance to a value of 50 per cent of pre-illness pay
□ 20 days' holiday.

These basic benefits continue to apply to all employees to ensure that no employee reduces his or her benefits to below a safety level. It is felt, for example, that all employees should have at least four weeks' holiday a year or they may suffer through overwork. At the same time, employees are allowed to convert a maximum of only 20 per cent of their salary into benefits in order to avoid over-purchase of items like pensions, cars and holidays. A safety net therefore exists at both ends.

What benefits are flexed?

There is a huge variety of benefits on offer across different organisations (see Table 22).

The last item listed in Table 22 may raise some eyebrows! In the Price Waterhouse scheme, employees may exchange their salaries to purchase vouchers for Tesco, Marks & Spencer and Argos at discounted rates. The benefits for those who choose to do so are high, because the vouchers can be purchased in bulk at between 5 and 10 per cent of face value (less for Marks & Spencer).

Table 22
LIST OF POSSIBLE BENEFITS TO BE FLEXED

Pensions	Life assurance
Private health insurance	Dental insurance
Child-care vouchers	Creche facilities
Mortgage subsidy	Company car upgrade or down-grade
Leased car facility	Elder-care
Holidays	Private petrol allowance
Long-term disability insurance	Discounted computer equipment
Discounted company purchases	Discounted training courses
Personal accident insurance	Travel insurance
Retail accounts – grocery, clothing and household	

Organisations usually start with a comparatively short list to which they may then add something each year, depending on the interests of staff as learned through an evaluation of the scheme.

Is it offered to all staff?

Logic would indicate that flexible benefits should be available to all staff or the system would become divisive. Admiral Insurance implemented the scheme for all staff to emphasise they were a single-status organisation (Merrick, 1994). Most organisations operate in this way, but not all. BHS, the retailer, introduced a scheme just for senior executives in 1991 and then extended it to 400 company car owners in 1994. There was no plan to extend it to the remaining 11,500 staff. Their view is that it is natural that there are fewer benefits further down the organisation, especially with part-time retail staff – but it is also the case that this decision is being kept under review.

Should a pilot scheme be tried first?

Given the initial complex administration arrangements, a pilot in one area would appear to be prudent, and it would also test the popularity of the scheme. Mercury's pilot took place in April 1993 and involved 400 employees, principally in the research and development area. EMAP, the communications group, went down the same road in 1995 with a similar-sized pilot group (Platt, 1994). Both schemes helped to clarify a number of debatable points and prepared the ground for the remaining employees to join when many more of their questions could be answered.

How many employees are likely to flex their benefits?

Not as many flex their benefits as one might expect, in truth. For example, only 15 per cent of Birmingham Midshires Building Society staff have chosen to vary their existing benefits package, and Mercury's percentage is around 35 per cent (Arkin, 1997).

How are schemes communicated to staff?

The success of schemes is influenced by the effort put in to communicate them fully to employees. Birmingham Midshires distributed a guide to all employees and operated a telephone helpline for several weeks at the crucial decision times. They found that their most successful method, however, was the 'road show' that travelled to regions and branches where employees had the chance to put questions to the flexible benefits team, which included members of those companies that were providing some of the benefits, such as insurance and vouchers.

National and Provincial Building Society incorporated the communicating of their scheme's introduction in 1993 into an on-going system called 'Understanding'. This integrated continuous moves to meet customer satisfaction – such as introducing flexible working hours – with a full explanation of the new flexible benefits scheme. Employees responded well and saw how it fitted in with the new organisational culture.

The Burton Group scheme was launched in 1992, and was accompanied by a 'branding' exercise. A range of items branded 'Flexible Reward' were produced. These included folders, pencils, letter-headed stationery and carrier-bags.

How often can employees flex their package?

The majority of schemes limit the changes to a once a year, fixed most commonly at the time of the annual pay review. On starting up schemes, organisations sometimes promise the opportunity of change within six months. This allows employees a chance to remedy rash moves or, more likely, to become more bolder in their choices.

An employee's personal situation may alter during the course of a year, and organisations usually allow changes to be made in the case of marriage, divorce, pregnancy, or the death of a spouse or close member of the family. In the case of other unexpected events (a house flooding, for example, for which additional expenditure may be required), an employee may be allowed to make changes by agreement.

Are there any legal problems?

The essence of flexible benefits is that employees are free to change their terms and conditions if they wish. There is no compulsion. Legal issues are therefore few and far between. But there is a degree of complexity when pension provision is included – for two reasons.

Firstly, there is not a great deal of flexibility that can be added to defined benefits schemes (also called 'final salary schemes') except by allowing an employee to purchase more years of service – which usually proves very expensive. That is why one or two organisations have switched to defined contribution schemes from when the flexible benefits scheme starts, which generally allows more flexibility for the employee as well as proving more cost-effective for the employer.

Secondly, some pension trustees believe that creating the provision of a reduced 'core' pension is not in their members' interest in the long term. There are differing views on this, as on all issues of pensions, and independent advice is almost impossible to obtain. Most commentators take the view that for the great majority of employees but especially for the young, any change to provision should be upwards and not reduced to a 'core', but it should be done by persuasion.

What's in it for the employee?

Quite a lot, really. It is highly regarded by employees working under the system and has a number of real advantages:

- □ Young employees with few commitments can choose to enhance their car, eliminate all their dependent benefits or take more cash or holidays.
- □ Employees with mortgages and young children can choose childcare benefits and better medical insurance, forgoing some of their salary, if necessary.
- □ Older employees can choose higher pension contributions and eliminate dependent benefits.
- □ Employees whose spouses are already covered for medical insurance will not choose this item.
- □ Allowing such a choice in the matter demonstrates that

the employer has a thoughtful, flexible and individual approach to employment situations.

□ When personal circumstances change, employees can change their benefits.

□ There are certain tax-efficiency advantages, particularly in the area of company cars.

□ Some benefits can be purchased at preferential rates through the scheme. For example, Luncheon Vouchers, nursery places and private health care at Admiral Insurance are all offered at group-discounted rates.

What's in it for the employer?

The system would appear to be a one-way benefit to employees – but there are advantages for the employer, even though they may be more subtle:

□ Giving a fixed-benefit plan to employees means that the cost to the employer *is* fixed for that year. There can be no unexpected cost increases.

□ Introducing a new benefit can be achieved without any cost by simply adding it to the list of benefits and putting a price against it. For example, a company that does not have any current provision for childcare can add this to the list at a particular price, choosing whatever discount to the market rate they have negotiated. Employees who choose to take up the benefit do so at the expense of another benefit or by deduction from salary.

□ In an organisation that emphasises the need for flexibility in work practices by employees, this can be a good 'quid pro quo'.

□ It is a very useful selling-point in recruiting staff because it sounds so attractive.

□ The awarding of company cars can become less of a divisive process. Employees can choose to enhance or downgrade their awarded car, which can diffuse the high-profile aspect that occurs when new cars are seen in the company car park.

A survey of employers' reasons for operating a flexible benefits scheme is shown in Table 23.

Table 23

ADVANTAGES IN OPERATING A FLEXIBLE BENEFITS SCHEME

		1997 (%)	1996 (%)	1995 (%)
1	Meeting diverse needs of employees	33.4	32.8	48.0
2	Containing future benefit cost increases	11.6	14.1	12.0
3	Increasing employee understanding of total compensation	16.9	18.9	12.0
4	Helping recruitment	10.5	8.8	6.4
5	Helping retention	13.7	8.9	6.4
6	Reducing the cost of total compensation	2.2	2.9	3.6
7	Harmonising total compensation arrangements	6.5	7.0	2.4
8	Removing/reducing status symbols	3.8	5.9	3.6
9	Other	1.4	0.6	0.8

Source: Hewitt Associates, Flexible Compensation Survey, 1997.

So what's the catch?

As often, there seem to be potential benefits for both sides – so why have fewer than 100 organisations actually taken up a formal scheme?

The first drawback is the administrative burden. It *is* a complex operation, particularly at the start of the scheme. Various consultants offer packages which ease the process, and which make good use of advanced computer systems. The start-up cost, however, remains high.

Most large organisations that could choose this path are continuing to downsize and therefore find it difficult to justify introducing such a scheme which has no immediate bottom-line benefit. The initial cost to smaller employees would be prohibitive.

There are some subtle costs involved. Take private medical insurance, for example. Let us assume that an organisation with 1,000 employees has negotiated a scheme with a provider to cover basic insurance for employees and spouses for, say, £500 per employee. This means a total cost of £500,000. This is based on the provider's total experience for a company that size and that organisation's claim experience. (No organisation would allow a customer to claim more than the contributions for more than two years without a severe hike in contributions!)

Now let us assume that the organisation goes over to flexible benefits. A number of employees – let us say 200 – choose not to take part but to take cash instead. They make, as the technical expression goes, adverse selection. They are principally the young and healthy, and those covered by insurance already under the name of their spouses. They have never made a claim previously. In theory, this should mean a neutral cost for the employer. But the provider will work out the likely number of claims for the reduced number of employees – and it is likely to be exactly the same as before. All those at risk – those who are not young and healthy – are still in the scheme. The insurance provider is therefore likely to put its rates up by 20 per cent, meaning an extra £100,000 cost to the organisation. The only way this can be countered is for the employer to charge a 20 per cent higher points fee on the menu – to which employees will respond that they are getting fewer benefits than before.

Thirdly , the tax efficiency can be changed each year in the national budget or by the high court which may catch out any employer who is involved in a complex wheeze devised by consultants (note ASDA's Executive Share Option scheme in 1996).

Fourthly, some employees may make bad choices. The young may not contribute to the pension scheme, which is very unwise of them. The value of the contributions they make before they are 30 is very high and can reduce the need to increase their contributions when they are older. The scheme really should have some independent counselling built in – and if it is truly independent (ie the counsellors are not selling anything), that means extra costs.

The successful scheme

An example of a successful flexible benefits scheme is described in the case-study below.

Case-study

FLEXIBLE BENEFITS AT THE MORTGAGE CORPORATION

In 1990 the Mortgage Corporation introduced one of the first flexible benefits schemes in the UK for its 400 employees. They called it 'Options' and it resulted from 18 months of planning, assisted by Hewitt Associates. Included in the flexible menu were private medical insurance, bonuses and pension. A year into the scheme, the opportunity to top up or reduce holidays was added, and dental insurance and company cars were phased in over the next two years.

The change in the pension was seen as a critical factor. It reflected the distinct shift away from the company's previous paternalism to an era of increased employee empowerment and responsibility in that it gave the employees significant investment decision-making powers.

The directors, who fully supported the concept, took an active part in the launch. Line managers ran a series of briefing sessions for their staff, helped by video clips and discussion guides. External consultants made presentations on the details of the pension changes and ran individual counselling surgeries during the initial choice-making period.

In 1995 an evaluation of the scheme took place through an independent employee attitude survey which had an 80 per cent response rate. Findings included:

☐ The scheme was well administered.

☐ Communication about the scheme by the organisation was effective.

☐ It was attractive to have a degree of flexibility in how the package was delivered.

☐ All of the options were valued.

☐ New options that employees wanted to see included childcare, insurance against car breakdowns, critical illness and travel accidents plus the opportunity to save up for sabbaticals.

Source: Hewitt Associates.

References and Further Reading

ARKIN A. 'Mutually inclusive'. *People Management*, 20 March 1997, pp. 32–34.

HEWITT ASSOCIATES. *Fundamentals of Flexible Compensation*. New York, Wiley, 1988.

JOHNSON R. *Flexible Benefits: A how-to guide*. Brookfield, International Foundation of Employee Benefit Plans, 1996.

MERRICK N. 'Benefits to suit all tastes and lifestyles'. *Personnel Management*, December 1994, pp. 46–47.

PLATT S. 'Take your pick'. *Personnel Today*, 13 September 1994, pp. 23–28.

12 FAMILY-FRIENDLY POLICIES

Introduction

We have seen that employers need a flexible workforce to meet the changing organisational needs in both the public and the private arenas, a skilled workforce willing to work hours outside those of the normal working day. Demographic forecasts show that the conventional nine-to-five workforce will begin a secular decline in the twenty-first century. The only sources of labour with an opportunity to grow (assuming there is no change in immigration policy) comprise the increasing proportion of women who are entering the workplace on a part-time or full-time basis and, to a smaller extent, the number of older employees who are continuing in employment which is more likely to be on a part-time basis.

There is a case that women are well adapted to flexible practices. In the workplace they often have to juggle careers, families and caring responsibilities. As the major consumers they are very attuned to customer-oriented activities.

So, given these two uncontested facts – that there is likely to be a severe labour shortage and that the only major source is women and older people – how can employers meet their needs and encourage them into the workforce?

Their greatest need is for the employers themselves to be flexible. They should be flexible in the hours of work required, through schemes such as *flexitime* or *flexible working hours*; they should allow careers to develop in a flexible way accommodating *career breaks* or *sabbaticals*; they should recognise the vital nature of various forms of *childcare* and *elder-care* in supporting individuals and families to cope with divergent demands; they should recognise that their needs change at different times of their working life; and that a form of *flexible benefits* would help them to accommodate these changes.

All of these subjects are covered in this chapter (except flexible benefits which was covered in Chapter 11). The common theme is that although the costs of being a family-friendly employer may make such an approach unattractive, the costs of *not* supporting employees with family responsibilities is far greater. The overall cost of replacing a junior manager who has to leave employment for reasons associated with family responsibilities has been calculated as over £7,000, which includes recruitment, selection, training, development and some temporary cover, all to get back to the previous situation. On this basis it would be far more logical to work out a solution to prevent losing all the skills and experience of the employee leaving. This becomes even more crucial as unemployment continues to fall and skills shortages become more severe.[1]

Flexitime

Twenty years ago, flexitime stood alone as the only system supporting any degree of employee flexibility in the workplace, and it still operates in a large number of workplaces. It is established most strongly in the public sector. The 1995 Labour Force Survey found 61 per cent of organisations operated a scheme, and it was especially popular in local authorities, where the figure was as high as 85 per cent.

Since the middle 1980s, however, the spread of take-up has slowed down considerably. This is strange in some ways because the strongest reason initially for implementing a scheme was to allow staff to stagger their starting and finishing times and so avoid the rush hours. As traffic has increased four-fold since 1980 and rush hours have reached horrendous proportions even in rural areas, one would have expected a gradual increase in its implementation. Flexitime continues to be popular with employees and appears to have a number of benefits for employers. So why has it fallen out of favour with employers? We shall look first at some of the different versions of operation, including its coverage, the varying rules, the monitoring system and the benefits before examining the major drawbacks. The most extensive recent survey was carried out by IRS in 1996 and much of the information below has been extracted from that survey, augmented by information from our own survey and from other occasional sources.

Whom does it cover?

Across the whole country, around 10 per cent of employees worked a form of flexitime in 1997: a total of 2.5 million employees (Labour Force Survey) involving slightly more women than men. It is most prevalent in clerical and secretarial (22 per cent), professional and technical occupations (19 per cent), and has much lower representation in the craft, operative and sales area (4–6 per cent). By industry, the service sector again takes the lead, with 18 per cent compared to less than 6 per cent in manufacturing. It is generally confined to the larger organisations in its formal setting, although small companies may operate an informal system for key staff. So no major surprises here: it is associated closely with white-collar workers in large offices in the service sector.

Normally, all employees in an establishment come under the scheme – but some organisations make exceptions. Manual workers at the London Borough of Ealing do not take part, nor staff on fixed-term contracts. Residential staff are usually excluded because they mostly live on site and have no traffic problems. Staff with a very close relationship with clients, such as care workers are often excluded, such as at Manchester City Council. School staff are generally excluded – one could imagine the chaos if teachers arrived at different times from the pupils! In the Nationwide Building Society the system applies at head office but not in the branches. Managers and senior staff are mostly excluded.

How does it operate?
Outline

Employees are contracted to work for a weekly or monthly number of hours. Under flexitime, within certain prescribed limits, they may vary their daily start and finish times as long

Table 24
EXAMPLES OF CORETIME

	morning	afternoon
London Borough of Croydon	9.45 am to 12.00 noon	2.30 pm to 4.00 pm
Wiltshire County Council	9.30 am to 12.00 noon	2.00 pm to 4.30 pm
Royal Insurance	10.00 am to 11.30 am	2.30 pm to 4.00 pm

as they work the total hours agreed for the accounting period. Certificated absence is counted as hours worked.

Bandwidth

The bandwidth is the period of the day within which the flexitime system works. The normal period is between 8 am and 6 pm, a total of 10 hours, but some organisations stretch the arrangement to start at 7.30 am (Cleveland County Council and the Employment Service) or to finish at 6.30 pm (Oxfordshire County Council and Ilford Films).

Coretime

This is the period when employees have to be in the workplace, and is normally from 10 am to 12 noon and from 2 pm to 4 pm. There are many variations, however, depending on local circumstances. Examples are set out in Table 24.

Arrangements may differ on a Friday, when the coretime may be shortened in the afternoon by 30 minutes or an hour.

Flexible periods

This is the bandwidth less the coretime – the time within which employees can choose to be at work or not, within the constraints of the rules. The normal period of flexibility is 6 hours, although with longer bandwidths or shorter coretime this can be extended to 7½ hours or longer. Almost without exception, organisations insist that an unpaid lunch 'hour' is taken – usually a minimum of 30 minutes, sometimes 45 minutes.

Accounting periods

The hours that employees actually work is totalled at the end of the accounting period: usually four weeks or a calendar month, occasionally eight weeks. Employees who work more than their contractual hours during that period may carry forward their surplus. How many hours they are allowed to carry forward varies greatly: the most common is eight or ten hours. Similarly, if employees work for a deficit of hours, they can carry this forward, although the amount of time allowed here is usually less than that of a surplus. Any surplus accumulated can be used by the employees as 'flexileave', which has a limit – usually around a day or possibly two days at most.

For example, Edinburgh City Council has a maximum *surplus* of 15 hours, a maximum *deficit* of ten hours and a maximum *flexileave* of 10 hours 53 minutes, whereas the London Borough of Ealing has 7 hours for each.

Monitoring

Technology has started to replace both the manual system by which employees recorded their hours which were then countersigned by their manager and the old-style clocking-in system, although these old methods are still very much in evidence. The IRS survey found that 75 per cent of organisations still operated such systems. New systems are more complex and usually combine security with time-monitoring, utilising an employee smart card. Employees use the card to enter and leave the premises and perhaps also to enter or leave laboratories or other restricted environments within the premises. The advantage is that the recording is automatic and print-outs showing attendance patterns are simple to produce. Porsche Cars in Reading have used such a system since opening their new high-tech British head office.

Medical absences

Some schemes make it clear from the outset that time off for routine medical and dental appointments must come out of an employee's surplus hours and must be taken outside the coretime. Not all organisations have been able to make this stick, and in any case the distinction between routine and non-routine appointments is not always clear. For example, a sequence of dental appointments which lead to an eventual decision to take out wisdom teeth, or a routine check-up which leads to a series of tests for heart abnormalities, presents difficulties here. Most organisations therefore allow such appointments to accumulate as part of an employee's hours, but employees are encouraged to make such appointments outside the coretime.

Other rules

It is made plain in the rules governing the schemes that all of these flexible arrangements are allowed subject to the overriding requirements of the organisation. Offices must have the required minimum manning levels; customers must be helped at all times; service delivery requirements must not be put in jeopardy; lunch hours, early and late times must be adequately covered.

Advantages to employees

□ Employees can clearly avoid rush hours, especially the morning rush hour, by using a later or earlier starting and finishing time. This is a key advantage for those working in large metropolises.

□ If there is a problem with transport – a car not starting, or trains cancelled – an employee is less likely to be held to be late, unless his or her eventual arrival stretches into coretime.

□ Employees have a much better opportunity to manage their work and personal commitments and interests than if they worked fixed hours. In simple terms, longer hours worked from Monday to Thursday will allow for a half-day on Friday to go shopping or play golf. Time can be accumulated to take an extended weekend break.

□ Employees in an office team often make arrangements between themselves to ensure at least the minimum office manning levels required and to accommodate leave needs, and this help the spirit of co-operation, teamworking and mutual assistance.

□ If an employee has a social or domestic problem – say a caring responsibility for an elderly relative which involves a morning visit each day – he or she can adjust work hours and still work full-time, rather than having to request unpaid leave or attempt to go part-time, or even having to leave the organisation altogether. More routine caring arrangements – like the school run rota – can be easily accommodated.

Advantages to employers

☐ Because of the benefits to employees, flexitime is clearly an aid to recruitment at most levels of an organisation. Employees who have worked under such a system will be attracted towards joining an organisation which has that benefit.

☐ Flexitime allows employees with family responsibilities to make work adjustments as detailed above and thereby stay with the organisation. Their skills and experience are retained. In an area where these skills may be at a premium or where labour is not easy to obtain, flexitime can be crucial.

☐ The operational hours are extended without having to pay overtime or bring in additional staff. Manchester City Council and Co-operative Insurance have both used this as a major reason for implementation.

☐ Lateness is abolished at a stroke. Organisations no longer have to pay staff that are late, which is the normal office staff procedure. Staff simply get credited for the time they are there and receive no credits when they are missing. Nor do organisations have to attempt to discipline those that are habitually late. All personnel staff know how difficult and unpleasant this may be, especially when the employee concerned has a special domestic situation. (If the organisation concedes a special allowance to one worker, it often antagonises other staff who have a similar cross to bear but have managed to cope with it!)

☐ The system can reduce absenteeism. The Salvation Army head office in London had relatively high rates of absenteeism in the late 1980s and an investigation disclosed that when employees had transport or domestic difficulties they would rather miss work than come in late. The introduction of flexitime reduced absenteeism immediately from 8 per cent to 4 per cent.

□ Committed employees will stay later one evening to complete an important piece of work, knowing that they can carry these hours forward and have a reduced day later. The organisation gets its work completed to deadline.

Disadvantages to employees

□ Some employees working under smart card systems resent the amount of monitoring. A few organisations, as part of their move to non-smoking environments, require an employee who goes outside the entrance for a quick smoke twice a day, to swipe his or her card, thereby coming off hours. Some alternatively resent doing so when entering the canteen.

□ The flexibility, although in general a considerable benefit, can present challenges at home if other members of the family try to impose more duties and responsibilities on an employee, knowing that he or she does not have a fixed starting or finishing time.

Disadvantages to employers

□ Sorting out what hours count as 'work' for accumulation purposes is complex. The employee who arrives at 8 am may read a newspaper for a while until other employees arrive. Lunch time can be equally difficult to assess: 30 minutes may be deducted automatically, but some employees may take much longer. Under a smart card system, an employee may eat sandwiches and read the paper in the office and then go out for the half hour allowed.

□ In the light of the extended hours of operation, it may be necessary for security or health and safety reasons for supervision to be in place over all of the hours. This puts an additional burden on managers and supervisors.

□ Management has an additional problem in attempting to plan the manning levels for the week. Although informal agreements are reached with staff on their planned starting and stopping times, employees are usually under no formal obligation to keep precisely to their plans. Excessive traffic or an unexpected domestic situation may mean the plans are changed at no notice.

☐ Staff arriving in the office at different times can be disruptive. Most staff, on arrival, engage in social conversation so that if an office opens at 8.45 am, it is accepted that not a lot gets done before 9 am. However, if the office opens at 8 am and staff are arriving all the time up to 10 am, the disruption can be excessive throughout that period. If it is all repeated from 4 pm, this can add up to a considerable amount of disruption for a manager to try to sort out.

☐ From the customers' viewpoint, flexitime has its limitations. Although they may be able to contact the office over a longer period during the day, they may not be able to talk to the member of staff they want or get the answer they want because that person is arriving later, leaving early or taking flexileave.

☐ In general, employees receive credit for every minute they are on the premises. There may well be situations when employees are not required on the premises – for example, before 9 am or after 5 pm – but an organisation with flexitime would find it difficult to force employees to leave. Without flexitime, this would not matter: they would simply come off pay at 5 pm. Employees who may choose, for whatever reason, to work the system to their benefit may work extra hours one week, when they are not required, to give them enough credits to take leave the following week. When they take that leave, the organisation may need to bring in temporary labour, thereby increasing the overall costs.

To sum up, flexitime can be a very good system for recruiting and retaining staff and, given committed staff, it will bring a great many benefits to both sides. However, it is not popular with management and supervisors, who carry the brunt of additional organisation but do not have the benefit of flexitime themselves. It also is not performance-related in any way. It is simply a system of recording employees' time in the workplace, not of measuring how productive they are. Directors commonly come to the conclusion that the benefits for the employees in general greatly outweigh the pro-portional benefits to the organisation.

In addition, it is often said that the longer employees work on flexitime, the more they get it to work in their favour, and this may not always coincide with the interests of the organisation. Proving this last point is difficult and evidence is only anecdotal. It has, however, been influential in the decision by organisations in the 1990s in general to steer clear of it. After all, once in, it would be impossible to wind up the scheme without a considerable effect upon morale.

Key points for introducing a flexitime scheme

In *Changing Times – A guide to flexible work patterns*, published by New Ways to Work (1993), there is a check-list for employers to help them introduce a flexitime scheme:

☐ Decide whether participation will be voluntary or not. Some schemes allow the option of remaining on fixed hours.

☐ Consider carefully which employees will not be able to join the scheme, such as managers, maintenance staff, etc. One approach is not to specify exclusions formally in the scheme but allow them to be agreed on by individual departments – but this brings the difficulties of inconsistency across the organisation.

☐ Decide what bandwidths, coretimes, flexible times and accounting periods are appropriate.

☐ Decide the maximum number of credit hours which can be carried forward.

☐ Consider what happens when staff are away from the office on business.

☐ Determine the system for doctors' and dentists' appointments.

☐ Consider how people who work at home can fit into the scheme.

☐ Decide how bank-holiday weeks are to be dealt with.

☐ Think about the timings of staff/team meetings.

☐ Sort out issues of supervising the scheme and organising the administration.

A couple of other important points can be added to this list:

❑ Consider associating its introduction with staff training so that a person who answers the phone at 8.15 am can deal with a problem there and then. It is far better than a person who says: 'The person you want will be in sometime later – not sure when – certainly 10 am or was she taking flexi-leave today?' Such training may be a costly process but it is vital to have the range of staff skills and knowledge to improve the flexibility.

❑ Make sure rules are in place for bereavements, especially those which are not close family ones.

Flexible working hours

There are a number of other arrangements that can be made which should meet employee needs in this area:

Term-time working operates in many organisations (including at Dixons). This may be an arrangement solely for parents of children at primary school or for parents of children aged between 5 and 14 (Alliance and Leicester). Employees are expected to take all or most of their holiday entitlement in this period. Pay is either averaged over the year or simply deducted for those periods they do not work. Employers often replace the employees with students or other temporary employees.

Compressed working weeks can be agreed by which employees work the normal total of hours over four or even three days. This is not uncommon in hospitals, where midwives work three shifts of 12 hours in a week. In 1996 Texaco introduced a pilot nine-day fortnight made up of eight eight-hour days and one six-hour day, which gave staff one Friday off a fortnight. Staff would cover for colleagues and learn about their jobs, and it also helped in family responsibility terms. About 2 per cent of all employees have compressed working week arragements (Labour Force Survey, 1997).

Staggered working hours operate where employees can start and finish later, ie 10 am to 6 pm or earlier from 8 am to 4 pm.

Employment breaks

There are a number of versions of this aspect of flexibility. The most common is a form of continuing *maternity leave* beyond the 'right to return to work' period such that the employee is free to return to work within a number of years, usually five. This is also called a *career break* by some organisations – although that may also include the situation where an employee's spouse is posted overseas for a fixed period and they decide to go abroad together. There are also versions of *paternity leave*, when it has been decided that the father will stay at home rather than the mother. *Caring leave* can be granted when a close relative has a life-threatening illness or accident, on the understanding that the employee will return after the recovery or death of the person concerned. There is also *sabbatical leave* which can be for a number of purposes including travel, study and research.

Formal schemes relating to employment breaks have been essentially restricted to the larger organisations. They are most commonly found in the service sector, such as in banks, insurance companies and building societies, with an equally strong representation in the public sector. Both groups employ large numbers of women to whom the schemes were first addressed as an alternative to returning to work after maternity leave. There has, however, been increasing interest in them on the part of smaller professional organisations, such as legal firms and accountants, who have rapidly increased their female intake in recent years and who want to ensure that their particular skills and knowledge – which have a high market value – are not lost to the organisation should they wish to stay at home after maternity leave.

A survey of nearly 1,000 organisations by *Personnel Today* in 1991 disclosed that 12 per cent offered different forms of breaks. In the local authority sector 22 per cent offered such breaks according to the 1993 survey by New Ways to Work. The Luton University survey in 1997 found that this number had increased to over 30 per cent. These surveys indicate a steadily growing trend.

The Abbey National's scheme allows a maximum break of five years which can be taken as two separate periods. Employees are eligible to apply if they have three years' service and an appraisal rating of 'Effective' or above for the past two years and been working for 16 hours or more a week. A further safeguard is that not more than one in eight employees in a department will be permitted to take a break at the same time (although this may be allowed if the department head feels confident that the department will not suffer). Employees may be asked to attend training courses while on the break, and there is an annual meeting in the region for all career-break employees. Two weeks' employment is also obligatory each year at current pay rates and break employees receive the normal in-house communication publications. Employees have to give at least 12 weeks' notice of their intention to return, and Abbey National will aim then to find a post as close as possible to the employee's former grade and location – although such a post cannot be guaranteed.

The vast majority of staff who take employment breaks are female. New Ways to Work found that there were only 142 (2.5 per cent) males out of a total of 4,961 staff on employment breaks in 30 large organisations, and only three males out of 647 in total who had returned from a break.

Essential features of employment breaks

The need to keep contact

First and foremost, good employers do not regard the scheme as a 'clean break' with all contact severed. The principal idea is that regular communication is maintained and that the employee will come back to the organisation for short spells at regular intervals. The most common arrangement is for the employee to work for a minimum period of two to four weeks in a year, usually in the summer months when temporary employment is valuable to the organisation. This benefits both sides. The employer has access to experienced labour at a time when it is required without paying agency rates. It enables the employee to keep his or her skills up to standard, and to catch up on the social scene. And it can provide an opportunity for a certain amount of training – for example, if new computer systems have been introduced. Behind these benefits is the sense of commitment on both sides. They both intend that full employee status will be returned to at a date in the future.

Returning to work

An agreement needs to be made about the 're-entry' arrangement. Some organisations are quite clear that employees will be offered their own job or a similar job at the same grade when they return to work. Others take a different approach. Some offer a two-tier system by which staff with key skills are guaranteed the same job back and others only a promise to make every effort to find a job at the same level. Commercial Union's policy is to take the guarantee of re-entry a stage further by making an offer of some compensation if the employee cannot be found a job at the same salary (see the case-study below).

Case-study

CAREER BREAK AT COMMERCIAL UNION

When I return, will I automatically get my old job back?

The Company would do its best to slot you back into the same job, at the same location. Failing this, we would try and provide a job at the same level as that which you left. This will be more feasible where there are a number of jobs of the same type – for example, clerical jobs or programmers. Greater difficulty will be faced slotting in specific title-holders such as Underwriters and Line Managers.

If it was not possible to restore your own job, we would try and offer alternatives. The suggested job might be in a different function or at a lower-evaluated level. ... Under these circumstances, we would provide a form of salary protection.

We would pay you at the level for your previous job for one year, at the end of which the 'excess' salary (the difference between your old and new jobs) would be the Excess Component I and would be reduced by one third. The remainder would be run off over the next two years in equal proportions.

As an example, if the initial difference was £1,500:

at the end of:	it would diminish to:
year 1	£1,000
year 2	£500
year 3	zero

During this period, you would gain any general increases based on your 'true' Component I amount.

Source: employee information leaflet

Employers usually take a flexible approach in these schemes towards employees who wish to return on a part-time basis at first or at lower responsibilities, although neither of these can be guaranteed by the organisation.

Length of break

Most schemes settle at a five-year maximum after which time the employee's right to a position is lost. Some are shorter, such as at Manweb, whose scheme specifies two years, whereas the British Council has actually extended its scheme to seven years.

Benefits to employers

- The scheme quite clearly demonstrates the employer's belief in a long-term commitment to employees, which should assist in improving relationships with employees.
- The scheme contributes towards an effective and active equal opportunities programme.
- It gives a real opportunity for female employees with serious career aspirations to manage to combine work and domestic responsibilities. Many are unwilling to forgo the close experiences of the early childhood years and recognise the possible difficulties with extended childcare. It is to be expected that these employees will make a continuing positive contribution to the organisation on their return and for some years afterwards.
- It provides a useful source of temporary trained staff at peak periods.
- Short-term contracts can be carried out by specialist staff who are likely to have more relevant experience than agency staff.
- Retention of trained and experienced staff is crucial, particularly in a tight labour market. Where investment is high, it is even more important to take every opportunity to try to retain such employees who choose to take breaks.
- It is a benefit to emphasise for recruitment purposes.

Benefits to staff

- Statutory maternity leave is considered not long enough by many mothers, so it is an attractive option to take a longer break, with a job to go back to at the end.

□ The occasional temporary work allows the employee an opportunity to update skills and knowledge and makes re-entry far easier. It allows confidence to be retained.

□ Under a flexible career break system, it allows the returner to come back when they are ready and not to lose many years from their career plan.

□ For spouses to be posted abroad presents a real dilemma over whether to give up the career and follow them, with the uncertainty that brings of getting a suitable job on return, or to stay at a distance with possible social and emotional difficulties. The employment break solves this problem.

□ Similarly, the need to look after a close relative can bring a career grinding to a halt. An employment break can allow a period of caring and time to reflect on the next stage, depending upon the health of the person being looked after and any other relevant factors.

Sabbaticals

There is a difference between sabbaticals and other employment breaks because employees are normally paid while they are on a sabbatical. For this reason, they are far less common in practice.

Only a handful of organisations operate them on a formal basis. The John Lewis Partnership scheme is the most quoted one: it was introduced in 1979 by the Chairman, Peter Lewis, as a way to celebrate 50 years of the Partnership. Employees have to complete 25 years' service, and around 100 employees qualify each year for this benefit, which takes the form of up to 26 weeks' paid leave. There are no restrictions on what they can do in this period – it is intended as a reward – and they return to the same position at the end of the period.

One has to say that the John Lewis Partnership is a most unusual organisation in many ways, and there are increasingly fewer organisations these days with employees who stay in excess of 25 years.

Legal aspects

In most of the contracts set up to include employment breaks, the employer makes it clear that there is no contractual responsibility involved. The employee ceases to be in employment during the break (except for the occasional short spell of employment) and has no legal right to a job at the end of the break. At least, that appears to be the current law, for no case has yet been tested at law in which the return situation has been in dispute.

Childcare provision

'Organisations are still coming to terms with a historically schizophrenic approach to return-to-work mothers, valuing them as a labour resource but shrinking back from any obligation to make the return easier.' So said Tom Shea, managing director of Jigsaw Day Nurseries, in 1995 (quoted in *On Flux*, Hewitt Associates, 1995, p. 9).

There is no doubt that the lack of suitable childcare has a detrimental effect upon both women in the workplace and those intending to return after maternity leave. A TUC survey (TUC, 1996) provides interesting and convincing evidence of this:

- ❑ 73 per cent reported that it had affected their job and career prospects in some way
- ❑ 20 per cent reported that it caused a break in their career
- ❑ 14 per cent reported that it made them less reliable and available for work
- ❑ 13 per cent reported that it had prevented them from seeking promotion.

There is no doubt that a growing number of women with young children wish to come into the workplace. Employers for Childcare in a 1994 survey found that 52 per cent of women with children under five now work compared to only 37 per cent in 1984.

Employers can make life easier in a number of ways. They can set up in-house nurseries or creches, get together with a group of other employers in the area to establish a nursery, provide vouchers or a childcare allowance, or be generally sympathetic in the workplace through time-off provisions.

The current situation was examined by the Policy Studies Institute (Forth *et al*, 1996) in a report sponsored by the Department for Education and Employment which showed:

- [ ] 2 per cent operated a workplace nursery (there are only an estimated 500 or so workplace nurseries in the UK)
- [ ] 1 per cent operated a nursery elsewhere
- [ ] 2 per cent operated a childcare allowance or voucher scheme
- [ ] 34 per cent covered time off at short notice for childcare problems with some form of special paid or unpaid leave provision
- [ ] 29 per cent mixed the provision of special leave with other arrangements which required the employee either to make up any time lost at a later date or to use his or her annual leave entitlement to cover the absence
- [ ] 25 per cent provided an opportunity for mothers to work at home if childcare arrangements broke down.

Nursery or vouchers?

At first sight, providing an in-house nursery would appear to be the best solution. A mother would not have to make an extra journey and would be able to drop in during the day. The staffing would come under direct control, so the quality of the childcare could be guaranteed and the size could be matched to the expected requirement. It would certainly promote a favourable corporate image. Nurseries are also a tax-free benefit for the employee. The Midland nursery scheme has proved a considerable success: it has been found that the proportion of women returners from maternity leave increased from 30 per cent in 1988 to 85 per cent in 1994.

However, there are snags to consider:

- [ ] Finding a suitable location on the premises is usually not easy, given the required health and safety standards and the need to be distant from circulatory areas due to noise levels. A temporary building in the car park rarely meets planning requirements these days.

- The operating cost per child per month is between £400 and £600, and to make it free to employees would be a very substantial expense. There is then the tricky decision on how much it should be subsidised – too much might result in resentment and a waiting-list; too little and it might appear that the company is not giving enough encouragement. Each year there would have to be a review of the fees, providing another possible area of disgruntlement.

- If there was a waiting-list, would applications be dealt with on a first-come first-served basis or would there be preferential treatment for seniority? If there were no current places, how would employees be able to return from maternity leave?

- There could be a natural temptation for mothers to drop in too often!

- If a mother did not get on with the nursery staff, she would be presented with a genuine dilemma. Should she withdraw the child and lose the benefit or soldier on with an arrangement which could affect her work?

- Less sympathetic fellow employees could resent the presence of children on the premises – some, apparently, come to work to get away from them.

- Managing the nursery is usually outside an organisation's experience and could divert managerial time and expertise.

- Any vacancies at the nursery would add substantially to the cost.

These are very substantial reasons and go some way to explaining why so few nurseries have been set up.

A *joint venture* overcomes some of these problems and is becoming more common. Employers, for tax reasons, have to be strategically involved with the management of the nursery, but not on a day-to-day basis, and the financial risks are far less. Children are not on the premises, and responsibility for difficult decisions on waiting-lists and fees can be shared.

Specific organisations have been set up to work with groups of employers, such as Kiddiflex, run jointly by Jigsaw Day Nurseries and Hewitt Associates.

The third alternative is *childcare vouchers* or *allowances*. They have a number of advantages:

□ They are currently exempt as a benefit in kind from National Insurance contributions and, for private sector employers, are corporation-tax-deductible.

□ It gives parents the freedom to spend the voucher or allowance as they wish and to choose the most appropriate care.

□ There is the psychological advantage that employees will be pleased when the level of the subsidy is raised and no money has to be collected from the employee. If necessary, the value can be pegged without too much discord.

□ No time is spent on searching for premises, running the nursery, deciding on waiting-lists, or any other organisational issues.

There is one somewhat unexpected cost in vouchers/ allowances. Although nursery provision has to be offered to all employees, male and female, it is still unlikely (not impossible, but unlikely) that fathers would bring in their children to the workplace, so they would be less likely to take up the benefit. If vouchers/allowances were offered, fathers would all accept gratefully, so the cost may well be doubled. A further factor is that vouchers are seen as a taxable benefit for the employee.

Employers provide a large variety of subsidies. North British Housing Association, winner of the 1995 Parents at Work Award, paid employees £77 a month towards their child-care costs, while the winner in the small organisations category, *Time Out* magazine, paid £50 a week at the full rate until the child's seventh birthday and then at 50 per cent until the child was aged 14. The IDS 1995 survey reported that for in-house nurseries costing around £150 a week, the Midland Bank and British Airways charged around half this cost, while ICI at Slough charged only one third, subsidising the remainder. Sometimes the degree of subsidy varies with salary.

Information and referral services

An increasingly popular option for employers is to offer some form of family care referral or information service so employees can arrange their own care. One such is the LV Group's Familylife Solutions. This is a nationwide telephone service that provides confidential information, help and advice on areas including:

☐ holiday activities for children
☐ detailed information on how to find the best care
☐ advice on contracts
☐ telephone counselling
☐ 24-hour emergency back-up.

Out-of-school schemes

Between 1993 and 1996 the Employment Department provided £45 million to pump-prime local out-of-school schemes which are supported by finance from local employers who take places for the children of their employees. Research has shown that this has been very valuable in helping employees to work full hours throughout the year, rather than having to finish early and work only during term-time. Longmans, in Harlow, provides funds for a four-week play scheme for 24 children aged five to eleven at a local leisure centre. In 1995 a group of London hospitals funded a summer scheme for 80 children costing around £6,000 (Hall, 1995).

In November 1997, Gordon Brown announced the government's intention to provide £300 million to support after-school clubs which would give single parents more opportunity to work conventional hours.

Supporting carers, elder-care

We've a big bulge of key people in their late thirties and early forties. They are currently concerned about childcare, schooling and so on. Within the next ten years they will be concerned about looking after their parents. These people will be difficult to replace and we have no choice but to be responsive and understanding about these issues.

Human resources manager, quoted in Bevan *et al* (1997)

All of the reasons given to support childcare provisions apply equally well to those provisions for caring for older relatives.

The proportion of adults (one in six) who provide informal care for someone sick, disabled or elderly is now identical to the proportion caring for children aged 16 or under. Forty-three per cent of married women carers manage to combine caring and employment, the majority of them working part-time.

The type of additional assistance can take the form of financial support for a day centre for elderly relatives. In November 1997, Peugeot will be opening a 'granny creche', supported by the Motor Industry Benevolent Fund. Employees will be able to entrust relatives to the care of the centre for £15 a day, and facilities will include bathing, laundry, hairdressing and chiropody. It came about through research by the Benevolent Fund and Help the Aged, who found that some employees were in physical danger because they were often exhausted by looking after elderly relatives at night and then having to come in the next day to operate dangerous machinery. Alternatively, they had a higher rate of absenteeism which built up over the years of caring (Wark and McGinty, 1997).

The legal situation

Aside from maternity provisions, which are outside the orbit of this publication, there are no current legal requirements to provide any family-friendly benefits. On the horizon, however, arising from the Labour government's decision to sign up to the Social Contract, there will be the Parental Leave Directive which will oblige organisations to grant unpaid parental leave for a period of up to eight years after the birth or adoption of a child.

Conclusion

Companies at the forefront of family-friendly policies usually combine most, if not all, of these initiatives. They do so for two reasons. Firstly, they believe that it is in the company's interest to be regarded as a 'good employer' so they perform better in the recruitment and retention marketplace. Secondly, they regard it as good bottom-line business practice. Boots, for example, estimate that they have saved

£1 million in recruitment and training costs by retaining employees through term-time working, paternity leave and career breaks (Welch, 1997). An American study showed that every $1 spent on caring and other support services yields $6 in direct savings from lower absenteeism and improved productivity.

Examples of organisations with a comprehensive policy include Price Waterhouse, who have introduced workshops for new mothers and fathers, on-line childcare information plus childcare allowances; British Airways (Crewcare), who introduced a support group called Working Parents which provides a parent network, newsletters, workshops and mentors for women returners; Heysham Power Station in Morecambe who launched a Childcare Charter which includes childcare vouchers and career breaks plus an encouragement to job-share. All of these were finalists in the 1996 Parents at Work Award.

Abbey National is another award winner in this field. The organisation has a wide set of flexible working initiatives, including career breaks, job shares and flexitime. The case-study below sets out their thinking behind this approach.

Case-study

ABBEY NATIONAL

Abbey National plc, based in Milton Keynes, has a set of flexible working options. John King, director, group personnel, explains the organisation's reasons for supporting the concept in a leaflet to managers:

As a progressive employer, Abbey National is constantly seeking to help staff achieve a balance between personal and career commitments, by offering new and flexible methods of working.

We recognise that more and more companies are beginning to move away from the traditional 9–5 five-day working week. One business reason for this shift is that customers are demanding service at times that are convenient for them – for instance at the weekend or in the late evening.

If staff can be more flexible in the hours that they work, the business can benefit. Flexible working will also give you more options in managing the peaks and troughs of day-to-day business needs. Flexible working allows you, as a manager, to retain and motivate experienced members of your staff in situations where they might otherwise leave the company. Finally, part-time does not mean part-commitment. If staff are able to combine more effectively their career and their personal life, experience shows that they are likely to be more motivated and committed to the company.

As a manager, it is up to you to utilise these new working methods when you judge that they are right for the business and benefit your staff. Flexible working will require your full co-operation and commitment as well as that of the members of staff if it is to be operated successfully.

References and further reading

BEVAN S., KETTLEY P. AND PATCH A. *Who Cares? The Business Benefits of Carer-friendly Practices.* IES Report No. 330. Brighton, Institute of Employment Studies/LV Group, 1997.

DALY N. 'Rigid NHS hours drive nurses from wards'. *Personnel Today*, 12 February 1998, p. 1.

FORTH J., LISSENBURGH S., CALLENDER C. and MILLWARD N. *Family-friendly Working Arrangements in Britain.* Policy Studies Institute Report No. RR16. London, DfEE, 1996.

HALL L. 'Happy families'. *Personnel Today*, 14 March 1995, pp. 27–28.

IDS. *Childcare.* IDS Study No. 54. London, March 1995.

IRS. 'Still a flexible friend – a survey of flexitime arrangements'. *IRS Employment Trends* 603, March 1996, pp. 5–16.

NEW WAYS TO WORK. *Changing Times – A Guide to Flexible Work Patterns.* London, 1993.

NEW WAYS TO WORK. *Taking a Break: Introducing employment breaks.* London, 1992.

TUC. *Childcare Survey – Summary Report.* London, Trade Union Congress, 1996.

WARK P. and McGINTY S. 'Double Whammy'. *Sunday Times*, 19 October 1997, p. 14.

WATSON G. 'The flexible workforce and patterns of work in the UK'. *Employment Gazette*, July 1994, pp. 239–247.

WELCH J. 'Parents' rights still in infancy, firms admit'. *People Management*, 7 August 1997, p. 11.

Further information

Employers for Childcare, Cowley House, Little College Street, London, SW1 3XS. Telephone: 0171 976 7374.
LV Group, 50 Vauxhall Bridge Road, London SW1V 2RS. Telephone: 0171 834 6666.
National Childminding Association, 8 Masons Hill, Bromley, Kent, BR2 9EY. Telephone: 0181 464 6164.
Parents at Work, 77 Holloway Road, London, N7 8JZ. Telephone: 0171 700 5771.
(Working for Childcare is at the same address – telephone: 0171 700 0281.)

End-note

1   For example, a 1998 report revealed that 60 per cent of nurses were prevented from re-starting work in the NHS because of the lack of flexible working hours and childcare facilities (Daly, 1998).

13 FLEXIBLE WORKING THROUGH EMPOWERMENT

Introduction: Empowerment and the 'in-house entrepreneur'

Over the last decade or so the term *empowerment* has become a much used and much maligned business buzzword. Numerous organisations have sought, with varying degrees of success, to introduce or support empowerment programmes as a way of improving competitiveness or of being able to deal with customers' requirements more effectively. For example, many retail organisations have empowered front line employees to make the decision themselves on whether a customer may be given a refund on a faulty product, rather than having to refer each such decision to the manager. Other organisations have taken the empowerment concept further and developed 'self-managed teams', in which decisions on shift patterns, sickness cover, even recruitment and staff development, are taken by the team members without reference to a higher level of authority.

No one definition of what empowerment is is likely to be sufficient to cover the variety of forms that empowerment can assume: each organisation, and each manager must make the call about what form or style of empowerment is right for them. Empowerment should not be seen as an all-or-nothing concept. Those managers who make the most of the opportunities that empowerment offer are usually those who recognise that willingness and ability to be empowered is unevenly distributed through their workforce. What might be seen by one set of employees as an opportunity to develop and grow might equally be seen as a major threat by those with less confidence and fewer skills. Managers seeking to implement empowerment in their teams or across whole organisations must balance the risks of giving employees greater freedom against the advantages that empowerment claims to offer.

The potential for achieving flexibility through empowerment depends entirely on the outcomes made possible by empowerment. The manager who is looking to introduce empowerment must also make a difficult judgement call on the acceptability of empowerment, and all its consequences, to the culture of the organisation. In many ways the empowered employee can contribute to flexibility by behaving as if he or she was an entrepreneur inside the organisation – an 'in-house entrepreneur' – thinking more carefully about the wider impact and consequences of each action or omission. Such a move requires an employee to use a wholly different and far more challenging set of skills than before: the empowered employee is as far removed as it is possible to imagine from the typical Taylorist vision of the worker as a mere extension of the workplace machinery.

In dealing with empowerment as a practical concept, the best method of explaining it is to take working examples from organisations that claim to use empowerment and develop from them a broader understanding of the myths and realities often associated with empowerment. Operating in a truly empowered environment is far from an easy ride for managers because it forces organisations to take risks that previously were not considered. Turning employees into 'in-house entrepreneurs' means changing the behaviour and mindsets of people alongside changing policies and procedures to support the empowerment process.

Why go for empowerment?

The logic behind the drive for empowerment is simple and compelling, at least on the surface. Empowerment claims to offer opportunities to 'supercharge' organisations, by driving decision-making down to lower levels than before and by vesting those nearest to the problem with the power, skill and ability to take effective action.

In this way empowerment has the potential effect of converting ordinary employees into a competitive resource, utilising their judgement and skills for the benefit of customers, workmates and, ultimately, the organisation. The empowered employee will be expected to question routine, to cut through poor procedures and eliminate low quality – in precisely the way that a typical entrepreneur might behave – in order to ensure that customers (internal and external) get the best value, and the best possible levels of service or product.

Hard evidence of the business benefits of empowerment is not easy to establish. Consultants the Bourton Group (formerly known as Ingersoll Engineers) nonetheless reported recently (*The Independendent on Sunday*, 28 December 1997) that they had developed a technique for assessing the 'empoweredness' of an organisation, and had found concrete evidence that those organisations which were judged to be empowered were outperforming those that were not. If their evidence and analysis is to be believed, then embracing empowerment should soon become less of an act of faith and more of a sensible business decision. The Bourton Empowerment Audit is based on a four-year study and uses four key themes to assess the degree to which employees are empowered: relationships, style of management, organisation structure, and communications. A databank of over 100 organisations has now been analysed, and a clear correlation between empowerment and the level of improvements in business performance experienced has been observed.

Mindful of the likely scepticism that some would have towards such results, the Bourton Group make much of the fact that measurement of performance was on a strictly financial basis, taking into account turnover, return on sales, return on capital employed (ROCE) and profit per employee. When the consultants then analysed the companies in the upper quartile of these performance areas, they found that there were significantly more empowered businesses present than those whose management style reflected very few or none of the principles of empowerment. Among the more empowered group of companies, above half had achieved increased sales revenue of 30 per cent and significant increases in ROCE, and profit per employee had increased by

Table 25
EXAMPLES OF EMPOWERMENT PROGRAMMES REPORTED IN *PEOPLE MANAGEMENT*, 1997

Example 1: Learning from the Bodyshop 'Lads'

Launched in 1995, the Learning and Development (LAD) section of Bodyshop has introduced self-managed learning for all the company's central staff and earned a strategic input to the company. Bodyshop's renowned culture will always need extensive reinforcement and support, and this unique learning mechanism fitted neatly with the desire to push decision-making and responsibility downwards.

The LAD initiative runs two types of empowerment-supporting programmes. It deals with the traditional organisational training needs such as induction and programmed management development, although no doubt in a highly non-traditional way, but it also offers customised internal consultancy for special learning needs wherever and however they might be identified. Learning for empowerment is delivered in a variety of ways, the crucial theme being that it is seen as a long-term process.

Because the goal of the programme is to support and encourage an empowered organisation, managers cannot just send employees to participate in the learning: employees have to identify and ask for the learning they need. It is then up to LAD to provide it.

Example 2: Rank Hovis leaders lead to empowerment

In 1996 Rank Hovis initiated a leadership development programme at the plant in Southampton which had the effect of turning 16 supervisors into team leaders. Along the way the company discovered empowerment as the chief means of unleashing employee potential. Supervisors whose primary function had been to control and check were now empowered to run budgets and haggle with suppliers over terms and conditions which had previously been dictated from on high.

Before embarking on the programme, all 16 assessed their own skill levels and identified shortfalls. Training in leadership performance objectives, teambuilding, coaching and commercial awareness was used to build confidence in the team leaders, and the changes which ensued caused a further shift in thinking at the company.

Managers at levels above the newly empowered employees were not keeping up; they too had to become versed in the new ways of working. They have since taken heart from the opportunities opened up for them as many day-to-day decisions are now devolved to those who are closest to each problem and its solution.

Example 3: Norfolk County Services empowered to clean up

When Norfolk County Services won a lucrative contract to clean schools they were surprised to see many of their employees heading for the door. Empowerment formed the basis of the company's successful turnaround of the situation, which led to their winning a National Training Award.

The cause of the mass departures was thought to be the cuts in pay that had been necessary to win the contract in the first place – but this was only part of the story. Exit interviews highlighted insecurity, low morale, and uncertainty about the new management structure as significant reasons for leaving. This meant that the company had to embark on a massive communications and development exercise to explain the new structures and reporting mechanisms to staff who remained.

The opportunity to change fundamentally the way the job was accomplished was also taken. Previously, all attempts by employees to use their initiative had been positively discouraged in the name of consistency. Under the new regime, initiative is encouraged and employees are invited to make their views known at consultative committees which meet four times a year.

The emphasis on general training has also led to more movement of staff within the organisation. Where once cleaners had no career prospects at all, thanks to the development of skill and confidence levels that a more empowered approach automatically generates it is not uncommon for those cleaning staff who wish to to move up to become senior cleaners, supervisors and even contract managers.

---

more than £5,000 – evidence of the potential rewards that empowerment can bring. Other benefits of empowerment programmes are set out in Table 25.

Restructuring for flexibility through empowerment

The potential change in the role, responsibilities and requirements of the employee is a significant – some would argue crucial – development in the way more flexible organisations are to be structured, managed and developed in the future. Estimates of the potential gains available vary, but anyone who has worked for an organisation of any size can usually relate tales of waste, poor practice or inefficiency, all of which might be significantly reduced by an empowerment programme. If employees are currently operating at only 60 per cent of their potential, the benefits to be gained, for no extra cost, are substantial.

What empowerment means to some organisations

One approach to using empowerment as a tool for flexibilisation is to see it as only one vital part of a broader organisational development strategy. An example of this approach was reported many years ago by renowned business guru Tom Peters, who told the story of Johnsonville Foods to illustrate this type of approach to empowerment. Peters (1989) recounts how the Wisconsin company, which makes sausages and meat products, has a conscious policy of encouraging all employees to put time and energy into company-financed self-development courses, job-related or not. Managers of Johnsonville Foods claim, however, that they are not acting out of altruistic motives. Peters reports that the company's empowerment philosophy stems from a belief that 'turned on', interested employees, whose brains are kept active outside the workplace, might just bring those lively minds into the workplace and use them to produce better-quality meat products – products that the company can more easily sell for a premium price and thereby make more money.

In the UK, a similar 'scatter-gun approach' to empowerment at front-line employee level is to be found in a number of organisations. Ford UK, for example, has for many years run an Employee Development Action Programme (EDAP) which gives all employees access to a company grant each year that can be spent on any aspect of self-development. Such an approach to empowerment is something of a hit-and-miss affair and is unlikely to be tied into identified business objectives, so the benefits that accrue to the organisation will be very difficult to accurately evaluate. Wherever the empowerment concept is not tied to specific organisational objectives and subject to individual choice, employees may well be developing or improving skills and taking action in non-relevant or even non-required areas.

At Elida Gibbs when it was introduced in the early 1990s, the empowerment programme was seen as a key feature of more general organisational development. Encouraging the self-development of employees was seen as crucial to a desired change in culture within the organisation, and the on-going commitment to becoming a 'learning organisation'. The company business plan for 1995 set ambitious goals for people development of 10 days' average training per employee, and a minimum of 3 days' for at least 90 per cent of employees. Elida Gibbs encouraged and supported employee self-development via a 24-hour employee learning centre operated by the company in Leeds, promoting both business-focused learning and learning *per se*. The company believes it has discovered previously hidden talent through its empowerment programme, and managers relate numerous success stories about empowered, committed workers. The resulting restructuring to use this newly discovered talent offers practical examples of self-managed work teams, fewer levels of management and greater delegation of decision-making.

Despite such a positive outcome, an illustration of the difficulties experienced by organisations in seeking to define empowerment precisely is contained in the draft Empowerment Vision for the personal products division of Elida Gibbs (as reported in the company magazine *Linkline* in March 1995):

> To establish an empowered organisation which allows self-managed teams and individuals to take ownership and responsibility within their own area of operation, with the prime purpose of meeting and exceeding both local Company and personal goals, consistently with the shared Personal Products Europe strategic objectives for the business.

Few would argue with such a vision, but its implementation is often way beyond management's ability or desire. After all, HR managers strive to tailor training programmes to business needs to justify the organisational and human investment. Removing this direct link means that not only is the strategic impact of empowerment diluted but the likely pay-off of the process will shift too far away from the organisation (ie the funders) and ever closer to the recipients.

A more common, and arguably more effective, approach to achieving flexibility through empowerment is to link it selectively to key performance areas or within clearly defined responsibility boundaries. This approach inevitably restricts the type or content of empowerment programmes – but it sits comfortably with organisation managers who are increasingly accustomed to seeking maximum organisational benefit from any new business initiative.

Birds-Eye Walls presents a clear example of this approach to using empowerment as a business tool. The company sees the value in pushing decision-making authority and responsibility down to the lowest practical level, but stresses the need for two distinct but related empowerment support mechanisms. Structural support and attitudinal changes are seen as essential to preparing and guiding the way to effective empowerment. Without a changed structure to allow newly empowered employees to perform effectively, the benefits of it will inevitably be restricted. The second support mechanism is for the managers to be strong enough to change their own attitudes towards employees and play down the control and direction function in favour of encouraging confidence, action and completion of tasks by employees closest by any problem. Employees who have bought into the empowerment concept and experienced personal or organisational development, can quickly lose enthusiasm if they are faced with an unyielding bureaucratic structure that is too inflexible to accommodate new practices or ideas.

In terms of attitudinal change, it is often argued that the strongest resistance to accepting empowerment and empowered action in organisations comes from middle and senior managers. Taking this into account, an organisation that seeks to successfully introduce empowerment must develop a strategy for minimising resistance from the existing holders of power.

Birds-Eye Walls saw empowerment as one vital piece in the much bigger jigsaw of general organisational development. It was improved operational efficiency that was perceived as the prime beneficial result of empowerment, through the increased use of new initiatives such as teamworking. As before, the company also boasts of having an employee learning centre on each site, to help empowerment to contribute, in a targeted way, to the company's critical success factors. These are identified (in the framework document *Category Development*, 1995) as:

□ *innovation* – innovative products, brands and services
□ *quality* – preferred product quality and brand image
□ *service* – best supplier to our customers
□ *cost* – low-cost base with continuous productivity improvement
□ *people* – competent and motivated people.

This vision of empowerment allows a greater role for specific, targeted training and development, managed directed and evaluated by the HR function, while still recognising the potential general benefits available to the organisation as a whole.

A final view of what empowerment means to the practitioner argues that the concept is merely 'old wine in new bottles' – a rehash of well-established employee involvement (EI) attempts updated from previous eras. The lowest level of empowerment may result in no more than an intensification of in-house training – ie providing employees with a wider range of more sophisticated skills. Evidence of the appeal of this approach can be seen in companies such as the Rover Group (case-study in Burnes, 1996), where the empowerment programme has been used as a successful and significant prop to support an organisational de-layering process.

Is empowerment just good HR practice?

It is arguable that all empowerment programmes will tend to slide in the direction of the 'in-house entrepreneur', consciously or not, because once employee behaviour goes beyond formally defined job roles it will become increasingly difficult to identify an employee's role boundary. But getting employees to use their best judgement and act accordingly in the interests of the business could just be seen as good employment practice, and this would mean that the advent of empowerment programmes is not a totally new or original HR development, merely an extension of the 'human relations school' approach to organisational development. If this view achieves greater credibility, empowerment will eventually come to be seen merely as one element of change management: one that gives both employees and managers greater freedom to act.

An example of this approach to empowerment can be found in the stance taken by the Whitbread Beer Company whose appreciation of the potential of empowerment started from an analysis of the company business plan. The potential contribution of the people to the business was measured and was then compared with the actual contribution. Shortfalls identified in this way became the subject of changes in working practices. Empowerment, where applicable, was merely one option among such changes; others were programmed improvements in levels of competence and in technology/ process. Empowerment for this company is just one of many possible sources of improvement, and may or may not be appropriate depending upon the business case. (See also Chapter 17.)

Most empowerment programmes could be said to embody the view that their aim is to enhance the value added by employees (especially at lower levels) by encouraging them to develop and exercise a greater range of personal skills and to take more initiative and responsibility in their work. The use of empowerment at NatWest's information technology support division provides a different focus for investigating the potential that can be unleashed by such policies. In an environment that needs fast-moving and supportive HR policies, the use of an empowerment approach to work has provided both stimulation and challenges to the organisation. The bank found that empowerment quickly became a strong driver towards multi-skilling and multi-responsibility team-working when they introduced a restructuring process which took them from 12 down to eight levels of management. But the approach adopted was to integrate empowerment with many other practices within the division. A top-down training programme was undertaken to facilitate the introduction of more empowered ways of working alongside a concept of 'career theming' by which some of the disadvantages of reduced promotion possibilities which inevitably stem from flatter hierarchies were replaced by career structures that encompass lateral or sideways promotions and role redesignation. Such developments were made possible only by the introduction of the necessary skills and abilities to support empowerment.

Varying degrees of empowerment

For all organisations that wish to introduce a more empowered way of operating the question for managers to address is how far the concept can be taken. Empowerment does not have to be an all-or-nothing feature of any organisation: some companies will embrace the philosophy and practices of empowered working in all its glory, while others will reject it totally after due consideration as not appropriate for them or their environment. The collapse of Barings Bank as a result of the empowered and less than adequately controlled actions of the Singapore-based futures trader Nick Leeson, widely reported in 1995, may serve as a warning.

All organisations have some degree of employee empowerment and autonomy, and it could be argued that the further down the empowerment road organisations travel, the greater the potential risks – and benefits – there are for organisations. In addition, the increasing use of empowerment will call for significant changes in behaviour and approaches on the part of organisational managers. At Grand Metropolitan, empowerment has resulted in devolving responsibility to the lowest practical level, to ensure customer interests are best served. The company's philosophy of empowerment may thus be seen as a business-driven one, following analysis of where Grand Metropolitan thought it might have a potential weakness. Interestingly, this approach to empowerment does not rule out the right of management to propose solutions to crisis situations which often need autocratic decisions; only if empowerment increases efficiency will it be supported.

Any introduction of empowerment, even where it has been tried only in a small section of an organisation, must deal with the cultural aspects not just of what the organisation does but also of how it is done, in terms of policies, values and, ultimately, business ethics. One distinct possibility, where empowerment is introduced in a limited way, is that the empowered section will develop a culture and *modus operandi* that sets itself apart from the rest of the organisation. This may be a positive development or it could equally lead to the formation of an elite, to perceived unfair treatment and to accusations of favouritism from other sections of the organisation.

Studies of empowerment programmes (see Steininger, 1994; Ellis 1996) regularly highlight one of the critical factors in the success or otherwise of a move towards empowerment as being 'the boundary factor', a term used to describe the extent and scope of empowerment. This boundary defines how far the empowered employee can go with his or her independent action before having to refer to some sort of controlling authority.

The 'fried egg' model of empowerment (Figure 2, page 266) was in use at Royal Mail (amongst other organisations). The model illustrates how jobs can be expanded to the limits of

Figure 2
BOUNDED EMPOWERMENT: IDEAL

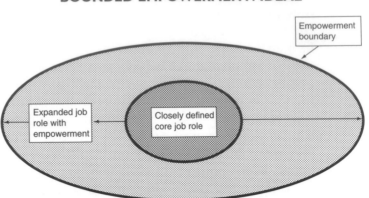

the empowerment boundary, with the assistance of trained and willing employees. Empowerment of this sort does not always engender flexibility: this sort of empowerment may rely on complicated sets of rules and procedures to define an employee's empowered action in a variety of situations.

Users of the model commented that it was too sterile to describe accurately the workings of an empowerment programme or philosophy. A more accurate and telling version

Figure 3
REALISTICALLY BOUNDED EMPOWERMENT

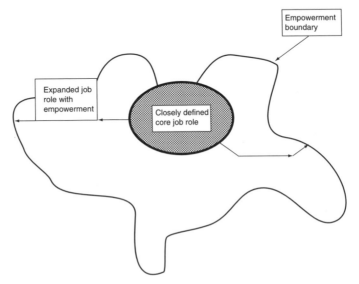

of the model would be like Figure 3, page 266, where the empowerment boundary is quite fluid and often difficult to predict or define.

Such an interpretation of the empowerment process not only allows for more flexibility and scope for individual differences in performance, it also allows managers to constantly and arbitrarily redefine and redraw the empowerment boundary, leading to confusion and frustration for the empowered employee.

The limits to empowerment are perhaps summed up by the following quote from a report by the Employment Department (1994):

> To get the benefits of employee involvement, it may well be necessary to change the culture of the organisation. For example, it is bound to be difficult to secure the full commitment of all employees in an old-fashioned structure where there are clear distinctions of status and employment conditions and benefits between management, white-collar and blue-collar employees.

As for decision-making and power the report continued:

> Successful employee involvement depends on mutual trust. Managers who give their staff the power to make decisions about the product or service have to trust them not to abuse that power.

Future development of the empowerment concept

In typical organisations subordinates must have very clearly defined roles. Large-scale empowerment is unlikely to flourish in an environment where both flexibility and initiative-taking (the cornerstones of any empowerment philosophy) are not part of the normal way of operating. Work of the human relations school suggests that empowerment might lead to increased employee motivation and release previously untapped potential within the organisation. But for some organisations (and managers) this might be a dangerous step to take, as empowered employees start flexing their wings and questioning previously accepted organisational policies.

Two extreme levels of ambition can be considered. At the most basic level empowerment may result in no more than an intensification of in-house training – ie the provision to employees of a wider range of more sophisticated skills. The elimination of the middle-manager cadre in many organis-ations has, *de facto*, pushed much decision-making and responsibility downwards – a situation of empowerment by default. This sort of experience is unlikely to prove the most effective because the resulting, unplanned empowerment will be generally be minimally prepared and structured.

At the other extreme, ambitious empowerment projects have proposed the development of the concept introduced in the introduction to this chapter: the 'in-house entrepreneur'. For this concept to work, organisations have to abandon for-mally defined roles and work as if they are merely an alliance of like-minded entrepreneurs, and not merely employees. Organisations as diverse as Hewlett Packard and Bodyshop provide benchmark examples to illustrate some instances of movement towards this concept.

To get the most from empowerment, managers must ensure that the newly empowered are given access to timely and adequate information and support mechanisms. A further factor to consider is the level of support and effort that those releasing power – the managers – are able to call on. Many empowerment programmes suffer as a result of the barriers (real and imaginary) put up by managers who see the process of empowerment as an erosion of their traditional-status pos-ition and authority.

Introducing empowerment: some practical steps

Firstly, be sure of the purposes and extent of the empower-ment programme. What are your objectives? (Cost reduction, increased innovation, increased flexibility, improved quality are typical examples.) Consider tying the programme into other organisational objectives and policies. (Many organis-ations have decided against using the term *empowerment*, even though they readily admit to utilising the concept, fear-ful that it will be seen as this year's fad which will soon go away.)

Secondly, identify a staged, workable, timetabled empowerment implementation strategy. This will largely depend on the organisational situation, but introducing empowerment to a small section or department might be more easily controlled and evaluated than a wholesale company-wide introduction. Consider the resources needed to introduce the programme, including time for staff retraining, inputs from internal and external trainers to introduce the new system, and the possible knock-on effects of job redesigns/redefinitions. Agree limits to the empowerment with employees and managers concerned so that both know the extent of their own responsibilities and those of others.

Thirdly, consult with those targeted for empowerment. Identify their needs and possible weaknesses; build a serious consideration of these into your implementation programme. Be ready for a backlash from those who do not see the need for empowerment. Embed the new practices at every opportunity to show how seriously you are taking the concept. For example, you could use the appraisal, reward and recognition systems to reinforce the objectives of your empowerment programme.

Fourthly, evaluate the progress and achievements of the programme, to provide feedback to those who were unsure about the benefits and costs of the new regime. Once the empowerment programme starts, those who embrace it will be on a never-ending journey constantly re-examining and redefining previously stable relationships and reporting systems. Those who are not happy with the new way of working will need to be considered and action taken either to bring them into line or to deal with eventual exit procedures.

The skills and attributes needed for effective employee empowerment

For empowerment to be effective, empowered employees are often required to act as if they were entrepreneurs because entrepreneurial skills involve exercising black-box areas of personal competence, such as judgement, intuition, vision, etc. Contrasts can easily be drawn between employees and entrepreneurs in terms of the range and depth of decision-making skills required, in addition to the level of commitment, engagement and performance required. In both these areas what an entrepreneur needs to do to be successful goes significantly beyond what is required to fulfil a formal (job) role in an organisation. In tabular fashion this can be conceptualised as in Table 26 overleaf.

Table 26
MOVING FROM EMPLOYEE TO ENTREPRENEUR

Employee package		Entrepreneur package
formal job role	⟶	boundaryless role
written job description	⟶	total engagement
rewarded for/judged on	⟶	rewarded for/judged on
obedience and conformity	⟶	risk/results
carry out duties	⟶	use creativity/initiative
follow procedures	⟶	develop procedures

Structural changes to support empowerment

The potential gain to organisations of exploiting entrepreneur-like qualities and skills in all their employees is easily recognised, but looking for such an outcome from an empowerment programme alone is simply not possible, not least because structural limitations in formal organisations physically prevent employees from performing the role of entrepreneurs. All empowerment programmes attempt to devolve decision-making to lower levels in the organisation, in sharp contrast to the classic organisational principle of information being funnelled up, decisions handed down. Empowered employees must be able to use the information available and their own judgement about a situation to make a decision at their own level instead of having to communicate the information to managers higher up the organisation and waiting for the decision to be delivered back down. They must realise that their position in the decision-making process is fundamentally changed and be able to accept that, on occasion, they will arrive at outcome decisions with which their superior may not readily concur. Unless this is accepted as a potential risk or cost to the organisation, employees will spend more time trying to second-guess the solution that the manager would like them to come up with in analysing the problem and trying to match a solution to organisational objectives and the resources available.

On the senior management side there is usually little incentive and no established mechanisms to challenge such collusion by subordinates to weave empowerment fantasies. In many large organisations the top management group often functions very much like an autonomous, empowered work-group (depending on the personality of the CEO and the general management style of the company). Within the group there is real decision-making discussion. High levels of personal trust are likely between the members, and conflicting views will therefore be openly discussed and argued out. All of this is of course underpinned by high levels of security (high salaries, high status, superior conditions of employment, pension rights, etc) which provide a shield against any significant risk of losing their positions. This group may be said to exist within a magic bubble of social and economic security, which truly does empower them.

The danger of shambolic empowerment is for top management, looking out from within its magic bubble, to imagine that it has created the same style of working life for the groups below it (a delusion that could easily be reinforced by the boss-pleasing employees). This situation is often illustrated when senior executives abruptly and without consultion declare a policy and retire expecting the policy automatically to be implemented, only to return some time later and wonder why the policy has never seen the light of day. Without the true structural reforms needed to support and promote empowerment, the real results in terms of improved organisational competitiveness will simply not materialise.

Where real decision-making devolution occurs in the name of empowerment, the consequences can be equally distressing, depending on what level of decision-making is involved. The major issue that arises is that of where the boundary (or frontier) of empowerment can be drawn. Subordinates are certainly encouraged to have a say, or even decide unilaterally, on the tactics of their team or unit, but what about its strategy? What about its objectives and mission? And then what about the tactics, strategy, objectives and mission of the subsidiary or division of which they are a part? At what point does the meaning of *empowerment* drain away on encountering the decision-making territory of those legally empowered to take the organisation's strategic decisions?

An example of these concerns comes from Clive Thomson, chief executive of Rentokil, who gives contemporary expression to the reality of strategic empowerment: 'Those managers who talk about total empowerment and who delegate fully cannot possibly be adding value.'

The resolution of such contentious issues of corporate governance in many organisations has been found in the deliberate policy of confining empowerment to lower levels of the organisation – even though the empowered few could be designated a closed system, and could be given a budget and access to a set of inputs around which they would be instructed to organise themselves independently to achieve certain objectives.

Entrepreneurial commitment, engagement and high performance through empowerment

Steininger (1994) considered the reasons behind the failure of many organisational quality initiatives; he claimed that:

> The real causes of our current struggle with quality lie deeper. There are certain philosophical and psychological assumptions about people that must be understood if a company is to be transformed into one that continually manages for quality. Unfortunately these assumptions cut directly against the prevailing management thinking and go against the deepest, ingrained paradigms held by the majority of our business leaders.

That the entrepreneurial characteristics are those of commitment, engagement and high performance leads to several problems with the idea that even the best and most supported programmes of empowerment can simply instil these in employees. The first problem is the issue of ownership. The classic trade-off of risk for return lies very close to the core of capitalism: entrepreneurs take risks investing time, energy and money in uncertain projects. If successful, they are rewarded with large personal benefits; if the project fails, they lose out. The structure underlying the role of the employee is completely different: like bureaucrats they can be certain that they will be punished for mistakes and equally certain that they will never be fully rewarded for the successes they achieve. Unlike entrepreneurs, therefore – and this is the key – risk avoidance is part of their role, which contrasts strikingly with one of the basic principles of empowerment by which employees are expected to make decisions and judgement calls personally, rather than waiting for an all-knowing and all-seeing manager on high to take the decision on behalf of the employee. Many employees in non-empowered organisations can recall, with some amusement and not infrequent anger, decisions or solutions proposed by managers too remote from the chalkface of the problem to understand the real issues. The empowerment tool aims to put a halt to this by enabling those best placed, at whatever level they might be in the organisation, to make the call, to take the responsibility and the action.

A further problem is that of employment security. Entrepreneurs cannot be separated from the projects to which they devote their lives: their ownership is as much psychological as it is legal. Employees in contrast have a much more tenuous, if contractual, relationship with the organisation. The willingness to commit deeply to an organisation, which is a pre-requisite for fully effective empowerment, accounts for the fact that in relation to the majority of organisation members, the chances of being dismissed from it are far higher for them than for the entrepreneurs. It is somewhat ironic that the contemporary drive to empower employees collides both philosophically and logically with the reduction of employment security generated by other recent organisational developments such as downsizing, de-layering and outsourcing.

An entrepreneurial lifestyle undoubtedly contributes to personal growth, but the decision to adopt it has to be a freely chosen personal decision, not one imposed from outside. Writing about the situation at Royal Mail, Ellis (1996) points out that organisations that abdicate responsibility for helping managers deal with employees encountering empowerment, do so with damaging results. 'A mechanism for supporting the managers of newly empowered employees must be devised. Roles and responsibilities need to be realigned in order to facilitate the release of power, authority and control to lower levels of the organisation.'

Conclusion: flexibility through empowerment

The case-study below illustrates how Tesco has used the concept of empowerment as a practical tool to develop more flexible customer service. The company believes that driving decision-making down to the lowest possible level offers many new opportunities to satisfy customers. Empowerment-enablers identified include training, teamworking and multi-skilling to ensure that the first person coming into contact with a customer has the skill and desire to 'own' the issue. Despite the problems revealed by this case-study – introducing empowerment is seldom easy – most people would agree that some degree of empowerment is essential as an adjunct to flexible working practices.

Case-study

EMPOWERMENT BENEFITS EXPERIENCED AT TESCO

In common with many retail outlets, Tesco has recently implemented a number of initiatives to increase flexibility and customer service. A vital enabling factor in achieving both of these objectives has been the introduction and support of increased opportunities for empowerment of staff. Although the use of the philosophy of empowerment is not openly declared, Tesco has successfully implemented a number of policies which lead one to conclude that the company recognises and capitalises on the potential benefits to be gained from allowing front-line staff to take and make decisions aimed at improving customer service.

Empowerment enablers identified at Tesco

In many of its in-store operations, Tesco has deliberately augmented the existing use of multi-skilled teams and introduced new areas of cross-functional teamworking. A distinct policy shift has seen the company change its emphasis, in certain areas, from a concentration on systems and procedures to a concentration on people. Staff areas in the stores are festooned with posters and examples of visual training materials which pursue the message that staff make the difference and people count more than systems. Company induction procedures in many stores now include discussion about and training on the concept and culture of empowerment, involving practical instances of how an employee can use his or her actions and abilities to assist customers. Employees are encouraged to see their role primarily as customer services providers who should be able to comply with customer requests and provide instant responses to the majority of typical in-store situations. On-going in-store training and development is used as a vehicle for sustaining and reinforcing the message. A typical example of the new approach is in the handling of many standard customer complaints. Traditionally, they would have been referred to the relevant manager and an appropriate response made. Under the more empowerment-oriented regime the complaint can be dealt with by whoever first picks it up, resulting in quicker action and less opportunity for dissatisfied customers. It also leaves the store management free to concentrate on non-standard issues and other management tasks.

Practical problems experienced with empowerment at Tesco

Rewarding empowered employees either individually or through the teams to which they contribute has proved to be a problem where reward systems are rigid and externally determined. In practical terms, the reward for an employee who performs well in this empowered environment is restricted to verbal or other non-financial measures. The company believes that there is further scope for recognition of those employees who embrace the empowerment philosophy, and is experimenting with non-traditional recognition schemes to highlight good practice. Some further scope exists for tying the performance of empowered employees to profit-sharing, but this is, at best, a distant connection and, at worst, seen by employees as irrelevant.

A further difficulty experienced – one that is common to many organisations where empowerment is introduced – is the conflict between completing essential tasks and projects under tight time pressure, and the tendency for many of the tasks required for empowerment to eat into the restricted resources available. In this situation the management of the organisation finds itself with difficult choices to make, for staff resources tied up in dealing (albeit in an empowered way) with one customer's problem cannot be used elsewhere in the store.

Benefits gained and lessons learned

The introduction of empowerment policies in many stores is seen as one small but significant element of a much larger organisational response to the need for increased flexibility and performance from all staff. In a situation where flexible contracts are increasingly common (one third of checkout staff at some stores are on flexible contracts), variable working hours are widespread, and an increasingly diverse employee group is being utilised, the use of an empowerment philosophy has both tremendous advantages and potential pitfalls. The danger of inconsistency of message between employee and customer requires careful training, and close monitoring. The employees expected to carry out empowered tasks need support and development in order to be clear about the boundaries of their role and the techniques of disengagement when problems have to be handed on to more senior members of the organisation.

While the reward for employees who effectively solve customers' problems can be immediate in terms of job satisfaction, the company is keen to avoid a situation where non-financial rewards such as being named 'employee of the week' are used in a token way, and seen as not meaningful.

The sensible approach to empowerment for most organisations would appear to be a step-by-step one. Some of the justifications for introducing empowerment are outlined in this chapter, and it is our belief that the great majority of HR policies can benefit from a reappraisal of organisational priorities and possibilities that empowerment can offer. Merely having a company policy on empowerment is clearly an insufficient and inadequate step towards a truly empowered organisation.

Even a well-thought-out, well-funded and well-managed empowerment policy may still leave vital questions unanswered – questions such as:

□ What incentive does an employee have to internalise and adhere to it?
□ Where does the boundary of empowerment lie?
□ What of an employee who does not wish (or is unable) to accept responsibility?

Recent times in the USA, though less so in the UK, have seen a pronounced upswing in the provision of individual self-development or self-support solutions from therapists and counsellors. Businesses are also increasingly turning to senior management performance coaches, consultants and advisers. There is a strong link between the upsurge in these development activities and the desire to develop an effectively empowered workforce. All these changes tend to assume that employees and managers alike will welcome all development opportunities with open arms – which may or not be the case.

Typical claims made for the enabling capacity of empowerment programmes can be found in Carlzon (1987):

> To free someone from rigorous control ... and give that person freedom to take responsibility for ideas, decisions and action releases hidden resources that would otherwise remain inaccessible to both the individual and the organisation.

Despite the more outlandish suggestions of such idealists, however, many businesses have understandably used the empowerment option as another tool to tighten their grip on efficiency and improve bottom-line results. The study carried out by the Bourton Group into the effects of empowerment on financial performance should encourage managers to at least consider the use of a more empowered workforce.

References and further reading

BURNES B. *Managing Change: A strategic approach to organisational dynamics.* London, Pitman, 1996.

CARLZON J. *Moments of Truth.* Stockholm, Ballinger, 1987.

ELLIS S. 'A study into strategic change management at Royal Mail', MPhil Dissertation, University of Luton, England, 1996.

HANDY C. *Gods of Management.* London, Random Century, 1978.

MACGREGOR D. *The Human Side of Entrepreneurship.* NewYork, Harper & Row, 1961.

MASLOW A. *Motivation and Personality.* New York, Harper & Row, 1970.

PETERS T. *Thriving on Chaos.* New York, Pan, 1989.

PETERS T. *Liberation Management, – Necessary Disorganisation for the Nanosecond Nineties.* London, Macmillan, 1994.

STEININGER D. J. 'Why quality initiatives are failing'. *Human Resource Management*, Vol. 33, No. 4, Winter 1994, pp. 601–616.

TAYLOR F. W. *The Principles of Scientific Management.* New York, W. W. Norton, 1967.

14 FLEXIBILITY AND THE PSYCHOLOGICAL CONTRACT

Introduction

We have seen that the theme of this book is flexibility, in many of its facets, applied to modern working conditions. A number of commentators have been very critical of the way that employers have imposed flexibility in recent years, and have even indicated that it should carry a health warning for employees; and that it serves to benefit only the employer; and that it demonstrates the end of the traditional balanced psychological contract and replaces it with a one-sided affair. This chapter attempts to give a even-handed view of the issue, beginning with an examination of the downside of modern flexibility practices for employees. It then looks at areas where employers need to act to ensure that employees are treated fairly and respond well to the new practices. Finally, some recent IPD research is summarised.

There has been a fundamental shift in the boundaries that shape the organisation and understanding of work over the last couple of decades. Employees now have different expectations of work. Overall, they are better educated and aware of their rights, possess higher skill levels and are more inspirational than the previous generation. Similarly, the swiftly changing economic and social conditions have forced employers to change both their focus and their approach to the organisation of work to effect suitable changes to the business infrastructure to survive and prosper within the turbulent times.

The major driving forces of change, summarised in Chapter 1, have resulted in a huge amount of organisational restructuring, the most prominent outcomes being the de-layering process and the reduction in administrative head-count. Kissler (1991) referred to aspects of the de-layering process as 'organisational liposuction' but suggested that brains as well as fat were often being lost. Certainly the heady days of the secure middle manager have passed, together with those of the mass union ranks of skilled workers in smoke-stack industries.

The changing employment contract

The changing dynamics and experience within the workplace have led to a questioning of the nature of the employment contract. There is a clear movement away from the long-term, stable employment commitment that was much in evidence in the post-war period. Today, from an employee's viewpoint, there are a number of clear downsides to the relationship:

Power shift

The decline of the unions and the available pool of labour in an economy where unemployment has averaged over 2 million since 1979 has tilted power very much in favour of the employer. This allows an employer to demand more and give less: a situation reminiscent of the depression years. Demands in flexibility, often forced through in times of crisis, can provide substantial benefits to the organisation, with few compensatory advantages for the employee. A further example is of businesses using the more advanced telecom-munications systems to relocate to areas with abundant and cheap labour which can be exploited on a 'green field' opera-tion. Companies starting up call centres in the north and in Scotland stand accused here.

Peripheral work

A number of organisations that have delineated their core and periphery place much less value on their peripheral activities. This is made clear by the use of short-term contracts, low pay, poor conditions and a lack of training and development. Employees can become enveloped in this cycle, unable to break out into a job that supports a reasonable standard of living for them and their families. The rise in Income Support payments shows that this is a growing problem, and one that comprises a cause of concern for society as a whole, in that it can lead to a permanent low-paid underclass associated with poor education, social deprivation, crime and drugs.

Increase in insecurity

Each successive round of restructuring in organisations provides less long-term security for the 'survivors'. In fact, the 'survivor syndrome' has become a well-accepted term indicating that morale takes a long time to recover. Any recovery is destroyed by a further round of changes. Insecurity leads to stress in the workplace, particularly among those with heavy financial and family commitments. The de-layering and administrative downsizing has hit middle management the hardest, and their fall is the furthest, in many cases with little to soften the blow. The legal environment has encouraged such action in the USA and the UK, where protection against job loss is minimal, especially at managerial levels. The continuing acceptance at tribunals that restructuring for the benefit of the business cannot be questioned, and the strange decision to limit the amount of compensation at unfair dismissal cases (perhaps to be remedied under the *Fairness at Work* White Paper proposals) all work against the vulnerable middle manager who must increasingly feel underpowered rather than empowered.

Although some employees may find the uncertainty affords a degree of excitement (why else would hundreds of thousands of temps temp when they can get permanent jobs?), there is a world of difference between being a part-time non-executive director of a FTSE-100 company on a one-year contract and a part-time industrial cleaner waiting for the cleaning contract to be renewed at the end of the month.

Longer hours

Flexibility in working hours has not always led to the expected reduction in hours, except in a few successful annual hours operations. In most cases, the requirement to complete jobs to tight timescales to satisfy the customer, and the empowerment process for managers and supervisors which has landed them with buying, recruiting, disciplining and customer-care responsibilities (and, by the way, another ten staff to run while they are about it), have together meant longer days. Add on to that the need for retail staff in the evenings and at weekends and it is not surprising that the British have the longest working hours in Europe.

Transactional contract

This expression means that employees receive pay and recognition for what they do, rather than for what they are within the organisation (Parks, 1994). *Transactional* contracts are short-term and closely define the roles and outcomes of both parts. Such contracts replace relational *contracts*, which are characterised by longer-term relationships and relatively unspecified obligations. In the latter, more traditional contracts, an individual's motivation stems from longer-term interest in the organisation's development and expansion, and commitment can often be of an altruistic nature. Under the former more modern approach, however, seniority and loyalty do not mean much: what matters is what you have achieved over the last 12 months in contributing to the organisation's bottom line.

For some employees who have worked hard to get to their current positions, it is a bitter pill to swallow that they need constantly to prove their worth, give full value every quarter, and are heavily criticised for current performance when their past performance has been well recognised.

Lack of career development

There is no doubt that, despite organisations' protestations to the contrary, strategy remains short-term in most industries (notable exceptions being in the pharmaceutical and motor industries). Long-term investment in career development has suffered considerably. This is demonstrated by the vastly reduced number of graduate training positions and the virtual disappearance of sponsorship for undergraduate courses, both of which have occurred at precisely the time that student numbers have exploded. In the workplace, employers may be loath to invest in expensive career courses except on behalf of the small core of key employees. 'There is no such thing as a career path any more. It's crazy paving – and you have to lay it yourself!' So said Robin Linnecar, partner at KPMG Career Consultancy Services (quoted in Caulkin, 1995).

In the complex business world, planning a career is becoming more – not less – difficult, and individuals have growing anxieties as to the appropriate moves once past age 35. The result of a false move is far more dangerous in terms of financial security than previously. In the 1960s and 1970s it was still possible to branch out from a long-term career with a large organisation to move to a smaller company or to self-employment and then move back within a couple of years if it did not work out. Not so today. Individuals have to live with their decisions, not knowing what the alternative action (or no action at all) might have brought.

Increased risk

But the risk is not just centred on whether the job is here to stay or not, or on whether to stay put or jump: other risks abound. Self-development, which can involve volunteering for a sideways move or taking on a medium-term project, has the same risk factor. Will the move produce a learning experience, increase skills and bring organisational approval? Or will it be a dead end, leading only to the exit? Is it worth developing through a qualification which can involve a considerable loss of reduced leisure time, a sacrifice of family life and the risk of not finishing? What type of rewards will it bring – and is there no progress without an MBA or Master's degree?

A further risk is involved in the payment system, where steady and predictable rises in basic pay on a published and understood pay system has increasingly being replaced with contingency pay, based on the performance of the individual, team or organisation, or sometimes that of all three. Bonuses based on organisational performance are fine when times are good, but a disappointment when the tap is turned off in harder times. Individual performance pay can provide opportunities but can also create disputes when external forces stop targets being achieved or when there is a difference of opinion over how competent an employee is in more nebulous areas such as communication or customer care. Take-home pay can therefore vary, involving risks in financial commitment. Furthermore, the pay can be less overall, particularly towards the periphery end.

Another risk occurs in specific flexibility initiatives. In zero-hours systems, for example, employees have no real idea of the work they will be doing in the week ahead, let alone the following 12 months. Those in the complementary labour force are often in a similar situation, being moved around to meet month-to-month requirements with no clear idea of their position 12 months hence. Employees outsourced have some protection under TUPE, but only for a few months before their new employer gets to work to change the working systems to a more efficient model – with the almost inevitable consequences for jobs, working conditions and pay.

No choice over involvement

There are some employees who have no great desire to be deeply involved in the organisation they work for. A job is merely a job to provide the wherewithal to live and the opportunities to participate in leisure pursuits. Organisations are increasingly eliminating this attitude and forcing employees to play a full part in the life of the organisational body. Teamworking and the associated empowerment puts an outsider at a disadvantage. Pundits popularise the *Kaizen* culture in which making suggestions for improvements is obligatory and non-participation is frowned on. There is a movement towards focused performance management where individuals help put together their targets and agree where their competencies should improve. All these serve to force employees to get involved in a far more intense way than in previous decades.

Management needs to act

The factors above provide a challenge for the organisation. It is simply not good enough to cut a swathe through employment costs, 'right-size' the organisation with 30 per cent less headcount, and then expect the remaining employees to carry on as before. Forcing flexibility through in crisis or by using dominant power simply fuels resentment and creates future difficulties. The new flexibility systems must be accompanied by an overall strategy to make use of employees' overt or latent skills, commitment and abilities.

Without action, key long-term requirements for business survival are missing. Firstly, there is a need for constant innovation, and existing employees play a key role here. Ideas can be bought from consultants, from head-hunted managers and read out of books, but the evidence has always been that a huge mass of small and medium-sized incremental innovations emerge from committed employees. The Japanese demonstrated this clearly in the 1970s and 1980s. Innovation requires both employees and employers to go the extra mile to deliver something beyond the letter of the employment contract.

An employer who relies on power superiority will get compliance and blind obedience – but the Russians found that although it may work in a wartime emergency when orders are not questioned, it fails slowly but comprehensively in peaceful competition. Communism failed because it did not harness those essential features of mutual trust and enthusiasm.

Secondly, employers need employees who are genuine in their customer relations. We have all met uncommitted organisational representatives who know their formal job but somehow just manage to find a way to avoid meeting our own immediate and long-term requirements while apparently doing their job competently. 'No, that item just isn't in stock – very sorry about this.' 'I'm sorry you have been hanging on so long – I just don't know where he is – very sorry about this.' 'We would love to deliver it as you want it but it just isn't in our delivery schedule.' And so on. Employees tired of a one-way flexibility system, cynical about the last two restructurings and a little exasperated with the extra responsibilities not commensurate with pay, will not respond in attempting – as it is described these days – 'to delight their customers'. It needs a fundamentally motivated employee to achieve this.

Thirdly, the creation of flatter structures runs the risk of depleting the stock of future leaders with experience of the business: those who aspire to promotion to board positions are far more likely to leave if the promotion opportunities are so depleted. Unless organisations think that most board roles can be filled from the ranks of consultancies (a most dangerous belief), they need to ensure that sufficient employees with talent and potential believe that the organisation will work for them if they work for it. If the reported comments of a city bond dealer are typical ('You want loyalty? Get a dog!' as he continued his job-hopping progress), then organisations do have a problem here. Microsoft is one of the few companies that has tackled this problem with a well-focused strategy. Their Career Development Programme was set up a few years back to put employees back in charge of their own careers, encouraging them in the processes of self-analysis, which included a clear and independent view on their current and future relationship with the organisation, and building up a CV that they would constantly develop while they continued to work with Microsoft. They were challenged to develop new skills and to become proactive in their own development. Although in theory this would make employees far more marketable and likely to leave Microsoft, the evidence to date is the opposite – that more employees are staying longer as they appreciate this stretching and challenging process (Ryves, 1996).

Finally, all organisations need genuine co-operation and communication to work effectively, but downsized ones need it more, because employees have less time to gossip and use the grapevine. Communicating and co-operating is a mindset as well as a science. Employees are simply not going to put in the effort in these areas in both an informal and formal way unless they want the organisation to succeed in the long term. If they believe their own future is limited, or they have a deep-seated belief that the organisation has not been fair to them or their colleagues and ex-colleagues, they will simply not bother.

So what is this psychological contract?

The concept first surfaced in the work of Schein (1970) who suggested that the individual 'has a variety of expectations of the organisation and that the organisation has a variety of expectations of him. These expectations not only cover how much work is to be performed for how much pay but also involve the whole pattern of rights, privileges and obligations between the worker and the organisation.'

In other words, the *idea* of a contract goes further than the paper the contract is written on. It is concerned with assumptions, expectations and promises as much as with mutual obligations. It goes further than the implied terms of an employment contract and includes those of mutual trust, honesty and a duty of care.

Previously, a contract was relatively simple. Employees worked hard, remained loyal, moved when asked to, passed the required qualifications, did what they were told, and in return the organisation rewarded them with security, a career, paid them fairly, generally looked after them and provided them with work that, at times, was quite interesting. Pascale (1995) compares the old-style business corporations and those in Japan today to ocean liners, in that if you secured a berth, it is possible to cruise through a career without changing ships and to disembark on retirement.

Today, the employee still wants the same rewards – but we have seen that they are becoming much less available, especially the concept of security. In fact, some question the whole concept of 'a job' at all. According to William Bridges (1995), the job is an artificial invention, created around 200 years ago so that tasks essential to the emerging industrial and commercial sector would in fact get done – tasks that could be 'boxed up' and given to several workers. Supervisors were needed to ensure they did the work, and managers were set to watch over the supervisors, thus creating a hierarchy of responsibilities and skills. Today's workplace has changed, says Bridges, to the effect that 100 per cent of all jobs have become temporary as the IT revolution does away with the conventional structures of the nineteenth and twentieth centuries. Manipulating information is the key skill, and certain sectors – such as communications and much of the media – have found traditional jobs too inflexible to cope with the constantly changing work.

So now the psychological contract has to apply in the context of flexibility – now that the boundaries are much wider than the employment contract and the workplace. It has to try to marry the different needs of the employer to the needs of the employee (who may not be an employee as such anyway). It has to create an understanding by which both parties are dependent on each other, but much more on a purchaser-supplier basis rather than as master and servant.

IPD research

The Institute of Personnel and Development (IPD) has commissioned two sets of research, in 1995 and 1996, into the current nature of the contract, from Templeton College, Oxford and Birkbeck College, London. The series of findings included:

- Low levels of trust in the organisation were linked to employees' experience of redundancy, and this – or the fear of redundancy – appeared to be a major driver in the employees' view of the contractual relationship.
- The psychological contract was in a better state than expected: 81 per cent of respondents believed that they were being treated fairly by their employer, and 72 per cent had some trust in their organisation to keep its promises and honour its commitments.
- The major factor associated with a psychological contract regarded as positive is the use of progressive HRM policies – including policies designed to provide jobs with interest and variety, a policy of avoiding compulsory redundancy and lay-offs, full provision of information on the organisation's performance and prospects, and the use of internal promotion in preference to appointing people from outside.
- Employees are working beyond contract, on average 9 hours above their contracted hours.
- Thirty per cent of senior managers work more than 60 hours a week.
- Job insecurity is less of a problem than expected: only 12 per cent are worried about being made redundant in the next two years.

Figure 4
MODEL OF THE PSYCHOLOGICAL CONTRACT

Source: Herriot and Pemberton, 1995.

Despite the surprisingly good news on the psychological con
tract from this random telephone sample of 1,000 employees,
the research gives clear messages to organisations who want
to retain the motivation and commitment of their employees.

Action to enhance the quality of the psychological contract

Herriot and Pemberton (1995) set out a model of four stages of
psychological contracting in Figure 4.

Inform

Given the business environment, ensure that employees are
quite clear about what the organisation wants and needs to
meets its business goals, particularly those goals for which
flexible working is essential. The organisation also needs to
be informed about what its employees themselves are looking
for, generally through attitude surveys.

Negotiate

Discuss the various styles of working on offer with employees
on an open basis and give a clear message on benefits and disadvantages. Make sure all employees have an opportunity to

consider the various options that exist and the conditions that accompany them. The most successful employers are able to offer the no-compulsory redundancy package in return for a large degree of personal mobility and the willingness to learn new skills and to use them to their best ability. In one of the most critical areas of flexibility, from an employee's viewpoint – outsourcing – there are a number of crucial elements where negotiating expertise can make all the difference to the careers of the employees concerned. One of the leading unions, MSF, has produced a 24-point checklist to assist negotiators to get the best deal. This includes requesting presentations from the bidding companies, negotiating for job security for an extended period, fully understanding TUPE, making strategic use of publicity, and carefully policing all the agreements once the successful bidder is in the saddle (Skyte, 1997).

Monitor

Because new ways of working are experimental, it is essential to carefully monitor progress and to ensure that the psychological contract is still on track, neither side taking an unfair advantage. For example, employers must take care that those employees with skills in very short supply are not exerting undue pressure on the organisation to ratchet up their rewards, or that the organisation is not taking advantage of a weak employment market to pay rates that could be considered to be less than a living wage.

Renegotiate or exit

Organisations should accept that many employees are happy to see their current post in their own minds as a temporary one, despite its officially permanent nature, and may be planning to move on (as is often the case with professionals in personnel, law and accounting). Such a move should therefore not be seen as a betrayal but as a natural progression by which mutual benefit has been achieved.

In this model, Herriot and Pemberton see the role of the HRM professional as well positioned to help guide employees through the model, pointing out the opportunities and the pitfalls, monitoring the entire process, and well positioned also to increase the organisation's awareness of the need for creating post-transactional contracts when they need renegotiating.

The HRM role could be further enhanced through an additional series of injunctions.

Involve

The vast majority of employees enjoy an involvement in the workplace. It is no coincidence that one of Karl Marx's main themes was the alienation of the worker from the workplace where ownership of all the means of work had been taken out of his control – tools, machinery, materials, direction and profit. The encouragement of a full involvement policy, through empowerment, teamworking, decision-making and ideas schemes as well as the financial involvement through profit-sharing and share option schemes, must be essential to improve the quality of the contract. The role of communicator here is vital.

Invite

Invitations should extend to a number of areas. Firstly, employees should be encouraged to appreciate the concept of 'employability' or ' lifetime learning' so that they take it upon themselves to develop skills which are useful to the organisation but also have a generic use. The obvious examples here are IT skills and knowledge, team-leading, project management, and making presentations all fit into the transferable skills pattern in terms of management quality. This is beneficial to both parties in the present, but beneficial also for the employee in the future should he or she become a victim of the latest batch of restructuring or market reorientation. Secondly, employees should be invited to see flexibility as an opportunity to grasp rather than an inequitable management imposition – one that can provide greater leisure, fit in with private life commitments, or allow for a career path that had not been considered. This is the role of an effective persuader. Employees should be encouraged to display a 'self-employment' mindset, delivering their work in terms of specification, not by a chunk of hours.

Enforce

Mutual trust is a crucial element in the contract, so HR professionals should make sure that promises are kept on both sides. The employer must keep promises on employability and flexibility terms, and the employee must keep promises on performance, whether at work or in attendance levels or in the details of the flexibility deal.

Excite

Change can be extremely invigorating. Each new generation of employees is more prepared to change its ways of working than the last. A real test of the planning and selling skills of the HR department is to make the changes exciting to employees. Sometimes this is not difficult – teleworking and teleconferencing *is* an exciting development. Other areas are more difficult – a new shift system, for example – but the accompanying flexible reward system can always provide opportunities to liven up a dull subject. For some jobs, especially in the media, it is the unpredictable nature of the work that provides the attraction: it is no coincidence that media studies is the fastest-growing undergraduate subject in UK universities.

Finally, there is the constant reminder that the factor that improves the psychological contract more than any other is the commitment of the organisation to the employee, which is demonstrated by training and development, even for temporary and part-time employees. For Manpower, this is what makes the competitive difference. Perhaps they believe another of Bridges' axioms – that in a post-job world, the only viable long-term career is to be a temp (Caulkin, 1995).

References and further reading

BRIDGES W. *Jobshift: How to prosper in a workplace without jobs*. London, Nicholas Brealey, 1995.
CAULKIN S. 'Take your partners'. *Management Today*, February 1995, pp. 26–30.
HERRIOT P. and PEMBERTON C. 'A new deal for middle managers'. *People Management*, 15 June 1995, pp. 2–34.

KISSLER G. 'The new employment contract'. *Human Resource Management*, 33, 1994, pp. 335–52.

PARKS J. 'Till death us do part: changing work relationships in the 1990s' in *Trends in Organisational Behaviour*, ed. COOPER C. and ROUSSEAU D. London, Wiley, 1994.

PASCALE R. 'In search of the new 'employment contract', *Human Resources*, 21, 1995, pp. 21–26.

RYVES D. 'Career development – climbing without the ladder'. *Flexible Working*, May 1996, pp. 36–39.

SCHEIN E. *Career Dynamics: Matching individual and organisational needs*. Reading, Mass., Addison Wesley, 1970.

SKYTE P. 'Outsourcing – What about the workers?'. *Flexible Working*, July 1997, pp. 24–30.w

15   SELLING THE IDEA OF FLEXIBILITY

Introduction: How flexible can you be?

Throughout this book we have given examples of the various types of flexibility being introduced to working practices in numerous and diverse organisations, and of the forms they might take. Some organisations have introduced flexibility strategically as a deliberate, planned step towards the goal of increased competitiveness, although many more have simply capitalised on the opportunities derived from flexible working practices as convenient answers to many of the challenging business questions faced by organisations. Some of the older, more traditional organisations which, like a graceful ocean liner, were designed in a world where the pace of change and adaptation was much more comfortable than it is today, are finding new ways to extend their useful lives using flexible working practices. Whichever way the organisation arrives at flexibility, the possible goal of an ultimately more effective customer response remains the same.

Flexible working should be seen as one option in the organisational development 'toolkit', but it is our view that once the 'flexibility option' is exercised, and the benefits are fully understood, it is one that will prove to be very hard to put down. The borders and constraints of flexibility have yet to be defined. The questions of just how flexible it is possible to be, and of what degree of flexibility is optimal, are still the subject of on-going research by ourselves and many others. Nonetheless, a crucial factor in the determination of how effective and successful an organisation's move towards greater flexibility will be is the extent to which those responsible can create support for flexibility, in both the practical and philosophical sense, within the organisation.

Like any new organisational policy, the move to increased flexibility will have its supporters and its enemies. To the manager who sees the benefits of flexible working, life is easier if the impact and power of those in favour can be augmented and the arguments of those opposing the changes can be diminished. The rest of this chapter is presented as a guide for the manager who wishes to ease the path of flexibility in his or her organisation and, at the same time, wring out the maximum benefits from flexible working. As for the extent or otherwise of flexibility achievable, perhaps in the circumstances of the intense competition that most businesses face, the more profitable question to ask is 'How *inflexible* can my organisation afford to be?'

Choosing the location and form of flexibility

The introduction of flexibility, perhaps more than any other policy change, requires support from others. Indeed, the success or otherwise of flexibilisation policies will ultimately depend on the extent to which those subjected to them (and those managing their implementation) understand, believe in, and welcome the benefits of flexibility. The task of the HR function is to try to help clarify the areas in which flexibility can make an effective contribution to the business, and the type of flexibility that should be used. It is also important to identify areas in which flexibility might be detrimental or harmful. For each business and in each sector of the business they will differ, but in general terms the most likely organisational areas in which positive benefits of flexibility will be obtained are the very top (the senior strategic management level) and the very bottom, the operational base of the organisation structure.

At its heart the organisation needs to attract and retain people who are willing and able to react and respond innovatively and quickly to changing scenarios and priorities. Typically, those operating at this level may themselves be accustomed to flexible working practices, perhaps holding executive directorships of several concerns in a portfolio of business commitments.

In the middle ground of the organisation, where strategy becomes interpreted into policy and activity, there is less need for flexibility and more concern for continuity. Functions and activities in this section of the organisation might be described as the stabilisers that operational and strategic flexibility require. This is the engine-room or powerhouse of the organisation, which can easily lose direction or focus if flexibility is taken beyond the organisation's capacity to cope.

The final area identified as likely to benefit from flexibilisation is at the edge or outskirts of the organisation. Some of the organisation's operational functions may be situated here – but more significantly, a number of support service or sub-assembly operations fall into this category: many examples exist of where such operations are effectively outsourced or sub-contracted away from the main body of the organisation. Such a development generally offers significant opportunities for increased flexibility.

Once the location of flexibilisation is determined, the type of flexibility to be introduced can be considered more closely. One of the determinants in this equation will be whether the introduction of flexibility is seen as a temporary, transitory stage in the development of the organisation or a semi-permanent (nothing in the modern business world can be permanently permanent) fix. A temporary shift will call for less effort to be put into organisational adaptation – policies and procedures may need to be altered in only a minor way – whereas a shift that changes work patterns and plans radically will require renegotiation of employee or supplier contracts, redrafting of manuals and procedures, and wholesale reconsideration of the organisational support mechanisms. Most, if not all, of the organisational fallout from the introduction of flexibilisation will involve the HR function's redrafting the necessary documentation, and supporting the introduction of training and reorientation programmes for the affected employees and managers. Table 28 indicates the relationships between various categories into which different types of flexibility might be grouped, and their possible impact on the organisation.

Table 28

WHAT TYPE OF FLEXIBILITY DOES AN ORGANISATION NEED?

Type of flexibility	Example	Likely impact
Reward systems	Flexible benefit packages	Behaviour modification, or motivation
Employment contracts	Zero-hours agreements	Changes in the employment relationship or psychological contract
Distancing	Outsourcing functions such as catering	Refocusing of the business on priorities or core processes
Employment practices	Teleworking	Changes in relationships, modification of styles of management

Selling the benefits of flexibility

As with many changes in organisation policy, extolling the benefits for the organisation may not be sufficient to convince the members of the validity of the changes. Perceived benefits to the individual or groups concerned must be identified and communicated. These benefits should include the enabling of organisational members to take some degree of control over work commitments – ie balancing work and non-work activities more evenly. Such balance has potential room for improvement where flexibility is introduced, and the work tasks that have to be completed can be accomplished in a variety of ways at a variety of locations at times that are convenient to both employee and employer/customer. Other benefits to be highlighted are the opportunities for developmental activities that flexibility offers, either through formal study or via experiential learning, leading to a broadening of skills and understanding. Employees who build up experience of working in a flexible way can also enhance their employability in such a way as to counter the uncertainty of employment relationships currently experienced in many industries. If the flexibility introduced offers those in employment the opportunity to acquire a wider range of skills and contribute to different tasks, a likely additional benefit is improved job satisfaction.

From the perspective of the manager, the benefits or advantages of flexibility will again need to be emphasised. On the surface, the introduction of flexible practices could entail more complicated managerial processes and increase the difficulty of the traditional managerial tasks in terms of communication, control, co-ordination and planning. To counter this, the benefits of flexibility to the manager may be pointed out in the increased range of problem-solving solutions that flexibility brings. Resources that were previously constrained by time, place or situation may now be freed up to become more available, more interchangeable and more effectively combined than before. If the new, flexibility-enhanced situation results in a better customer response, the big advantage to the manager concerned will be the increased ability to hit performance targets and to deliver effective solutions to organisational problems which were not previously possible.

Handling typical objections to flexibility

A key factor here will be an assessment of the organisation's readiness for flexibility. A manager who is thinking of introducing major steps towards flexibility will need to judge the likely impact on procedures, practices and the organisation culture. Organisations in which resistance to change and fear of new ideas is commonplace may find the move towards flexible working a giant leap of faith. Organisations with a change-welcoming and supportive culture are more likely to be open to try new ideas of flexibility.

To assist in this assessment, readers may want to devise questionnaires in order to provide managers or department heads with guidance on the likely readiness of their organisation for flexibility. The HR manager who is looking to implement some or all of the flexible policies and concepts described so far needs to be an expert communicator of the benefits of flexibility, both to the organisation and to the individuals concerned. Resistance to organisational change in most cases has to be expected and planned for. In some organisations the culture factor or 'the way we do things around here' will be the biggest barrier to change and flexibility. Effective movement from a traditional, highly structured organisation to a position where flexible working can be introduced, developed and enhanced will not be easy and will have to be a managed process.

An organisation that is looking to support the introduction of flexible working must first have an idea of the extent to which flexibility will be welcomed, desirable or downright impossible. Areas of probable high resistance will need to be identified and singled out for special treatment, training needs must be assessed and support mechanisms have to be developed. Only when the existing picture is accurately described can the march towards flexibility begin. To assist in this process some internal analysis is vital, and a realistic assessment of the organisation's current and potential capability for flexible working is a valuable and logical starting-point. This may take the form of an organisational flexibility survey, the results of which can be compared with published reports of current flexibility in a wide range of organisations.

Preparing for the journey towards flexibility

The journey towards flexibility has already begun in most sectors of society, but some organisations are having to catch up with those who already embrace and enjoy the benefits of flexible working. Nonetheless, the journey is likely to be a long and tough one, often prompting strategic level discussions around such issues as:

☐ What is our real reason for introducing flexibility?
☐ Are we in a market that demands or is best served by flexible working?
☐ What are the expectations of our customers? Do we really know who our customers are?
☐ Which organisational stakeholders do we need to satisfy or prioritise?

Only when the organisation agrees positions on these and other strategic issues can the flexibility strategy be fully considered. One of the strongest driving forces behind the introduction of flexible working is the unpredictability of many business and service environments, which suggests that organisations looking to develop grand strategic plans over the long term might ultimately be deluding themselves. Work by Stacey (1994), amongst others, suggests that chaotic environments cannot be catered for by the traditional application of strategic management techniques, and that planning approaches effective in the past may well have had their day. For organisations that face this sort of challenge, the option for flexibility is an option no more, for without flexibility it will become increasingly impossible to achieve any sort of strategic fit with the market.

The first step towards a successful journey must begin with a clear picture of the (intended) ultimate destination. That is not to say that the final arrival point will be the one originally envisaged, but a flexible strategy will be able to allow for this. In order to prepare for flexible working, the organisation and its managers must identify the types and extent of flexibility that are both desirable and achievable, and rule out the types of flexibility that are inappropriate and not applicable in their market environment. Further preparatory work must include consideration of the effects of the flexibility on the business's identified stakeholders – effects both positive and negative – with a plan for supporting or countering these effects.

The concept and role of leadership and management in the flexible organisation is a vital consideration. Where flexibility is introduced, the so-called soft indicators of performance and quality can often assume more significance than hard statistical or financial ones. This change will alter the role of organisational management and require new support and reporting mechanisms. Once the journey is under way, there must be close monitoring of the effects of flexibility on organisational performance indicators such as customer feedback and the project deadlines met. Even the traditional but much maligned staff morale surveys should give an indication of the effectiveness or otherwise of the new policies.

Choosing the right vehicle for flexibility

The shape or form of the organisation and the relationships between the people within it is the crucial issue here. Flexible practices will dictate that the organisation itself adapts to accommodate the requirements of flexibility – eg 24-hour opening, resource mobility, greater sophistication in communication channels, etc. The definition, grading and assessment of convenient and repetitive parcels of work we used to call jobs, and the concept of an organisational career, are likely to be redefined, if not completely eradicated. Organisational developments such as the use of 'portfolio workers', short-term flexi-contracts or outsourcing, and those which capitalise on the technology that supports 'virtual business parks', 'hot-desking', 'teleworking' and telecottages', are all possible vehicles for more radical flexibility. The organisation's managers have to decide which vehicle or vehicles are available and which are appropriate, and which are not.

Getting the most out of flexibility

Flexible working practices will not work if they are not keyed into, and integrated fully with, business requirements, resulting in the potential for a positive impact to bottom line performance measures. This does not mean that flexibility has a guarantee of success if its practices do fulfil these criteria. Many attempts to introduce flexibility have failed because they have been badly conceived, planned haphazardly, sold ineffectively and not evaluated at all. Our research leads us to believe that there are seven key stages to the successful introduction of a flexibility programme:

1   Research relevant flexibilisation practices to ensure that a powerful business case can be constructed based upon real evidence in your own or other industries. This must include internal research on managerial and employee attitude to the programme.

2   Design your flexibility to integrate with existing business practices where possible, so that you can prove to any doubters that the flexibilisation will make a major contribution to long-term survival and the success of the organisation. For example, for assessing current and future staff you will need employees who are willing to work flexibly. This aspect of their personality can be measured in different ways by a number of psychometric tests. For example, Saville and Holdsworth's Perspectives on Management

Competencies (PMC) measures 'flexibility' among a group of interpersonal competencies, and in their Inventory of Management Competencies 'flexibility' is again measured among a group of personal qualities. These tools are directed at managers and above, and are part of a group geared to self- and peer assessment under the general heading of '360-degree development'. Similarly, the California Psychological Inventory (published by Oxford Psychological Press) has a key scale for flexibility.

3   Check the new processes for possible conflict and contradiction with old ones, especially in the HR arena, and then propose compromise solutions or prepare a plan for the eradication of the old policies.

4   Sell the new practices to the whole workforce, with the full weight of a wholesale marketing and communications campaign.

5   Support the implementation phase with further communications and repeated explanation of the benefits of flexibilisation.

6   Have clear and effective proposals to deal with the practical (transaction) problems of managing flexible workers.

7   Monitor the progress and regularly evaluate the success of the new practices.

Conclusions and further considerations

All the approaches to increasing flexibility discovered and described in this research cannot ultimately generate more time: they are all aimed at increasing the productive use of a finite resource. And as with much research in the social sciences, our work has raised more questions and controversies than it has derived answers, insofar as the concept of flexible working can and must be studied at a number of levels. For organisations there are compelling economic arguments for increasing flexibility, especially when the policies and procedures used are tied to a mission that requires the creation of a responsive capability leading to sustained competitive advantage. For individuals the flexible working promise offers both opportunities and threats. Those who are able to take advantage of working effectively in a flexible environment can enjoy the benefits of increased earning potential, more variety and individuality, and space for their own creative and intellectual development. The threat of flexibility lies in the increased potential for employee exploitation, unregulated sweated labour and the end of meaningful long-term employment relationships. At the societal level, flexibility in the post-industrial era has consequences for a whole range of public and private service providers – transport, media and telecommunications being prime examples of those services which need to radically update their offerings to take account of unpredictable and increasingly lumpy product and service demand patterns.

The powerful effects of increasing workplace flexibility may call into question a whole range of social boundaries, such as the changes being experienced and encouraged in education. The traditional view that learning ends when one leaves school or college is gradually being replaced by the concept of flexible, lifelong learning (essential to drive the flexible organisation forward and prevent rapid skill obsolescence). In the public sector the demand for ever greater flexibility will prove hard to resist. Someone will soon be demanding to know why, if I can enquire about my bank balance 24 hours a day, I can't enquire about my children's school grades, or contact my GP, in a similar way?

The evidence adduced in this research strongly suggests that flexible working practices are on the increase and the snowball effect is well under way. The trends identified include strong evidence that organisations see flexibility as a high priority, and are looking for more creative and original approaches to introducing flexible working practices. The march towards flexibility does not, however, offer the promise of a leisure-filled Utopia. The pressures of flexible working are experienced at one extreme by managers who have survived de-layering and downsizing, and at the other by workers who have lost security of earnings, stability and programmed career progression. The phenomenon of 'presenteeism' – staying in the office even when the work is done – has been one reaction to the fear and uncertainty caused by increasing flexibility. Others have taken the opposite stance and opted to downshift – that is, to take a deliberately less active part in working life in return for less (financial) reward.

The impact of flexibility on quality and overall organisational performance is an area worthy of further research. Although the introduction of 24-hour services appears to offer increased access opportunities, the quality of what is on offer is much more dependent upon outcomes and impact. The danger of increasing flexibility without adequate consideration of HR and other resource implications is that the end user may well get easier access to a diluted and ultimately dissatisfying version of the service he or she really wants. Communication problems and poor satisfaction levels from the recent phenomenon of call centres provide some evidence for this, although as yet it is largely anecdotal.

The HR response holds many of the keys to the flexibility kingdom. The HR professional needs to be at the centre of developments in his or her own organisation, and in touch with flexibility initiatives that other benchmark organisations are trialling. It is likely that the development of flexible working will result in an enhancement of the role of (and of the demands on) the HR function. Flexible workers must be recruited, managed and developed in order to be effective contributors to the cause. In addition, a whole range of HR systems surrounding performance, reward, discipline and grievance will need to be reassessed and developed to take account of the new situation.

Flexibility in the workplace is nothing if it is not a crucial HR issue, and one that will be a major agenda item for senior strategic managers for the foreseeable future.

References and further reading

HANDY C. *The Age of Unreason*. London, Arrow Business Books, 1995.

HUWS U. *Teleworking in Britain: A Report to the Department of Employment*. London, Employment Department Research Management Branch, 1992.

KINSMAN F. *The Telecommuters*. London, Pitman, 1990.

MULGAN G. (editor) *Life After Politics*. Demos, London, Fontana Press, 1997.

STACEY R. *Managing Chaos*. London, Kogan Page, 1994.

STANWORTH J. and STANWORTH C. *Telework: The HR implications*. London, Institute of Personnel Management, 1991.

16 EUROPEAN LEGISLATION ON FLEXIBILITY

Introduction

For almost 20 years there have been movements in the European Union to legislate to protect employees who are involved in various elements of flexibility. These have been referred to, somewhat clumsily, as 'atypical' workers. There was considerable optimism in the early part of 1997 among the bodies representing trade unions that an agreement would be reached for a general Directive covering part-time, contract, freelance, outsourced employees and teleworkers (Welch, 1997) that would cover minimal contractual terms and health and safety issues.

As with much of European discussions, the outcome was a much reduced agreement in May 1997 which covered only permanent part-time employees. This represented a considerable watering-down of the Commission's original proposals, both in scope and content. The agreement between various bodies representing employers and trade unions was turned into a Directive late in 1997 by the Council of Ministers who gave it a deadline for introduction by the year 2000.

The main points of the Directive are:

- The Directive establishes the legal principle of equal rights for part-time staff, male and female, without their having to demonstrate indirect sex discrimination.
- Equal access must be given to part-time workers to pay, bonus, shift and other extra payments for comparable staff, and equal contractual terms must apply, such as sick pay and paid holiday.

☐ Benefits, such as share options, staff discounts and pensions, must apply in the same way.

It is of interest that little overall protection is implied. Discrimination against part-time employees can still take place if it can be justified objectively. Casual part-time workers can be excluded altogether by member states. Moreover, discrimination, if justified objectively, can be applied on the basis of length of service, time worked or earnings qualifications – which leaves the door wide open (IRLB, 1997).

Possible future measures

Whether further action in this area will follow is debatable. There continues to be a fine balance of views in Europe between improving competitiveness and de-regulation on the one hand, and still attempting to improve employees' working conditions and protect jobs on the other. Hans-Olaf Henkal, president of the BDI (the German equivalent of the CBI), spoke at the 1997 CBI Conference on his lack of success in persuading the German government to accept the need for lower labour costs and greater labour flexibility. There is considerable admiration in German business circles of the British flexible labour market (Overell, 1997). The Socialist French government's views are very different from this. That is why progress is slow in this area and has led to fairly harmless Directives, such as that on parental leave.

The Green Paper, *Partnership for a New Organisation of Work*, which completed its consultation period in November 1997, may lead to further action.

One other possible area of legislation is in the area of protecting teleworkers. Instigated by the European Commission, talks are due to start in 1998 involving representatives of the European Trade Union Confederation (ETUC) and the pan-European employers' bodies UNICE and CEEP. Currently, the Commission is indicating that the most likely outcome is a Code of Conduct, rather than a formal Directive. These discussions form one of a set of 'key actions' proposed by the Commission to advance teleworking in the EU. Others include more research into working conditions and a feasibility study of teleworking in the Commission itself, probably leading to pilot projects next year.

References and further reading

INDUSTRIAL RELATIONS LAW BULLETIN 571. June 1997, p. 16.
OVERELL S. 'Germany staggers as UK flexes its markets'. *People Management*, 20 November 1997, p. 18.
WELCH J. 'EU plans directive to protect "outworkers" '. *People Management*, 6 February 1997, p. 9.

17 TWO CASE-STUDIES

Whitbread Beer Company

Whitbread have always been a company at the forefront of flexible working. They were featured in a case-study as part of the 1986 IPD book and have made considerable strides since that time. This study concerns three aspects of their practices.

Brewing is sometimes considered a very stable industry with a captive market, a cartel-like industry structure, and utilitarian products. Nothing could be further from the truth. Their corporate environment is now one of a fickle and constantly changing marketplace for which a collection of products, some very fashionable and liable to disappear without trace in a very short period of time, are produced by highly competitive suppliers from all around the world. Moreover, operations have a seasonal element but are also moving towards seven-day operation – a combination which could lead to a logistics nightmare. However, a recent development in logistics is the Efficient Consumer Response (ECR) system which involves category management (replenishments, promotions, assortments and introductions) to bring together the efforts of manufacturers and retailers to optimise consumer sources of value. Through a complex interactive relationship, an on-line information flow allows a swift, accurate and flexible reaction to meet the changing consumer needs in all the retail outlets (pubs, off-licences, supermarkets, clubs, etc) and also to influence those needs through efficient marketing methods.

Servicing these requirements in a flexible labour force which includes a full complement of temporal flexibility: multi-skilling, teamworking and outsourcing. This study concentrates on three aspects only:

- □ the Tiverton bottling factory labour system
- □ committed hours in the logistics area
- □ competencies for managers and 'job fingerprinting'.

The Tiverton bottling factory

Up until the end of the 1980s, Tiverton concentrated on short runs of specialised bottles, such as for the export trade, and non-standard sizes for the home market. By 1991, however, the market for bottled beers had declined so much that the plant was closed. Within four years, this decline had reversed and a fashion evolved for drinking premium beers direct from the bottle, especially the dumpy 25-centilitre lager bottle. There was an immediate need to recommission a bottling line, but also uncertainty over its long-term future, so in 1995 the plant reopened with a single shift of 12 employees on temporary contracts. Events moved swiftly, and as demand rose, a second shift was opened, so that by 1997 the plant was bottling export ale and stout, premium ciders and beers under licence, and some 'designer drinks' all with a workforce of only 78.

To achieve this flexibility, employees work under unique contracts which essentially cover only 35 weeks but which can be extended over the full year should demand for the products justify it. The hours in a week can also vary, from a minimum of eight to a maximum of 72, although there is a guarantee that the average will be 39 hours over the 35 weeks. At the beginning of each quarter, a forecast plan is issued giving guidance on which shifts an individual or team must be prepared to cover. Employees are allocated a set of core weeks and may be called in for further weeks at a minimum of one week's notice.

A three-shift system now operates involving days, double-days, and nights, and employees are given one month's notice of change from, say, days to nights, and a week's notice of roster changes of the seven-day working system. A loyalty bonus (currently £250) is paid to employees who return to the company at the end of the lay-off during non-core weeks.

Multi-skilling is a vital element of the contract: operators are required to learn routine maintenance, quality-control systems and bottle size change procedures on top of their basic packaging-plant operations. Remuneration is based on the skills accumulated through a job matrix system.

Already the capital expended to set up the second bottling

line has been recovered, and costs per barrel are only a fraction of those of contract bottling.

Committed hours in logistics

The commitment to seven-day deliveries led Whitbread in 1993 to introduce revised working schedules in both their warehouses and distribution networks based on a form of annual hours.

Employees in the warehouse receive a fixed monthly payment based on a 45-hour week – although the actual hours worked can vary between 35 and 55, depending on demand, shift allocation, and the actual task on which an employee works. These shifts are on a Monday-to-Friday basis (except for one section of the night shift which provides the service to the 'On-trade' and which is required to attend on a Sunday-to-Thursday pattern).

The hours are totalled during the course of the year. The total hours cannot exceed an average of 45, and if they turn out to be less than 45 on average (excluding absence, of course) employees are not asked to make up the additional hours. In addition, there is an obligation to be available to attend for ten Saturdays or Sundays and five Bank Holidays, if required. If employees are called in for these days, they receive an additional shift payment.

The arrangements are the same for the delivery force except that the monthly payment is based on an average 50 hours a week, with a minimum of 35 hours and a maximum of 55 (11 hours per day).

It is made clear that the pattern of hours may be subject to variation depending on business needs, and as much notice of such changes will be given as is practically possible.

Competencies for managers and 'fingerprinting'

In 1993 Whitbread Beer Company introduced a system of management competencies to replace the list of 'management skills' which had formed the basis of training and assessment for a number of years. The research carried out over a year had made it quite clear that although a number of competencies were generic (ie they covered all management functions), they varied in application and importance in respect of individual

Figure 5
COMPETENCY MODEL

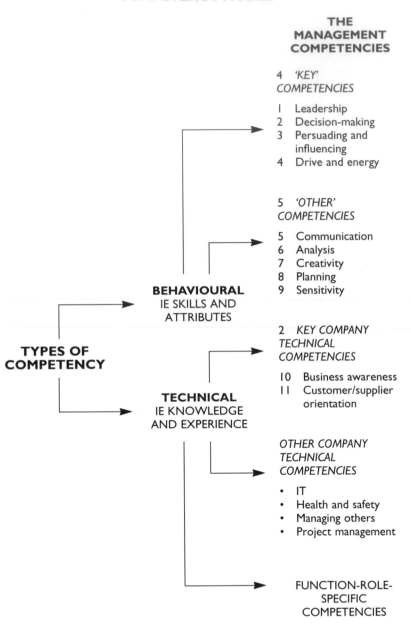

**THE
MANAGEMENT
COMPETENCIES**

4 *'KEY'
COMPETENCIES*

1 Leadership
2 Decision-making
3 Persuading and
   influencing
4 Drive and energy

5 *'OTHER'
COMPETENCIES*

5 Communication
6 Analysis
7 Creativity
8 Planning
9 Sensitivity

2 *KEY COMPANY
TECHNICAL
COMPETENCIES*

10 Business awareness
11 Customer/supplier
    orientation

*OTHER COMPANY
TECHNICAL
COMPETENCIES*

• IT
• Health and safety
• Managing others
• Project management

FUNCTION-ROLE-
SPECIFIC
COMPETENCIES

**TYPES OF
COMPETENCY**

BEHAVIOURAL
IE SKILLS AND
ATTRIBUTES

TECHNICAL
IE KNOWLEDGE
AND EXPERIENCE

Figure 6
JOB FINGERPRINTING

a	**INVESTIGATION AND FACT-FINDING**

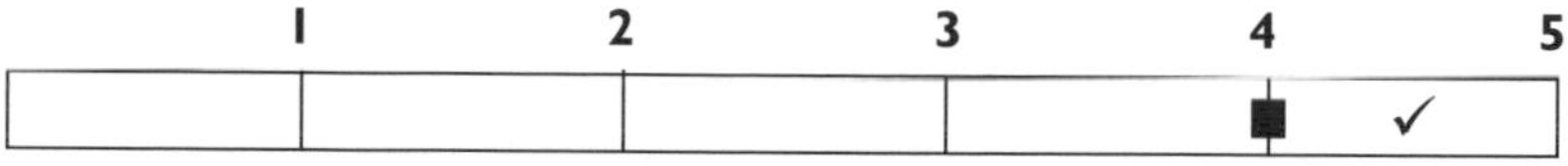

1	2	3	4	5

1. Has a basic understanding of the customer structure and can identify key decision-makers.
3. Can identify specific customer needs and wants and understands the business context.
5. Has a detailed understanding of the customer's market-place and strategies and is able to identify the strategic value to WBC.

b	**PLANNING AND FINANCIAL AWARENESS**

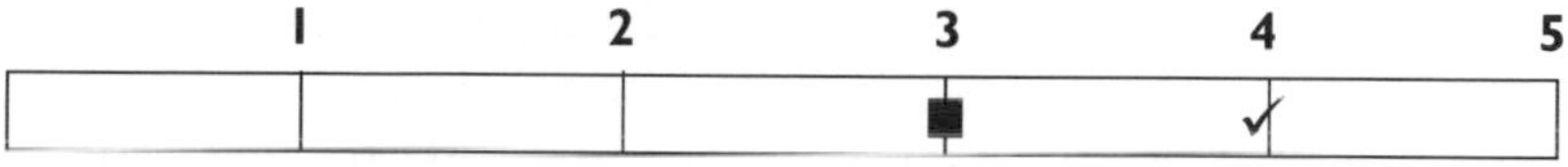

1	2	3	4	5

1. Is able to identify low-cost/high-value concessions and their financial implications at a basic level.
3. Is able to identify and cost more complex sanctions and incentives which may fall outside functional guidelines.
5. Is able to identify the strategic value of the negotiation/relationship.

jobs. To train, develop and assess all managers in the same skills therefore produced a rigid system, far removed from the business needs of flexibility and creative leadership required.

The competency system is divided into two parts:

□ the *model* (see Figure 5 opposite), which shows the two distinct types of competency (behavioural and technical) and the division into 'key' and 'other' competencies

□ '*job fingerprinting*' (see examples in Figure 6 above), which breaks down the competencies into bite-sized pieces relating to each individual, unique position.

Once each management role has been 'fingerprinted', the information is held on a database where it may be used for any of four main reasons:

□ to provide the basis for a personal development handbook for each individual

□ to be incorporated into the management performance reviews, so that managers are assessed primarily against the four key behavioural competencies

- □ to generate job profiles for selection purposes
- □ to provide the framework for a common management skills programme.

Each individual manager is profiled against the fingerprint of his or her position and, if he or she moves function, against that of the new position. Development gaps become far more easy to identify, development plans become more focused, and the selection procedure can incorporate assessment centres which concentrate on the key competencies that have been identified for that role.

Overall, the system is in place to meet the changing needs of the organisation. As the needs of each position alters, the competencies can be changed and the ensuing training requirement quickly identified. It matches the flexible needs of the business. Peter Radcliffe, human resources director, is convinced that flexibility is one of the key factors for his company in maintaining market position:

> We know that our customers' tastes are changing with increasing rapidity. Our successful Tiverton and Logistics operations show that it has been possible to introduce flexible practices into operations which had previously been seen as fixed and unyielding – and practices geared to the immediate needs of business economics rather than those of the customer. Identifying management competencies, and then training managers for those competencies that are key to the business, will ensure that future changes will be made to encourage and support flexibility throughout the business.

Lundbeck A/S

Lundbeck is a pharmaceutical group owned by a Danish foundation specialising in the development of new products for the treatment of illnesses of the central nervous system – schizophrenia, anxiety, depression and dementia. The British subsidiary operates from Milton Keynes, where 120 are employed. Around two-thirds are on the sales side, with the remainder in marketing, finance and administration.

The appointment of a new managing director in 1996 led to a number of new initiatives associated with a more open and co-operative culture tied in with the international vision statement. Here is an abstract from that statement concerned with the flexibility element:

> We must build our specialist knowledge and experience together with our (external) partners in primary and specialist health care. As specialists, we are closer to our partners than our competitors. Integration with our partners is our goal. To be closer to our partners, we must be more integrated internally. We have to bring down the barriers between ourselves before we can bring down the barriers with our partners.
>
> We need to break down the barriers between the centre and the individual operating units. We need to break down the barriers between departments. We need to create skilled, effective, multifunctional and multicultural teams. Teams that are integrated internally and externally, teams that are faster and more flexible than our competitors.

Initiatives have taken a number of forms:

Empowered teams

Project groups that are set up for specific purposes have become self-managed. In 1997, for example, five administrators were given the responsibility of looking at the use of office space, and a budget to work with. They examined the current situation, discussed the options and came up with a draft solution based on the needs of staff rather than status. It was presented to all the staff at head office, including their managers, and accepted (with some small revisions). Part of the successful implementation involved the removal of walls or, as it was called, the removal of barriers.

Another project involved the planning and implementation of a CD-ROM as a diagnostic tool for depression. Again, this was effected by a self-managed group from a number of functions. A further example was the Intranet project team who, once external training was provided, have successfully implemented an excellent Intranet service with the benefit of improved communication.

To support these activities, all staff have been involved in teambuilding training which has included outdoor exercises and role-plays.

Job descriptions

It has become increasingly important that staff carry out responsibilities outside their immediate job, so, to reflect this, it was decided to abolish formal job descriptions and, in most cases, to introduce brief summaries of essential job requirements instead. These stress the necessary flexibility to tackle any relevant problem and to make as large a contribution as possible to the whole company operation.

Self-development in a learning organisation

Staff are encouraged to develop their potential and to add at least two lines to their CV each year. For example, being involved with a project team and contributing original ideas that they have seen through from proposal to implementation are seen as important elements in enhancing the value of an investment in an employee. It is also recognised that this produces a well-rounded individual with more self-confidence.

Breaking down walls

Each Friday is a 'dress-down' day, when staff meet in the canteen. There is a short talk from an employee about a current project or the outcome of a recent medical conference. To improve overall communications, staff are encouraged to mingle with the people that they tend not to work too closely with.

To maintain the theme, the Danish managing director came to open a new medical wing and broke down a wall into the wing. As the staff followed him through into the wing, a jazzband played at the champagne reception.

On Lundbeck's twenty-fifth anniversary in the UK, a trip was organised for the whole company to visit the Copenhagen headquarters on a privately chartered plane. Events included presentations on new products, sightseeing and meals out, a light-hearted group-recording of the company song and, most important, a series of teambuilding exercises with joint Danish and British staff.

As Carol Holmes, company personnel manager explains:

companies in the pharmaceutical industry generally pay very well, so it is difficult for a small organisation to compete on the reward front. We need to make the positions intrinsically attractive, to make working at Lundbeck an experience, to encourage all staff to perform above their own expectations and to get a great sense of achievement out of the workplace. We do all we can to support this approach: organise flexible hours, encourage working mothers, pay for self-development, create the situations where staff can be creative themselves. This benefits all sides in practice: we have lower staff turnover costs, and employees enjoy their work – it's the best of both worlds!

INDEX